T0137058

Lecture Notes in Information Systems and Organisation

Volume 49

Series Editors

Paolo Spagnoletti, Rome, Italy

Marco De Marco, Rome, Italy

Nancy Pouloudi, Athens, Greece

Dov Te'eni, Tel Aviv, Israel

Jan vom Brocke, Vaduz, Liechtenstein

Robert Winter, St. Gallen, Switzerland

Richard Baskerville, Atlanta, USA

Lecture Notes in Information Systems and Organization—LNISO—is a series of scientific books that explore the current scenario of information systems, in particular IS and organization. The focus on the relationship between IT, IS and organization is the common thread of this collection, which aspires to provide scholars across the world with a point of reference and comparison in the study and research of information systems and organization. LNISO is the publication forum for the community of scholars investigating behavioral and design aspects of IS and organization. The series offers an integrated publication platform for high-quality conferences, symposia and workshops in this field. Materials are published upon a strictly controlled double blind peer review evaluation made by selected reviewers.

LNISO is abstracted/indexed in Scopus

More information about this series at https://link.springer.com/bookseries/11237

Luca Solari · Marcello Martinez ·
Alessio Maria Braccini · Alessandra Lazazzara
Editors

Do Machines Dream
of Electric Workers?

Understanding the Impact of Digital
Technologies on Organizations and Innovation

 Springer

Editors
Luca Solari
Department of Social and Political Sciences
University of Milan
Milan, Italy

Marcello Martinez
Department of Economics
University of Campania Luigi Vanvitelli
Capua, Italy

Alessio Maria Braccini
Department of Economics
Engineering
Society and Business Organization
Tuscia University
Viterbo, Italy

Alessandra Lazazzara
Department of Social and Political Sciences
University of Milan
Milan, Italy

ISSN 2195-4968 ISSN 2195-4976 (electronic)
Lecture Notes in Information Systems and Organisation
ISBN 978-3-030-83320-6 ISBN 978-3-030-83321-3 (eBook)
https://doi.org/10.1007/978-3-030-83321-3

This Springer imprint is published by the registered company Springer Nature Switzerland AG
The registered company address is: Gewerbestrasse 11, 6330 Cham, Switzerland

Introduction: Do Machines Dream of Electric Workers? New Frontiers in the Debate on Technology, Structure, and Strategy

Abstract For a long time, the variable of technology has been a relevant dimension on the debate around organisations and organising. Technologies are the many resource organisations used for generating value, and since the Industrial Revolution to the digital revolution, technologies increased their importance for organising. The debate on the implications of technology use in organisations has strong roots in the organisation studies literature. Diffusion and adoption of digital technologies pose new opportunities and challenges to organisations and present new avenues for research to organisation scholars. The 2020 edition of the annual workshop of organisation studies scholars invited researchers to reflect on the relationship between technologies and to organise from a new and critical perspective. This book is a collection of the best-extended works presented at the conference discussing several aspects of impact, innovation, change, challenges, and performance of digital technologies and organisations. This introduction chapter draws a common framework presenting the different contributions and introducing how they investigate relevant phenomena and raise implications for managers and future research.

Keywords Organisation · Digital technologies

Androids, Machines, and Humans

Do androids dream of electric sheep? The wondered question is the title of a famous sci-fi novel authored by Philip K. Dick in 1968. The organisers of the 2020 edition of the annual workshop of organisation studies scholar took the question as an opportunity for inviting researchers to reflect on the implications of digital technologies for organising.

Dick's novel describes a dystopian future located in a post-apocalyptic San Francisco of 1992. A global war has significantly damaged the Earth's life, and most animal species are either endangered or extinct. The human beings live depending on machines in a world crippling under *kipple*, a sort of rubbish that builds up without any human intervention. In such a world poor of organic wildlife, owning a real pet and not just an electric replica, is a dreamed status symbol and existential accomplishment target. The life of humans on Earth largely depends on machines. Humans live under the influence of machines they use to tweak their feelings and emotions. They are incentivised to move to off-world colonies by the possibility of counting on personal androids and robotic replicas of human beings with the role of serving humans in their needs. However, some of these androids rebel and escape to Earth, hiding from the retaliation of humans who, frightened by machines when they are no longer under their control, hunt and terminate them. In a context where mechanic life is designed to imitate organic life, the novel throws the question of the difference between nature and nurture.

Machines and Electric Workers

This book's title builds a metaphor inspired by Dick's novel, replacing androids with machinery, and electric sheep with electric workers, revamping the debate on technology and organising. The book contains a collection of original research papers authored by Italian scholars who participated to the annual edition of the organisation studies workshop and who discussed in their contributions several aspects on the implications of digital technologies for organising.

Technology has always been a central variable in organisation theory [1]. The study of the implications and relationships between the technology variables and other organisational-related variables depends on the fact that each organisation uses one or more technology to generate value transforming inputs into outputs [2]. However, technology has changed profoundly over the past years, raising many research implications for organisation theory. According to Perrow [3], technology summarises operations performed on objects through tools or mechanical devices to transform things. Innovation has pushed the nature of technology way beyond the original definition of Perrow. Technology is a variable under which different sets of tools, pieces of machinery, computers, competencies, techniques, and knowledge are used to pursue individual and organisational goals.

Digital technologies, in particular, are profoundly different from process technologies used to transform inputs into outputs, for three main reasons [4]. First of all, digital technologies are part of complex systems that do not behave linearly but present the user to continuous interrupts and changes of states with intricate patterns that make the understanding of how the overall system works complex for users. Secondly, digital technologies work continuously but need continuous updates and adaptations. Digital technologies are hence in an enduring state of constant becoming from a current state to a future state. Finally, digital technologies work at a high level of abstraction. Users interacting with digital technologies can form abstract maps of how digital technologies work. Nevertheless, these maps hardly ever perfectly match the internal processes under which the technology works, with unexpected effect, errors, and drift between expected use and use in action.

Organisation scholars studied technology from different points of view. Depending on how technology-related variables were included in the research designs, the literature has seen three approaches [5]. The first saw technology as the primary driver of changes. The second considers the social structures and agency as forces shaping technology in use. The third considers the emergent process of mutual interaction between technology and the surrounding social and organisational environment.

Three Perspectives on the Study of Technology and Organisation

The research papers selected and published in this book analyse digital technologies and organisations from three different perspectives, each discussed in the subsequent subsections.

The first perspective of analysis is that of the relationship between the technical and social sides in the socio-technical interplay inside organisations. The androids that dream of electric sheep and the humans of the dystopian future live in a sort of equilibrium. Humans resort on machines for help in their living, but at the same time depend on them, and rely on them when they have no other options from reality. Androids are designed to be as human as possible until they rebel searching for emancipation from oppressing humans. We are not at the point of the human vs robot conflict described in Dick's novel. However, for large extent organisations rely on technology, and the use of technology comes with rules, actors, routines, and values that have to coexist with existing organisational structures [6]. Section "Technology and Organising" introduces the chapters in this book discussing the implications and consequences of technology and organisation's mutual adaptation.

The second perspective of analysis is that of innovation. In Dick's novel, androids and machines, in general, represent new solutions to humans' existential problems. Living in a post-nuclear war Earth, where the planet is short in natural resources and where the alternative is an off-world colony, machines are the solution to human life in general misery. Being dystopian, the novel captures the darkest side of technology innovation and raises concern on the potential negative implications of excessive technology exploitation. The chapters in section "Innovation" discuss possible negative consequences and new opportunities and venues for organisations resulting from the exploitation of digital technologies.

Finally, the third perspective is on the debate between the virtual and the actual dimension of organising. The discussion of what is nature and what is nurture is central in Dick's novel. The electric sheep is not only the surrogate of a pet that humans hardly strive to find, but also a faithful replica of an organic form of life almost indistinguishable from a real animal. Dreaming of an electric sheep is the unknown desire of androids being more human than humans, but also the doubt of not knowing exactly what happens inside the mind of a replica machine. Current digital technologies are less sophisticated than these androids but for other aspects are instead way more complicated. The digital transformation adds the cyber dimension to the organisation [2], potentially not just replacing, or changing ways of organising, but throwing other forms of organising that raise several challenges on the opportunities and limitations of using digital technologies in the organisation. To this regard, the chapters in section "Nurture and Nature" discuss several aspects of the virtual dimension of organisations.

Technology and Organising

Philip K. Dick's androids are at the same time both similar but different from humans, and this difference is a source of contrast. Like the technology and the humans in Dick's novel, technology and organisations are different but tend to show similar characteristics emerging from mutual adaptation and imitation processes. The problem of combined technology and organisation adjustment is the cornerstone of the sociotechnical system studies [7, 8]. These flows of studies consider technology as a source of structures that constrain or empower human agency. At the same time, in society or organisations, the human agency creates structures and frames, giving meaning and legitimation to the way people use technology [9, 10].

Digital technologies affect organising in different ways, also producing profound changes in the very concept of organisation [11, 12]. The use of digital technologies affected organisational size and control, fostering better horizontal coordination, vertical control, and new forms of inter-organisational coupling. At the same time, digital technologies afforded increased visibility and control over organisational actions, enabling real-time, flexible, virtual, and mass size collaboration among organisational actors and different organisations. Concerning the implications of technology for organising five chapters in this book studies the consequences of digital technology adoption on different organisational variables.

The chapter of Maimone "Organizing for Industry 4.0" reflects on the organisational implications of Industry 4.0 technology adoption. Instead of focusing on the technological perspective like many other studies, the chapter addresses the impacts of these technologies at the meso-organisational level, exploring commonalities of strategies and practices by firms adopting Industry 4.0 technologies. The chapter discusses how semi-autonomous systems that allow a certain degree of self-organising are better suited for Industry 4.0 technology adoption.

Like the topic, the chapter of Margherita and Braccini "Consequences in the Workplace After Industry 4.0 Adoption: A Multiple Case Study of Italian Manufacturing Organisations" further explores the organisational implications of Industry 4.0 technology adoption. The chapter explores the relationship between capital and labour, particularly addressing the potential implications of job losses consequent to increased automation in manufacturing organisations. Adopting a multiple case analysis, authors discover mixing results with forms of labour disruption coexisting with forms of emancipation and empowerment. The chapter further highlights the positive outcomes of Industry 4.0 technology adoption and formulates managerial implications on mitigating the potential disruption due to automation.

The chapter by Curzi et al. "Remote Locations Are not All the Same: Determinants of Work Well-Being Among Home-Based and Mobile e-Workers" analyses instead the impact of remote e-work on workers' well-being. They address an aspect of technology with which several people worldwide had to feel under their skin in the exceptional events of the year 2020 linked to the diffusion of the COVID-19 disease. They study the perception of work-related stress and job satisfaction on remote workers, exploring how these perceptions change depending on the type of location chosen for remote work. Their work highlights that workers who autonomously decide the location of their job show reduced work-related stress. Once the world has the pandemic beyond its shoulders, the work of Curzi et al. will be relevant to exploit real value out of smart and remote workers when the choice of the location will no longer forcedly restricted to workers' homes.

The chapter by Fabbri et al. "Work Datafication and Digital Work Behavior Analysis as a Source of HRM Insights" reflects that digital transformation on the workplace increases networked collaboration and makes it observable with unprecedented timeliness and detail. The data tracked by virtual collaboration software represent valuable pieces of information from an HR management standpoint. The chapter discusses the results of an exploratory empirical analysis of data extracted from an enterprise collaboration software. It identifies a correlation between behavioural and digital work patterns and employees' attitude. Their work implies that an algorithmic model of analysis of electronic collaboration platform data would be valid to detect and represent employees' attitude.

Finally, the chapter of Gianecchini et al. "Shaping the Future of Work", the last one of this group, tackles the need of workers to update their competencies to remain attractive on the labour market with the diffusion of digital technologies. The focus is on workers' need to show adequate competencies for being still valuable on the workplace. Their work contributes to the T-shaped professional theory. They perform a quantitative analysis through a survey, and they find four different shapes of competency combinations in their sample of workers.

Innovation

Digital technologies are a potential source of organisational innovation processes. Digital technology adoption leads to different forms of transformation by introducing new structures, actors, practices, and values that can be part of organisational innovation processes [13]. At the same time, digital technologies are the driver of several forms of disruptions, and organisational actors have to continuously engage with the new and the unexpected, balancing forms of exploration and exploitation to seize future opportunities and to drop dead ends [14, 15].

Concerning the different dimensions of organisational innovation, five chapters in this book discuss the implication and consequences of digital technologies for different forms of organisational innovation and performance improvement.

To this regard, the chapter by Acciarini et al. "Blue Ocean or Dry Desert? Blockchain and Bitcoin Impact on Tourism Industry" focuses on the potential innovation in a relevant industry, the tourism industry, as a consequence of the diffusion of blockchain technologies. Analysing social media data, authors map the current discussion on the diffusion of cryptocurrencies and blockchain-based technology in the industry. Their analysis shows a rise of interest in the potential benefits of applying these technologies to travels and tourism and identifies the presence of influencers and dissemination brokers in such public debate.

The chapter by Bolici et al. "Ecosystems in Blockchain Competence Certification: An Explorative Multi-Perspective Analysis" explores the same kind of technology, blockchain, but in a different context, studying how the blockchain can play a role in the high education industry to generate value for all interested stakeholders. They present an exploratory study in which they interviewed key informants in two Italian universities, early adopters of blockchain certification systems.

The chapter by Todisco et al. "Building the Digital Public Administration: The Impact of Social Media in the Public Sector. The Perception of Public Employees in Italian Local Context" focuses instead on public sector organisations and their potential innovation in the ear of social media diffusion. In a world where people communicate and interact through social media platforms, the chapter focuses on the implications for the public sector organisations in transparency, information diffusion, and effectiveness. In the chapter, the authors study the perceptions that civil servants have on the impact of social media on the transparency and quality of services for citizens, discovering how perceptions change with the age of civil servants, with younger groups more inclined to accept this form of innovation positively. The chapter also discusses how the differences in digital literacy levels between the two subgroups might influence their perceptions.

The chapter by Romanelli and Ferrara "Museums Driving Innovation by Technology, People and Organization" studies how knowledge-intensive organisations such as museums adopt innovation. In particular, they aim at exploring how technologies enable museums to drive innovation for creating value for their stakeholders. Their work highlights how museums can foster engagement of users through technologies and promote innovation by stimulated shared re-understanding of the museum's collection and how technologies boost museums' role as an information provider and information mediator.

The chapter by Cristofaro et al. "Measuring Healthcare Performance in Digitalization Era an Empirical Analysis" develops on performance measurement and performance measurement systems. They study how digital technologies can help healthcare organisations monitor and measure the performance of healthcare services through an exploratory study on one hospital ward that implemented such a system to improve the quality of the services offered.

Nurture and Nature

One aspect that digital technologies introduce in an organisation is the simultaneous presence of a physical and of a virtual dimension. Resorting on electronic forms of information transformation and transportation, organisations introduce the virtual dimension into their structure with virtual teams, online electronic communities of practice, and new digital collaboration forms [12]. Digital technologies afford organisations these forms of cooperation and afford increased visibility over organisational-related phenomena up to the point that they can be simulated or virtually reproduced.

Digital technologies hence afford organisations with new forms of digital cooperation. Members of virtual teams cooperate on a shared objective, regardless of the lack of proximity and synchronicity in their actions [16]. Just like the androids in Dick's novel show behaviour akin humans, but not identical, these virtual forms of organising raise new challenges for new forms of cooperation or impact traditional forms of cooperating when translated to the virtual dimension.

In this regard, three chapters in this book explore implications on the virtual dimension of organisations by introducing digital technologies.

The chapter by Bianchi "Practice Enterprise and MOOCs in Higher Education Real and Perceived Performances" focuses on both the simulated and the virtual dimensions of cooperation with the higher education industry, exploring the implications of combining simulation-based learning for management with massive open online courses. In the chapter, the author discusses how to assess such settings' performance, exploring how and if a common approach to assess performance is desirable, especially considering the differences between reality and simulation.

The chapter by Adinolfi et al. "Organizational Followership: How Social Media Communication Affects Employees' Behavior" studies the innovation in the communication process between organisations and their employees and explores the implications on the perception of reality when communication happens through digital platforms. Drawing from the literature on social network and organisational behaviour, their chapter aims at rethinking the concept of organisational followership as a consequence of the adoption of digital technologies. Their empirical study runs an experiment on Instagram, showing the persistence of potential cognitive biases in communication on social media between leaders and followers, and reflects on the organisational implications of such a result.

On a complementary perspective in relationship to the previous chapter, the chapter by Collino and Lauto "Reducing Cognitive Biases Through Digitally Enabled Training. A Conceptual Framework" studies the potential role of advanced digital technologies in reducing cognitive biases when used during training. Their work is conceptual, and authors draw a framework for studying the relationship between training, cognitive biases, technologies, and task performance.

Luca Solari
Luca.solari@unimi.it
Marcello Martinez
Marcello.martinez@unicampania.it
Alessio Maria Braccini
abraccini@unitus.it
Alessandra Lazazzara
alessandra.lazazzara@unimi.it

References

1. Orlikowski, W. J. (1992). The duality of technology: Rethinking the concept of technology in organizations. *Organization Science, 3*, 398–427.
2. Hatch, M. J. (2013). *Teoria dell'organizzazione.* Bologna: il Mulino.
3. Perrow, C. (1967). A framework for the comparative analysis of organizations. *American Sociological Review, 32*, 194–208.
4. Weick, K. E. (1990). Technology as equivoque: Sensemaking in new technologies. In: P. S. Goodman (Ed.), *Technology and organizations* (pp. 1–44). San Francisco: Jossey-Bass,.
5. Martinez, M. (2004). *Organizzazione, informazioni e tecnologie.* il Mulino.
6. Niederman, F., Briggs, R. O., de Vreede, G.-J., Kolfschoten, G. L. (2008). Extending the contextual and organizational elements of adaptive structuration theory in GSS research. *Journal of the Association for Information Systems, 9*, 633–652.
7. Trist, E., Murray, H., & Trist, B. (Eds.) (1993). The social engagement of social science, a Tavistock anthology. University of Pennsylvania Press.
8. Emery, F. E., & Trist, E. L. (1969). Socio-technical systems. In: F. E. Emery (Ed.), *Systems Thinking.* Harmondsworth: Penguin.
9. DeSanctis, G., & Poole, M. S. (1994). Capturing the complexity in advanced technology use: Adaptive structuration theory. *Organization Science, 5*, 121–147.
10. Markus, L. M., & Silver, M. S. (2008). A foundation for the study of IT effects: A new look at DeSanctis and Poole's concepts of structural features and spirit. *Journal of the Association for Information Systems, 9*, 609–632.
11. Fulk, J., & DeSanctis, G. (1995). Electronic communication and changing organizational form. *Organization Science, 6*, 337–349.
12. Zammuto, R. F., Griffith, T. L., Majchrzak, A., Dougherty, D. J., Faraj, S., Dogherty, D. J., & Faraj, S. (2007). Information technology and the changing fabric of organization. *Organization Science, 18*, 749–762.
13. Hinings, B., Gegenhuber, T., & Greenwood, R. (2018). Digital innovation and transformation: An institutional perspective. *Information and Organization, 28*, 52–61.
14. Kumaraswamy, A., Garud, R., & Ansari, S. (Shaz) (2018). Perspectives on disruptive innovations. *Journal of Management Studies, 55*, 1025–1042.
15. Wenzel, M., Krämer, H., Koch, J., & Reckwitz, A. (2020). Future and organization studies: On the rediscovery of a problematic temporal category in organizations. *Organization Studies, 41*, 1441–1455.
16. Adamovic, M. (2018). An employee-focused human resource management perspective for the management of global virtual teams. *International Journal of Human Resource Management, 29*, 2159–2187.

Contents

About the Editors

Luca Solari is Professor of business organisation at the University of Milan, where he holds the role of President of Unimi Foundation and Director of the School of Journalism Walter Tobagi. He deals with the transformation of organisational functioning models between design, human resources management, technology, and organisational behaviour. He edited with Filomena Buonocore and Fabrizio Montanari an innovative volume for the teaching of contemporary business organisation.

Marcello Martinez is Professor of business organisation in the Department of Economics, Università della Campania Luigi Vanvitelli; Founding President of ASSIOA, Association of Italian Organization Studies Academic, Catholic University of Milan; Member of AIDP, Associazione Italiana Direttori del Perosnale Campania; President of the Scientific Committee of SDiO Studi di Organizzazione Aziendale; Leader of research and training projects on the topics of business organisation and human resources management; Author and Co-author of more than 140 publications; Director of the journal *Prospettive in Organizzazione*; Co-director of the journal *Studi Organizzativi, Franco Angeli*; and Coordinator of the Doctorate in Entrepreneurship and Innovation, University of Campania.

Alessio Maria Braccini is Professor of business organisation at the Tuscia University, Viterbo, Italy, where he is also the coordinator of the bachelor and master courses in economics and coordinator of the curriculum in digital transformation of the doctorate in economics management and quantitative methods. He leaded and participated in several research projects funded by the EU and the Lazio region. He is currently Vice-President for publication of ItAIS, the Italian Chapter of the Association for Information Systems, and Member of ASSIOA. He co-authored about 90 publications which appeared in journals such as *Information & Organization* (I&O), *Information Systems Journal* (ISJ), *International Journal of Accounting Information Systems* (IJAIS), *Government Information Quarterly* (GIQ), and the *Communications of AIS* (CAIS).

Alessandra Lazazzara is Associate Professor of organisation theory and human resource management at the University of Milan. Her research interests focus on job crafting, e-HRM, and diversity and inclusion. She has authored several publications in national and international journals and co-edited four books of the *LNISO* Springer series, and is editorial board's Member of *The International Journal of Human Resource Management, Industrial and Commercial Training, SN Business & Economics, Baltic Journal of Management,* and *Prospettive in Organizzazione.* She serves as Vice-President of ItAIS, the Italian Chapter of the Association for Information Systems, and she is Board Member of ASSIOA, the Association of Italian Organization Studies Academics.

Organizing for Industry 4.0

Fabrizio Maimone

Abstract The present paper is aimed to provide a theoretical framework for better understanding the relation between Industry 4.0 and organizing processes. The paper is based on a conceptual exploratory study and uses literature review to shed light to organizational strategies and configuration that may favourite the development of the so-called smart factory. Even though there are several articles and chapters on Industry 4.0, main works are focused on technology and operations. The analysis at meso-level of effective organizational strategies and practices seems to be still overlooked. This paper tries to feel this gap, trying to find out convergent elements between different organizational configurations, in order to highlight common strategies and practices. The findings of the exploratory study support the assumption that organizing and digital transformation associated with Industry 4.0 are entangled by a two-way relation: smart factory requires specific organizational strategies, model and practices. Moreover, organizational design impact of the level of digital readiness of firms and on the success of digital transformation. It is assumed that networked, flexible and semi-autonomous organizational systems that allow a certain degree of self-organization and internal/external networking seem to be more apt to face the challenge of industry 4.0. At the same time, it is possible to assume that there is not an "ideal" organizational form for Industry 4.0. The theoretical, methodological and practical implications of the main findings are discussed in the final part of the paper, and suggestions for future research are provided.

Keywords Industry 4.0 · Lean manufacturing · Networked organization

1 Introduction

According to Hess et al. [1, p. 124], digital transformation "is concerned with the changes digital technologies can bring about in a company's business model,

F. Maimone (✉)
Associate Professor of Organization Studies, LUMSA University,
Via Marcantonio Colonna 19, 00192 Rome, Italy
e-mail: f.maimone@lumsa.it

© The Author(s), under exclusive license to Springer Nature Switzerland AG 2022
L. Solari et al. (eds.), *Do Machines Dream of Electric Workers?*, Lecture Notes
in Information Systems and Organisation 49,
https://doi.org/10.1007/978-3-030-83321-3_1

which result in changed products or organizational structures or in the automation of processes. These changes can be observed in the rising demand for Internet-based media, which has lead to changes of entire business models (for example in the music industry)".

Industry 4.0 is a particular approach to digital transformation that was defined for the first time in a German government programme, aimed to increase the level of competitiveness of manufacturing industry [2]. Industry 4.0 programme was presented at the Hannover Messe in 2011 [3]. According to Buer et al. [4, p. 3], "The concept of Industry 4.0 describes the increasing digitization of the entire value chain and the resulting interconnection of people, objects and systems through real time data exchange. As a result of that interconnection, products, machines and processes are equipped with artificial intelligence and get enabled to adapt to sponta- neous changes of the environment independently. Furthermore, smart objects become embedded in broader systems, which enhance the creation of flexible, selfcontrolling production systems".

Moreover, Sanders, Elangeswaran e Wulfsberg [5] affirmed that: "Industry 4.0 is the fourth industrial revolution applying the principles of cyber-physical systems (CPS), internet and future-oriented technologies and smart systems with enhanced human–machine interaction paradigms. This enables identity and communication for every entity in the value stream and leads to IT-enabled mass customisation in manufacturing [6–8]".

Salkin et al. [9, p. 4], then, pointed out that the term Industry 4.0 includes different concepts, such as improvement in mechanization and automation, digitalization, networking and miniaturization Moreover, Industry 4.0 (Ib.) implies the integration of dynamic value creation networks and it is (Ib.) "…operationalised as the usage of intelligent products and processes, which enables autonomous data collection and analysis as well as interaction between products, processes, suppliers, and customers through the internet".

According to Mrugalska and Wyrwicka [10, p. 470], that commented the results of the study "Industry 4.0", published by the Fraunhofer Institute, it is possible to find out six emerging design principles: "… interoperability, virtualization, decentralization, real-time capability, service orientation and modularity".

Industry 4.0 is considered the new "technological imperative" [11] of the first century the new millennium.

This conceptual paper begins with a critical analysis of the concept of Industry 4.0 and of the so-called technological determinism and then addresses the analysis of the emerging organizing strategies and practices that may contribute to the development of Industry 4.0.

And tries to provides a contribute to answering the following research questions:

RQ1: Does "Industry 4.0" represent a real disruptive innovation in contemporary manufacturing?

RQ2: What are the main pros and cons of Industry 4.0?

RQ3: What are the main organizing strategies and practices that emerge from the analysis of the literature review?

RQ4: What are the convergent and divergent elements that rise from this analysis?

RQ5: Is there an emerging organizational configuration that can be deduced by the analysis of the literature review?

This conceptual paper, based on the analysis and re-elaboration of the scientific literature, tries to answer these research questions, providing a complex theoretical framework.

Even though there are few articles and chapters on Industry 4.0, only [12, p. 17]: "Few contributions go into any detail on issues concerning the pure management and governance of firms, all without a comprehensive approach which is absolutely necessary in management studies (i.e., impact and changes in human resources, sustainability issues, social innovation lens)". This paper tries to give a contribution to fill this gap, providing an analysis at meso-level, of most effective organizational strategies and practices, that can be applied in different organizational configurations.

This paper, hence, is aimed to feel this gap, finding out convergent elements between different organizational configurations, in order to highlight common strategies and practices. The originality of the paper is related to the approach that is aimed to find out a set of organizational strategies and emerging practices that may be used to implement Industry 4.0 like organizational systems, adopting specific combinations that may meet the unique needs of one organization.

The originality of the paper is related to the approach that is aimed to find out a set of configurational trends and dynamic evolutionary processes, more than a set of stable organizational solutions that are difficult to be implemented in a dynamic and continuous transforming system, as it is supposed to be Industry 4.0. Therefore, the analysis is mainly focused on processes more than on structures, and therefore, the central focus of the paper is organizing.

2   The Research Methodology

The literature review has been designed following the indications provided by Webster and Watson [13]. According to these authors (Ib., p. xv): "A high-quality review is complete and focuses on concepts. A complete review covers relevant literature on the topic and is not confined to one research methodology, one set of journals, or one geographic region". Moreover (Ib., p. Xvi), "A literature review is concept-centric. Thus, concepts determine the organizing framework of a review".

Relevant articles were chosen searching the keywords "industry 4.0" and "smart-manufacturing" on the Google Scholars website and on the Scopus and JSTOR search engines. The searching was not limited to titles and abstracts but included also the body of text of the resources.

The works were selected on the base of the relevance of the contents reported in the works respect the main topics addressed in this paper and grouped on the base of the key concepts emerging from the paper analyzed.

The approach is qualitative and focused on descriptive rather than statistical methods [14, p. 1157].

Therefore, the literature review was aimed to develop a conceptual analysis in order to contribute to theory building.

3   Antinomies and Paradoxes of New Organizational Forms

Before addressing the key issues discussed in this paper, it is perhaps necessary to clarify a few crucial points, for the analysis to be followed.

Many authors have argued that there is a gap between the evolutionary trends of organizing and the theoretical models elaborated by organizational scholars. Daft and Lewin [15], for example, remarked regretfully that new organizational forms "...seem far removed from academic research".

The overlooking of contemporary organizational forms it is not only a matter of lack of attention, but also the negative of the lack of focus. In fact, in the last decades many organizational models were elaborated and proposed, but mainly by practitioners and managers. For example, holacracy, an organizational approach based on self-organizing and management of a team-based organization, was elaborated by Brian Robertson [16, 17], the founder of a software company, in order to provide a systematic description of the organizational practices adopted in his own company. TEAL was conceived too by a non-academic, Frederic Laloux [18, 19], a former associate partner with McKinsey & Company and business coach. In both cases, the focus of the models is not on "organizational solutions" that, according to Puranam et al. [20], may be defined as a set of solutions conceived to face universal problems, but on an alternative conception of organizing, which is considered as ongoing, dynamic and evolutionary process, influenced by complex system dynamics [21–23] and interconnected with a wider ecosystem.

The traditional approach assumes that organizational design should be aimed to find out organizational solutions for the four "universal problems" of organizing: task division, task allocation, reward provision and information provision [20]. It is very hard to say that contemporary organizational models (such as Industry 4.0) could be described only by using these four dimensions that presumes the assumption that organizational systems are hierarchical and centralized structures based on prefixed and stable goals, roles and tasks. According to Child and McGrath [24. P. 1137], among others, new organizational forms are instead characterized by decentralized goal setting, distributed power, flexibility, horizontality, relational orientation, fuzzy roles adaptation, adaptation, impermanence and orientation towards innovation. Therefore, it is very difficult to describe them adopting classic organizational design dimensions.

Moreover, Puranam et al. [20] assumed that organizational systems are characterized by identifiable boundaries, which is another statement that is very hard to be sustained, in the age of digital networks, globalized work teams and temporary jobs. In fact, Child and McGrath [24, p. 1137] affirmed that in the new organizational forms boundaries are permeable and fuzzy.

Finally, Schreyögg and Sydow [25] discussed critically the theoretical perspective of organizational fluidity, addressing the paradoxes of new organizational forms that need to conciliate organizational flexibility with the counter-need of assuring a certain level of stability and routine, in order to achieve a good rate of efficiency and functionality.

According to the same authors (Ib., p. 25), to unlock the apparent paradoxical dynamics of new organizational forms, it is necessary "…to develop an organizational framework which allows for conceptualizing contradictions and paradoxes. Most organization theories—explicitly or implicitly—are still based on a linear logic. Consistency is still among the predominant design principles. However, we need a non-linear logic in order to capture countervailing processes".

Moreover, it is assumed that organizational hybridism [26–28] characterizes new organizational forms that have to conciliate the need for decentralization, adaptation, self-organization and management with the necessity of assuring standardization, integration and coordination at systemic level. According to Powell and Sandholtz [27], hybrid organizational forms are characterized by the recombination of existing organizational elements and by the transposition of organizational solution from one sector/organization to one another.

Finally, it is argued that [29] a combinatory design may assure to Industry 4.0 the right organizational configuration, apt to conciliate stability that is necessary for the requisite rate of standardization and flexibility, needed to facilitate continuous adaptation. According to Grandori and Furnari (Ib., p. 22), it is possible to assume that there are a set of rules that may generate organizational configurations, on the base of the combination of different organizational elements that may lead to a "chemistry of organization".

4   What is Industry 4.0 and What are its Pros and Cons

Industry 4.0 is a very popular expression, but there is a lack of consensus about the same definition of the concept. Discussing the results of a systematic review, Piccarozzi et al. [12, p. 16] pointed out that "there is no consensus about the definition of Industry 4.0. In other words, quite a lot of definitions have appeared in literature focusing on various issues, but none of them put managerial aspects at their very core, nor is there consensus about tools and/or issues and/or processes necessary to clearly define the boundaries of Industry 4.0". The same authors proposed a definition, that is, the synthesis of various perspectives emerging from the systematic review (Ib., p. 16): "Industry 4.0 refers to the integration of Internet of Things technologies into industrial value creation enabling manufacturers to harness entirely digitized, connected, smart, and decentralized value chains" … able to "deliver greater flexibility and robustness to firm competitiveness and enable them to build flexible and adaptable business structures, [acquiring] the permanent ability for internal evolutionary developments in order to cope with a changing business environment (…) as the result of a purposely formulated strategy implemented over time".

So, the key implicit assumptions that stay behind the conception of Industry 4.0 may be reassumed in a few points:

- Industry 4.0 is ineluctable since it is technologically determined.
- AI and machine learning consent to obtain better decisions in a shorter time, respect human decision making, and therefore the combination of IoT and Data Analytics technologies may favourite the design of more efficient and effective factories, that enable an increase in quality of products/service and a decrease of costs.
- Automatic (and progressively unmanned) production systems may produce better products at lower costs and respect human labour-based production systems.

These assumptions, nevertheless, may be argued for different reasons.

For what concerns the first point, it is possible to argue that, in spite of the lack of systematic definition of the concept of Industry 4.0, this approach is considered a sort of new "technological imperative". According to Markus and Robey [30, p. 585], "The essence of the technological imperative is conveyed by the word "impact." This perspective views technology as an exogenous force which determines or strongly constrains the behavior of individuals and organizations". Therefore, the technological imperative could be considered as a corollary of the perspective of technological determinism [31]. Salento (Ib.) citing Berger [11] assumed that technology, especially during times of crisis, is represented in terms of linear progress and teleological expectations.

Industry 4.0 was clearly presented as a form of promise of a better and brighter future. Industry 4.0 and smart working are supposed to be the "One Best Way" [32] of the first century of the new millennium.

In fact, the mainstream literature assumes that Industry 4.0 is the Fourth Industrial Revolution (see [5]) and leads towards a radical change (not only) in manufacturing.

The assumption that "Industry 4.0" is the outcome of deterministic change represents a disruptive innovation and can be considered also a sort of technological imperative was criticized by a few authors. Salento [31], among others, argued that Industry 4.0 cannot be considered as a sort of deterministic change, for two reasons: (a) it is not the consequence of radical change, but it can be considered the next step of the transformation process enacted by technological innovation and particularly by informatics revolution. (b) Industry 4.0 is also a space for decision-making: the development and implementation of Industry 4.0 do not follow deterministic paths, but it is also a matter of choices and therefore is strictly related to decision-making. Furthermore, the author (Ib.) highlighted the nature of self-fulfilling prophecy of the rhetoric of Industry 4.0: the same fact that experts, politicians and decision-makers promote the "magnificent and progressive fate" in smart manufacturing is able to produce real effects and to foster the diffusion of new productive model.

Also, Masino (Ib., p. 26) argued that Industry 4.0 does not correspond to a real revolution, but it is simply the next step of the transformation that began with the informatic revolution. Moreover, the author criticized the two assumptions of Industry 4.0:

(a) the conception of social, economic and organizational progress based on technological change and (b) the faith in the positive development of artificial intelligence and machine learning.

For what concerns the second point, the assumption of the superiority of machine intelligence, respect human intelligence, may be criticized for different aspects. The assumed superiority of AI respect human intelligence is based on the capacity of Artificial Intelligence to overcome the problem of bounded rationality [33]. According to Scherer [34, p. 364], "This points to a fundamental difference between the decision making processes of humans and those of modern AI—differences that can lead AI systems to generate solutions that a human would not expect… The computational power of modern computers (which will only continue to increase) means that an AI program can search through many more possibilities than a human in a given amount of time, thus permitting AI systems to analyze potential solutions that humans may not have considered, much less attempted to implement. When the universe of possibilities is sufficiently compact… the AI system may even be able to generate an optimal solution rather than a merely satisfactory".

Nevertheless, the application that is generally considered "intelligent" belongs to the so-called category of "artificial narrow intelligence" (ANI). As Gurkaynak et al. [35, p. 3] pointed out, "ANIs are AIs specialized in a specific area, such as IBM's Deep Blue®, the supercomputer that beat Gary Kasparov, the reigning World Chess Champion in May 1997… (they) can solve complex problems in the blink of an eye but they do not have any preconception of things other than the information provided to them by their creators. In a sense, ANI's reality is limited to their pre-determined capabilities of observation". The so called "General Artificial Intelligence", that regards machines able to replicate the human intelligence, covering a wide range of complex tasks remains mainly still in the future agenda of computer scientists [36]. Therefore, the ability of artificial intelligence to process information and solve problems depends, at the moment, mainly on the ability of the humans to program the artificial system. Moreover, the development of artificial intelligence may lead to the risk of the so-called maximum expected utility: one intelligent machine, able to learn from the experience, discover new and unexpected solutions and formulate autonomously goals and set of actions, in order to maximise the results, may produce [37, p. 6]—"unintended, potentially serious, negative side-effects if the utility function being maximized is not aligned with human interests (for example if some relevant criteria are not included in the utility function)". Finally, complex evolutionary systems are structurally unpredictable, in the long term, and future change of states and, hence, behaviours in those kinds of systems can be foreseen only in probabilistic trends and in the short term (see [38, 39]). This characteristic of complex systems is independent from the computational power, since it is a matter of structure of the system, not of calculation. Therefore, when the decision regards the behaviour of a complex system, such as social, economic or financial behaviours, the blind faith in artificial intelligence may lead to disasters. Moreover, it is very difficult that AI may replicate human abilities like empathy, creativity and intuition that are involved in complex human decision-making processes.

For these reasons, at least at the state of the art of the development of digital technologies, the implementation of Industry 4.0 needs the cooperation between machine and humans, and therefore is still far to push humans out from the stage.

The last issue concerns the assumption that automatic (and progressively unmanned) production systems may produce better products at lower costs and respect human labour-based production systems. Obviously, automatic production may facilitate a cost decrease, due to the cuts of labour costs and to the standardization of processes and products. Nevertheless, the assumption of the presumed higher quality of "smart-manufactured" products is more controversial. If the quality of product is measured in terms of standards or of intrinsic qualitative factor, then it is possible to assume that an automated and even unmanned smart production system may lead to an improvement of the overall quality of products. If, instead, we measure the quality also in terms of subjective customer needs, expectations and satisfaction (see [40, 41]), then it is possible to argue that in some cases "human factor" may impact positively on the perceived quality of some products, for example, in the case of "Made in Italy". Also because sometimes the success is also the outcome of serendipity, as it happened in the cases of Sony's Walkman or 3 M's Post-It, the success of a product may occur against all odds or by casual discovery. And no intelligent system may predict the unpredictable.

Also, these considerations support the assumption that it is likely that the evolution of Industry 4.0 will lead to a certain degree of cooperation/integration between humans and machines.

In any cases, there are pros and cons related to the implementation of smart manufacturing.

According to De Castro Fettermann et al. [42], Industry 4.0 may provide many advantages to production systems: better product quality, time reduction of processing, cost reduction, integration of value chains, process flexibility, improvement in the quality of customer service, product customization. The implementation of Industry 4.0 technologies may help production systems to better conciliate standardization and customer focus, in large-scale production, at least in many industrial sectors. And it facilitates processes of continuous adaptation and improvement (see also [12, 43, 44]).

At the same time, Industry 4.0 may bring also a few risks: skills shortage, unemployment (caused by the progressive substitution of human workers with machines), attempts to social and environmental sustainability. Moreover [42], the huge investments in technological capital may be a barrier for the implementation of Industry 4.0 models in SMEs and in developing economies.

In order to reduce risks and increase benefits, it is necessary to go beyond technological determinism and to adopt ad hoc regulation, governance, organizational design and management strategies (see among others [31]).

5   Organizing for Industry 4.0

5.1   Emerging Approaches

Industry 4.0 [12] "is based on the horizontal and vertical integration of production systems driven by real-time data interchange and flexible manufacturing to enable customized production".

According to Oztemel and Gursev [44, p. 134], "The fourth industrial revolution encourages the idea of unmanned factories and promotes global understanding to emerge along this line day by day through recommending more firmly connected companies and countries worldwide through supply chains and sensor networks".

Hermann et al. [43, p. 10] highlighted the emerging design principles implemented to develop Industry 4.0 (Table 1).

The smart factory is an integrated system. According to the results of a systematic review on the scientific literature about Industry 4.0 and smart manufacturing [45, p. 13], Industry 4.0 approaches are based on the following integration features:

- Horizontal Integration: integration of IT systems within a company and between companies (value networks).
- Vertical Integration: integration of IT systems at the different hierarchical levels.
- End-to-End Digital Integration: process integration within and across companies (value networks).

Moreover, it is possible to define the following priorities for action (Ib.):

- Standardization and Reference Architecture: Standardization of infrastructures, processes and products plays a critical role in the development of smart manufacturing.
- Managing Complex Systems: The rising complexity of Industry 4.0 systems fosters the need for planning and control.
- Delivering a Comprehensive Broadband Infrastructure: Digital infrastructures are fundamental to make the smart factory work.

Table 1 Design principles of Industry 4.0

	Cyber-physical systems	Internet of things	Internet of services	Smart factory
Interoperability	X	X	X	X
Virtualization	X			X
Decentralization	X			X
Real-time capability				X
Service orientation			X	
Modularity			X	

- Safety and Security: Smart manufacturing makes rise the concern on security, safety and privacy issues.
- Work Organization and Design: Industry 4.0 needs more responsible, autonomous and proactive workers, and therefore, it is necessary to find out ad hoc organizational strategies and solutions, aimed to facilitate smart organizing.
- Training and Continuing Professional Development: Industry 4.0 requires continuous learning, and therefore, ad hoc training and organizational learning strategies and systems are required.
- Regulatory Framework: Normative adaptation is necessary to align legislation with the evolution of productive system.
- Resource Productivity and Efficiency: Resources management is critical to achieve efficiency and cost savings.

Even though there is a common agreement on general requirements for the implementation of Industry 4.0, the analysis of scientific review permitted to find out that there is not some kind of one best way for smart manufacturing. If we analyse actual industrial practices, it is possible to observe that smart manufacturing usually implements already existing organizational approaches, adapting them to the needs of Industry 4.0.

According to the results of the literature review, it is possible to find out a few different emerging organizational approaches, commonly associated with Industry 4.0.

The first approach is lean manufacturing. In fact, Wang et al. [46] argued that industrial organization that has already implemented lean manufacturing is more ready to become "smart factory".

Moreover, Sanders, Elangeswaran e Wulfsberg [9] assumed that lean manufacturing is the emerging organizational model of Industry 4.0 (see also [47]). According to the authors (Ib., page 814), "Lean Manufacturing can be described as a multifaceted production approach comprising a variety of industrial practices, directed towards identifying value adding processes from the purview of customer and to enable flow of these processes at the pull of the customer through the organization" [48, 49].

This organizational approach is based on the following elements (Ib.):

1. Supplier feedback;
2. Just-in-time (JIT);
3. Supplier development;
4. Customer involvement;
5. Pull production;
6. Continuous flow;
7. Set-up time reduction;
8. Total productive/preventive maintenance;
9. Statistical process control;
10. Employee involvement.

The same authors (Ib.) argued that Industry 4.0 and lean manufacturing could be easily integrated, in order to improve the effectiveness of the two approaches.

Another emerging organizational model, associated with Industry 4.0, is Agile Organization. Erol et al. [50, p. 411] affirmed that organizational agility is one of the key drivers of Industry 4.0. Yusuf, Sarhadi and Gunasekaran [51, p. 17], moreover, defined organizational agility as "an effective integration of response ability and knowledge management in order to rapidly, efficiently and accurately adapt to any unexpected (or unpredictable) change in both proactive and reactive business/customer needs and opportunities without compromising with the cost or the quality of the product/process".

According to Wendler [52], the agility model is based on the following elements:

- Agility prerequisites: agile values and technology;
- Agility of people: workforce and management of change;
- Structures enhancing agility: collaboration and cooperation, and flexible structures.

The role played by the agility model in the smart factoring is pointed out by several authors [53–55].

Other authors have, instead, emphasized the role of network structures and assumed that smart production networks are characterized by a high degree of fragmentation (see [50, 56–59]).

According to Brettel et al. [58, p. 51], "Collaborative Manufacturing [60] and Collaborative Development Environments [61] gain importance especially for Small and Medium Enterprises (SME) with limited resources. Within a collaborative network, risks can be balanced and combined resources can expand the range of perceivable market opportunities…The organization in networks multiplies the available capacities without the need of further investments".

Networked configuration is based on "Integrated Engineering" 8Ib.), which facilitates the coordination of the whole value chain, within and across organizational boundaries. Production networks are seen as one of three key elements of Industry 4.0 [62, p. 556–557].

Warnecke [63], then, proposed the model of "fractal enterprise" that includes the organizational elements of: self-similarity, self-organization, self-optimization, goal orientation and dynamics. Fractals "are a high-level abstract idea of an infinite structure obtained by recursive application of the same pattern" [64, p. 667].

According to Olaniyi and Reidolf [65], the fractal organization may represent a model for Industry 4.0. Peralta et al. [66, p. 928] affirmed that "The objective of fractal manufacturing is to develop a framework for the planning, design, modelling, simulation, optimization, management and assessment of processes in analogy with the forms of organization of fractal natural entities; natural fractal objects adjust their functions, features or principles according to the context demands (environment pressure)". Moreover, Bider et al. [64] proposed a model based on three key features: business processes, assets and relationships between the same key elements.

Self-organization, flexibility and networking play a critical role also in this organizational structure. It is important to notice that, even though they could be similar (and obviously they have common traits), networked structure and fractal structure may differ, since the latter tries to replicate recursively the same patterns (business/operational process) in all autonomous sub-units that compose the fractal system; meanwhile, instead the former may also interconnect different organizations and sub-units, specialized in one of more phases of the productive process, and therefore, it could be characterized by a certain degree of network diversity.

5.2   Organizing for Industry 4.0: Convergent Tendencies

As it is assumed from the analysis of scientific literature, there is no best way of organizing for Industry 4.0. But, it is possible to highlight a few convergent tendencies.

Shamim et al. [67, p. 5311] pointed out that Industry 4.0 is characterized by continuous change, instability and evolutionary patterns. Therefore (Ib.), smart manufacturing is supposed to be compatible with an organic design of organizations [68], characterized by decentralization, post-bureaucratic, horizontal leadership and collaborative team working.

Sanders, Elangeswaran e Wulfsberg [6], then, argued that there is not an ideal organizational model for Industry 4.0, because smart factories need to be organized in order to meet their specific needs, and therefore, it is not possible to find out a single approach that is able to satisfy the exigencies of every smart factory. And they suggest (Ib.) the following emerging organizational solutions for Industry 4.0:

- Matrix structure
- Project teams
- Flat hierarchy.
- Decentralization.

Also in this case, the authors support an organic approach to organizational design, characterized by few elements of organizational flexibility.

It is possible then to argue that many authors support the idea that Industry 4.0 is characterized by the emerging of organizational hybridism, and it implies the need of a change of paradigms and mindset and the necessity to facilitate a process of upskilling and reskilling, not only in terms of digital competences.

Moreover, the analysis of the scientific literature on Industry 4.0 permitted to find out a few key elements that are considered critical for the organizational configurations analysed and are more frequently associated with smart factoring. The following tables report the organizational configurations that are more frequently associated with Industry 4.0 and the organizational elements more commonly associated with the same organizational configurations (Table 2).

Table 2 Key elements of smart organizing

	Self-organization	Organic structure	Horizontal leadership	Flexible organization	Networking	Values and mindset	Centrality of people
Lean manufacturing	X	X	X	X	X	X	X
Networked production system	X			X	X		
Agile organization	X	X	X	X	X	X	X
Fractal organization	X			X	X		

The emerging elements highlighted in the table can be arguably observed in all the organizational configuration analysed, but in the matrix proposed above, in each line is indicated only the key element that is considered critical and fundamental for the specific organizational form. May be a networked structure could attribute a central role to values and mindset and also to people, but the prevailing framework gives emphasis to engineering integration and knowledge flows through IoT and AI. Obviously, also digital lean manufacturing could lead theoretically to the emerging of the "dark factory", capable to operate virtually unmanned, but in this case it is possible to argue that this form is some kind of extreme configuration of an organizational approach that more frequently is based on the integration between digital intelligence and human intelligence. In any case, the table presented above is not universal, but it simply tries to provide a picture or the state of the art.

It is possible to assume that all the elements included in the above table are present, with different weights and combination, in at least two of the four organizational model generally associated with Industry 4.0: lean manufacturing and agile organization. That are also the organizational configuration most frequently cited in the literature, in association with Industry 4.0.

For what concerns the other two organizational forms studied, networked and fractal organization, only organizational flexibility and networking are included in all the works analysed.

Self-organization, flexible organization and networked structure seem to be the three organizational features that are observable, with different combinations and weights, in all the organizational models associated with Industry 4.0, according to the outcomes of the study of the scientific literature. Clearly, each of the three features seems to be related to each other: network systems, in fact, are based on self-organization and are flexible by default. What differs in each organizational model, associated with Industry 4.0 production systems, is the weights of each element within the same models and the different combinations to these organizational elements at meso- and micro-level.

This tendency is associated with the emergence of hybrid forms that seems to represent one of the most significant trends in Industry 4.0.

Moreover, it is possible to argue that there is a sort of meta-model emerging by the analysis of the scientific literature. This model is relation centric. Relation centric (see [69]) means that coordination mechanisms should allow the full integration between machine and human agents, horizontal and vertical process, across hierarchies and organizational boundaries. Relations create connections and therefore foster the level of interdependence among different elements of the organizational systems. And it facilitates self-organization: the relation and interconnections among organizational elements; in fact, it is supposed to be (at least partially) the result of the emerging patterns of interaction, driven by circular feedbacks. At the same time, since even flexible organizations need a certain degree of centralized coordination and stability (at least in the short term), the implementation of Industry 4.0 production systems requires ad hoc governance and interlocking organizational solutions.

Hence, it is argued that the key to unlock organizing for "Industry 4.0" is the ongoing processes of interaction and connection among the different parts of the organizational systems. The effectiveness of Industry 4.0 is not simply related to the adoption of certain organizational solutions, but it is the outcome of the dynamic configuration emerging from the continuous interplay between top-down and bottom-up processes, planned and emerging pattern of behaviours, flow of information and knowledge exchange.

Even though the three organizational elements indicated above are present in all different organizational configurations analysed, there are other aspects related to Industry 4.0 that, according to many authors, should be included in the general plan for the development of smart manufacturing: organizational culture, people's mindset, competence shortage and the needs to facilitate upskilling and reskilling processes.

Therefore, the implementation of Industry 4.0 may involve also the soft dimension of organizing. According to Picarozzi et al. [12], who cited De Sousa Jabbour et al. [70], "for the successful implementation of Industry 4.0 and environmentally-sustainable manufacturing, the first is management leadership followed by readiness for organizational change, top management commitment, strategic alignment, training and capacity building, empowerment, teamwork, organizational culture, communication, project management, national culture, and regional differences". Therefore, the implementation of Industry 4.0 requires the implementation of change management processes, the development of organizational capabilities, people's knowledge and competences and more generally a cultural change.

Therefore, it is possible to argue that, according to the outcomes of this exploratory research, there is not a universal "ideal" organizational model for Industry 4.0 and that different organizational strategies and practices are implemented in smart industries, combined in different configurations and with diverse weights. According to the outcomes of the exploratory research, new organizational configurations are characterized by a relational focus and therefore dynamic interconnections tend to replace rigid predefined structures. Hybrid forms seem to be an emergent feature in Industry 4.0 development. Moreover, since Industry 4.0 is a mix of standardization and specialization, coordination and self-management, it is possible to interpret emerging 4.0 organizational configurations as innovative forms of chaordic systems [71] that operates at the edge between order and chaos. Finally, the organizational approaches studied are characterized by a rising level of complexity and co-evolutionary patterns.

6 Discussion, Suggestions for Future Research and Open Conclusions

According to the outcomes of the literature review, it is possible to argue that Industry 4.0 is not technologically determined, but it is an emerging model that has its pros and cons and should be implemented adopting ad hoc regulatory systems, governance, organizational design and managerial systems, in order to reduce risks and maximize benefits, not only for the business, and therefore to make Industry 4.0 be more sustainable.

The cooperation between human and artificial agents seems to be the more promising perspective, in order to humanize smart factory, avoid the risks of disentangle smart factoring and human needs and avoid risks related to the limitations of big data analytics and AI that are not conceived to predict and prevent the unpredictable, especially referring to complex phenomena, and to cope with sudden crisis like corona virus pandemic that obliged social and economic systems to cope with a new global and almost unknown threat.

The findings of the exploratory study support the assumption that Industry 4.0-like firms do not present unique and specific organizational forms. The cases studied reported in the scientific literature show that Industry 4.0 is implemented adapting existing organizational models to the needs of smart factoring.

The framework emerging from the analysis of the scientific literature is permitted to highlight a few elements that may be observed in the so-called smart factory: flexible organization, self-organization [72], networked dynamic structure [73–75]. Moreover, it is possible to describe smart manufacturing flexible structures as chaordic systems [71, 76] that may be present in different combinations [29]. And it is possible to argue that there is a certain tendency towards the emerging hybrid configurations.

Then, it is possible to assume that smart organizations may show complex dynamics [76] and co-evolutional path [77]. Furthermore, Industry 4.0-like firms need to facilitate coordination, manage external and internal complexity and achieve a dynamic equilibrium between integration and diversity, continuous change and identity saving (see [78]).

The meta-model emerging from the analysis of the scientific literature is relation oriented [69], chaordic, hybrid, and it is based on dynamic configuration. The ability of adapting its configuration, combining different organizational elements and facilitating the dynamic interconnection among human and artificial agents, may be considering as the emerging key organizational competence of smart factoring.

The findings of the exploratory study support the assumption that organizing and digital transformation associated with Industry 4.0 are entangled by a two-way relation: smart factory requires specific organizational strategies, model and practices. On the other hand, organizational forms impact the level of digital readiness of firms. It is assumed that networked, flexible and partially autonomous organizations that allow a certain degree of self-organization seem to be more apt to face the challenge of Industry 4.0. At the same time, it is possible to assume that there is not an "ideal" organizational form for Industry 4.0.

The findings of the exploratory study suggest that digital transformation is not only a matter of technology and that the implementation of Industry 4.0 requires a complex change management process, that entails the necessity to analyse organizational needs (see [79]), adopting ad hoc strategies and actions, that meet the exigencies of the target organization, following a specific transformational path, that should facilitate upskilling, reskilling and a complex change management process.

The study presented in this paper is conceptual and has a few limitations. More empirical research is necessary to explore and study organizational strategies, models and practices, enacted by smart factories. Then, it is suggested to study different approaches and organizational configurations implemented in Industry 4.0, in different productive sectors and markets.

Moreover, it would be worthy of interest to study organizational strategies, configurations and practices enacted by smart factories that adopt strategically and purposely a mixed model that implies the collaboration between human and non-human agents.

References

1. Hess, T., Matt, C., Benlian, A., & Wiesböck, F. (2016). Options for formulating a digital transformation strategy. *MIS Quarterly Executive, 15*(2).
2. Kagermann, H., Helbig J., Hellinger, A., & Wahlster W. (2013). *Recommendations for implementing the strategic initiative INDUSTRIE 4.0: Securing the future of German manufacturing industry*. In Final Report of the Industrie 4.0 Working Group. Berlin: Acatech.
3. Drath, R., & Horch, A. (2014). Industrie 4.0: Hit or Hype? *IEEE Industrial Electronics Magazine, 8*(2), 56–58.
4. Buer, S. V., Strandhagen, J. O., & Chan, F. T. (2018). The link between industry 4.0 and lean manufacturing: Mapping current research and establishing a research agenda. *International Journal of Production Research, 56*(8), 2924–2940.
5. Sanders, A., Elangeswaran, C., & Wulfsberg, J. (2016). Industry 4.0 implies lean manufacturing: research activities in industry 4.0 function as enablers for lean manufacturing. *Journal of Industrial Engineering and Management, 9*(3), 811–833.
6. Lasi, H., Fettke, P., Kemper, H.G., Feld, T., & Hoffmann, M. (2014). Industry 4.0. *Business & Information Systems Engineering, 6*(4), 239.
7. Posada, J., Toro, C., Barandiaran, I., Oyarzun, D., Stricker, D., de Amicis, R., Pinto, E.B., Eisert, P., Döllner, J., & Vallarino, I. (2015). Visual computing as a key enabling technology for industrie 4.0 and industrial internet. *Computer Graphics and Applications, IEEE, 35*(2), 26–40.
8. Valdez, A. C., Brauner, P., Schaar, A. K., Holzinger, A., & Zieflea, M. (2015). Reducing complexity with simplicity-usability methods for industry 4.0. In *Proceedings 19th Triennial Congress of the IEA,Melbourne, Australia* (pp. 9–14). Germany: RWTH Publications.
9. Salkin, C., Oner, M., Ustundag, A., & Cevikcan, E. (2018). A conceptual framework for Industry 4.0. In Ustundag, A. & Cevikcan, E. (Eds.), *Industry 4.0: Managing the Digital Transformation* (pp. 3–23). Springer.
10. Mrugalska, B., & Wyrwicka, M. K. (2017). Towards lean production in industry 4.0. *Procedia Engineering, 182*, 466–473.
11. Berger, P. L. (1974). *Pyramids of sacrifice*. Basic Books.
12. Piccarozzi, M., Aquilani, B., & Gatti, C. (2018). Industry 4.0 in management studies: A systematic literature review. *Sustainability, 10*(10), 3821.
13. Webster, J., & Watson, R. T. (2002). Analyzing the past to prepare for the future: Writing a literature review. *MIS quarterly*, xiii-xxiii.
14. Crossan, M. M., & Apaydin, M. (2010). A multi-dimensional framework of organizational innovation: A systematic review of the literature. *Journal of management studies, 47*(6), 1154–1191.
15. Daft, R. L., & Lewin, A. Y. (1990). Can organization studies begin to break out of the normal science straitjacket? An editorial essay. *Organization Science, 1*(1), 1–9.

16. Robertson, B. J. (2007). Organization at the leading edge: Introducing Holacracy™. *Integral Leadership Review, 7*(3), 1–13.
17. Robertson, B. J. (2015). Holacracy: The revolutionary management system that abolishes hierarchy. *Penguin UK*.
18. Laloux, F. (2014). *Reinventing organizations*. Nelson Parker.
19. Laloux, F. (2015). The future of management is teal. Strategy and Leadership, Autumn.
20. Puranam, P., Alexy, O., & Reitzig, M. (2014). What's, "new" about new forms of organizing? *Academy of Management Review, 39*(2), 162–180.
21. Dooley, K. J., & Van de Ven, A. H. (1999). Explaining complex organizational dynamics. *Organization Science, 10*(3), 358–372.
22. Moldoveanu, M. C., & Bauer, R. M. (2004). On the relationship between organizational complexity and organizational structuration. *Organization Science, 15*(1), 98–118.
23. Maimone, F. (2017). Post-bureaucratic organizations as complex systems: Toward a co-evolutionary and multiparadigmatic perspective. In *Evolution of the post-bureaucratic organization* (pp. 152–179). IGI Global.
24. Child, J., & McGrath, R. G. (2001). Organizations unfettered: Organizational form in an information-intensive economy. *Academy of Management Journal, 44*(6), 1135–1148.
25. Schreyögg, G., & Sydow, J. (2010). Crossroads—organizing for fluidity? Dilemmas of new organizational forms. *Organization Science, 21*(6), 1251–1262.
26. Powell, W. W. (1987). Hybrid organizational arrangements: New form or transitional development? *California Management Review, 30*(1), 67–87.
27. Powell, W. W., & Sandholtz, K. W. (2012). Amphibious entrepreneurs and the emergence of organizational forms. *Strategic Entrepreneurship Journal, 6*(2), 94–115.
28. Bruce, K., & Jordan, J. (2007). Between markets and hierarchies: Towards a better taxonomy of hybrid organizational forms? *Technology Analysis & Strategic Management, 19*(1), 7–16.
29. Grandori, A., & Furnari, S. (2008). A chemistry of organization: Combinatory analysis and design. *Organization Studies, 29*(3), 459–485.
30. Markus, M. L., & Robey, D. (1988). Information technology and organizational change: Causal structure in theory and research. *Management Science, 34*(5), 583–598.
31. Salento, A. (Ed.). (2018). Industria 4.0. Oltre Il Determinismo Tecnologico. In *Ebook of the research program the organization workshop*, University of Salento.
32. Taylor, F. W. (1912). *Scientific management*. Harper's.
33. Simon, H. A. (1972). Theories of bounded rationality. *Decision and Organization, 1*(1), 161–176.
34. Scherer, M. U.: Regulating artificial intelligence systems: Risks, challenges, competencies, and strategies. *Harvard Journal of Law & Technology, 29*(2), pp. 353, Spring.
35. Gurkaynak, G., Yilmaz, I., & Haksever, G. (2016). Stifling artificial intelligence: Human perils. *Computer Law & Security Review, 32*(5), 749–758.
36. Müller, V. C. (2014). Risks of general artificial intelligence. *Journal of Experimental & Theoretical Artificial Intelligence, 26*(3), 297–301.
37. Vamplew, P., Dazeley, R., Foale, C., Firmin, S., & Mummery, J. (2018). Human-aligned artificial intelligence is a multiobjective problem. *Ethics and information technology, 20*(1), 27–40.
38. Thompson, J. M. T. (1988). The principia and contemporary mechanics: Chaotic dynamics and the new unpredictability. In *Notes and Records of the Royal Society of London* Vol. 42, No. (1), pp. 97–122.
39. Zwirn, H., & Delahaye, J. P. (2013). Unpredictability and computational irreducibility. In *Irreducibility and computational equivalence* (pp. 273–295). Springer.
40. Wicks, A. M., & Roethlein, C. J. (2009). A satisfaction-based definition of quality. *The Journal of Business and Economic Studies, 15*(1), 82.
41. Kotler, P., & Amstrong, G. (2012). *Principle of marketing* (14th ed.). Prentice Hall.
42. Fettermann, D. C., Cavalcante, C. G. S., Almeida, T. D. D., & Tortorella, G. L. (2018). How does industry 4.0 contribute to operations management?. *Journal of Industrial and Production Engineering, 35*(4), 255–268.

43. Hermann, M., Pentek, T., & Otto, B. (2015). Design principles for industrie 4.0 scenarios: a literature review. Dortmund: Technische Universität Dortmund.
44. Oztemel, E., & Gursev, S. (2020). Literature review of industry 4.0 and related technologies. *Journal of Intelligent Manufacturing, 31*(1), 127–182.
45. Liao, Y., Deschamps, F., Loures, E. D. F. R., & Ramos, L. F. P. (2017). Past, present and future of Industry 4.0-a systematic literature review and research agenda proposal. *International Journal of Production Research, 55*(12), 3609–3629.
46. Wang, B., Zhao, J. Y., Wan, Z. G., Ma, J. H., Li, H., Ma, J. (2016). Lean intelligent production system and value stream practice. In *Paper presented at the 3rd international conference on economics and management* (pp. 442–447). ICEM 2016, Jiangsu, China.
47. Nicoletti, B. (2013). Lean and automate manufacturing and logistics. In Advances in production management systems. Sustainable production and service supply chains (pp. 278–285). Springer: Berlin Heidelberg.
48. Shah, R., & Ward, P. T. (2007). Defining and developing measures of lean production. *Journal of Operations Management, 25*(4), 785–805.
49. Womack, J. P., Jones, D. T., & Roos, D. (1990). *The Machine that changed the world.* Simon & Schuster.
50. Erol, S., Schumacher, A., & Sihn, W. (2016, January). Strategic guidance towards Industry 4.0–a three-stage process model. In *International conference on competitive manufacturing* Vol. 9, No. 1, pp. 495–501.
51. Yusuf, Y. Y., Sarhadi, M., & Gunasekaran, A. (1999). Agile manufacturing: The drivers, concepts and attributes. *International Journal of Production Economics, 62*, 33–43.
52. Wendler, R. (2014, September) Development of the organizational agility maturity model. In *2014 Federated conference on computer science and information systems* (pp. 1197–1206). IEEE.
53. Matthiae, M., & Richter, J. (2018). Industry 4.0-induced change factors and the role of organizational agility. In *Twenty-Sixth European conference on information systems (ECIS 2018)* (pp. 53). Portsmouth, UK.
54. Akkaya, B. (2019). Leadership 5.0 in industry 4.0: Leadership in perspective of organizational agility. In *Managing operations throughout global supply chains* (pp. 136–158). IGI Global, USA.
55. Sony, M., & Naik, S. (2019). Ten lessons for managers while implementing industry 4.0. *IEEE Engineering Management Review.*
56. Dujin, A., Geissler, C., & Horstkötter, D. (2014). INDUSTRY 4.0: The new industrial revolution. Roland Berger Strategy Consultants: Munich.
57. Schuh, G., Potente, T., Wesch-Potente, C., Weber, A. R., & Prote, J. P. (2014). Collaboration mechanisms to increase productivity in the context of industrie 4.0. In *Proceedings of the19th robust manufacturing conference (CIRP)* (pp. 51–56). Bremen, Germany, 7–9 July, 2014.
58. Brettel, M.; Friederichsen, N.; Keller, M., Rosenberg, M. (2014). How virtualization, decentralization and network building change the manufacturing landscape: An industry 4.0 perspective. *International Journal of Engineering, Science and Technology, 9*(8), 37–44.
59. Barata, J., Rupino Da Cunha, P., Stal, J. (2018). Mobile supply chain management in the Industry 4.0 era. *Journal of Enterprise Information Management, 31*, 173–192.
60. Lin Hao W., Nagalingam S. V., Kuik S. S., & Murata T. (2012). Design of a Global decision support system for a manufacturing SME: Towards participating in collaborative manufacturing. *International Journal of Production Economics, 136*(1), 1–12.
61. Mendikoa, I., Sorli, M., Barbero, J. I., Carrillo, A., & Gorostizan, A. (2008). Collaborative product design and manufacturing with inventive approaches. *International Journal of Production Research, 46*(9), 2333–2344.
62. Veza, I., Mladineo, M., & Gjeldum, N. (2015). Managing innovative production network of smart factories. *IFAC-PapersOnLine, 48*(3), 555–560.
63. Warnecke, H. (1997). *The fractal company: A revolution in corporate Culture.* Springer.
64. Bider, I., Perjons, E., Elias, M., & Johannesson, P. (2017). A fractal enterprise model and its application for business development. *Software & Systems Modeling, 16*(3), 663–689.

65. Olaniyi, E. O., & Reidolf, M. (2015). Organisational innovation strategies in the context of smart specialization. *Journal of Security & Sustainability Issues, 5*(2).
66. Peralta, M. E., Marcos, M., Aguayo, F., Lama, J. R., & Córdoba, A. (2015). Sustainable fractal manufacturing: A new approach to sustainability in machining processes. *Procedia Engineering, 132*(2015), 926–933.
67. Shamim, S., Cang, S., Yu, H., & Li, Y. (2016, July). Management approaches for Industry 4.0: A human resource management perspective. In *2016 IEEE congress on evolutionary computation (CEC)* (pp. 5309–5316). IEEE.
68. Burns, T., & Stalker, G. M. (1961). *The management of innovation.* Tavistock.
69. Grandori, A., & Soda, G. (2006). A relational approach to organization design. *Industry and Innovation, 13*(2), 151–172.
70. De Sousa Jabbour, A. B. L. Jabbour, C. J. C., Foropon, C., & Godinho Filho, M. (2018). When titans meet—Can industry 4.0 revolutionise the environmentally-sustainable manufacturing wave? The role of critical success factors. *Technological Forecasting and Social Change, 132,* 18–25.
71. Hock, D. W. (1999). *Birth of the Chaordic Age.* Berrett-Koehler.
72. Kauffman, S. A. (1993). The origins of order: Self-organization and selection in evolution. OUP USA.
73. Bughin, J., & Chui, M. (2010). The rise of the networked enterprise: Web 2.0 finds its payday. McKinsey quarterly Vol. 4, pp. 3–8.
74. Mahutga, M. C. (2014). Production networks and the organization of the global manufacturing economy. *Sociological Perspectives, 57*(2), 229–255.
75. Satell, G. (2015). What makes an organization "Networked". Harvard Business Review.
76. van Eijnatten, F. M., & Putnik, G. D. (2004). Chaos, complexity, learning, and the learning organization: Towards a chaordic enterprise. *The Learning Organization, 11*(6), 418.
77. Volberda, H. W., & Lewin, A. Y. (2003). Co-evolutionary dynamics within and between firms: From evolution to co-evolution. *Journal of Management Studies, 40*(8), 2111–2136.
78. Volberda, H. W. (1996). Toward the flexible form: How to remain vital in hypercompetitive environments. *Organization Science, 7*(4), 359–374.
79. Pilati M., & Tosi H. L. (2017). Comportamento organizzativo. Individui, relazioni, organizzazione, management, EGEA, Milano.

Consequences in the Workplace After Industry 4.0 Adoption: A Multiple Case Study of Italian Manufacturing Organisations

Emanuele Gabriel Margherita⊙ and Alessio Maria Braccini⊙

Abstract In this study, we explore the consequences of Industry 4.0 adoption in the workplace. Industry 4.0 refers to a set of technologies for the assembly line, which allows increasing automation on operational and decision-making activities. The literature agrees on the positive impact that Industry 4.0 technologies have on the production process. We find in the literature contradictory results on the role of labour and the changes consequent to the adoption of the technologies. To address this gap, we performed a multiple case study of three Italian manufacturing organisations. Findings show the positive consequences of Industry 4.0 technologies and how the management addresses the negative social consequences of Industry 4.0.

Keywords Industry 4.0 · Social implications · Workplace consequences · Multiple case study

1 Introduction

Over the last years, manufacturing organisations started adopting Industry 4.0 (I40) technologies for optimising the production process and responding to low-cost competitors from developing countries. They consequently innovated their assembly lines deploying leading-edge technologies such as big data, robotics, Internet of things and additive manufacturing. The interconnection of these technologies enables the cyber-physical system (CPS), which provides self-decision-making. That is a new feature for the technical infrastructure, which allows to automate the production process detecting and addressing mechanical issues without human interaction [1]. Industry 4.0 potentially delivers outcome changes in the economic, ecological and social context [2]. I40 is known for delivering higher productivity, higher-quality products and valuable services enhancing production process efficiency [3–6]. I40

E. G. Margherita (✉) · A. M. Braccini
Department of Economics Engineering Society and Organization—DEIM, University of Tuscia,
Via del Paradiso, 47, 01100 Viterbo, Italy
e-mail: emargherita@unitus.it

technologies provide better usage of natural resource during the production, allowing a better energy saving and the reduction of CO2 emission [7–9].

Nevertheless, there is a consensus regarding the I40 benefits on the production process thanks to the increasing automation in terms of increasing productivity and higher-quality products. There is a contradiction in the literature about the consequences of I40 adoption on the workplace, namely the consequences on worker conditions and changes of organisational structure after I40 adoption.

On the one hand, researchers raised scepticism regarding positive benefits of I40 adoption in the workplace arguing that I40 is a means to reduce the number of employees and the employee activities within manufacturing organisations due to the increasing automation [10, 11]. On the other hand, researchers stated that the management of I40 automation leads to a positive impact on the workplace, improving work conditions and work environment for the employees [12, 13]. To address this gap, we propose an exploratory multiple case study analysis of three Italian manufacturing organisations which effectively adopted I40 technologies delivering workplace issues, and they have maintained stable the employment level. The study aims at answering the following questions: *"How does the adoption of Industry 4.0 deliver positive consequences on the workplace?".*

Our contribution to the literature is twofold. We present consequences on the workplace of I40 adoption and how the management handled I40 adoption avoiding negative consequences on the workplace.

2 Theoretical Background

In this section, we present the Industry 4.0 initiative and state of the art regarding consequences on the workplace of Industry 4.0 for organisations.

2.1 Industry 4.0

The integration of I40 technologies on the assembly line aims at improving the production processes affording manufacturing organisations to produce small-sized lots of customised and high-quality products [14]. Digital technologies used in I40 usually go under the name of I40 technologies [13]. I40 technologies are a cornerstone of several industrial initiatives—mainly European, but also worldwide—for boosting competitiveness and sustainability of manufacturing industry. The I40 technologies are:

- Robotics: devices which operate autonomously or in collaboration with the workforce to achieve a set of tasks. Different types of robots exist, from mobile robots to mechanical arms. Mobile robots flexibly handle and move materials in the warehouse. Mechanical arms can perform any desired manipulation tasks: modelling, welding, gripping and cutting [15].

- Cloud manufacturing refers to a virtual network in which supply chain actors provide resources and customers can access their services on demand. The manufacturing resources available become services displayed on a platform. The purpose of cloud manufacturing is to share resources and enhance manufacturing service provision [16, 17].
- Internet of Things (henceforth IoT): a dynamic networked infrastructure composed of several physical devices of any kind equipped with sensors and data transmission capabilities. IoT devices allow to capture, process and communicate in real-time data on how machines and humans perform tasks [11].
- IoT-based Logistic Solutions: IoT solutions for automated warehouse management. These technologies automatically manage inbound and outbound logistics and optimise the storage of products in the warehouse autonomously [18].

The use of I40 technologies takes the form of interconnected cyber-physical systems which can be programmed and automated and produce a digital trace of all the activities performed in production integrated with the traditional information systems in the organisation [19]. These machineries can also be autonomous as they can detect issues and take actions to solve them without any human intervention [1].

2.2 Consequences of Industry 4.0 in the Workplace

I40 technologies potentially deliver organisational benefits in the form of more efficient workflows, more efficient production processes using less natural resources and energy, and a better workplace for workers [13].

I40 is known for improving workflow delivering higher productivity-enhancing production process efficiency and flexibility [12]. A consensus in the literature states that IoT applications improve the efficiency and effectiveness of the supply chain management, reducing the inventory inaccuracy and the time to market [18]. In line with this, organisations employ IoT in the assembly line inventory management and warehouse management [18]. I40 increased data granularity of technologies which enables a better usage of natural resource during the production, allowing a better energy saving and the reduction of CO_2 emission [7].

Although empirical studies stated that I40 adoption delivered improvements on the workflow, pieces of evidence regarding the consequences of I40 adoption in the workplace are contradicting. On the one hand, scholars consider I40 as a technocentric initiative where the main focus is on the integration and automation of different technologies. The increasing automation allows organisations to reduce staff [10, 11, 20, 21]. Consequently, scholars argued that the role of the workforce in an I40 context could be extremely marginal because several decision-making activities are passed on to the technology [10, 11, 20, 21].

Table 1 Summary of the consequences of I40 adoption on workplace

	Attributes	References	Short description
Positive consequences on the workplace of I40 adoption	Reduction of work accident	[13, 22, 23]	I40 technologies automate unhealthy and dangerous production phases
	Improved workforce morale	[12, 13, 24]	Workforce experiences a better workplace oriented towards workforce needs
	Increasing safety at work	[13, 22, 25]	The implementation of I40 technologies increased safety over the production process
Negative consequences on the workplace of I40 adoption	Workforce substitution	[10, 11, 20, 21]	I40 technologies reduce workforce number employed within the production process by automating the production process
	Reduction of workforce core activity	[10, 11, 20, 21]	I40 technologies allow accomplishing core tasks in which workforce was previously in charge

Some studies revealed that I40 technologies allow automating unhealthy activities reducing increasing safety at work. I40 technologies allow automating repetitive tasks reducing the number of accidents in the workplace. Finally, the workforce shows improved morale in an I40 workplace since they are in charge of creative tasks. Table 1 summarises the current state of the art of the consequences of I40 adoption in the workplace in the literature.

3   Research Design

To answer the research question, we performed a multiple case study of three Italian manufacturing organisations. The method is recommended to investigate contemporary phenomenon within a particularly contextual setting in order to develop an initial understanding [26]. The method consists of selecting multiple cases, triangulating data during collection as well as analysing the data both within cases and across cases [26, 27].

We completed an organisation visit of 3 h for each case unit, observing both the traditional and the I40 assembly lines. During these visits, we collected semi-structured interviews with key informants of the I40 adoption (CEO, CPO, CIO) and with the supervisor of workers affected by the adoption of the new technologies. The interviews covered the following aspects: details of I40 technologies, adoption process, benefits on the assembly line and consequences of the adoption of the workplace. We enriched the data with observations—collected in field notes—and other materials, such as articles and interviews, available on the institutional website of the organisations [27].

We consider these specific settings as revelatory cases [27] since the organisations are pioneers in the adoption of I40 technologies. Therefore, these settings allow us to explore how I40 adoption currently and potentially changes the workplace.

The three cases share common similarities. First of all, they all implemented the technologies for achieving better control over the production process and increasing product quality. The cases have similar workplace issues which encouraged the management to adopt I40 technologies. All the organisations had a traditional, labour-intensive—as workers manually move products from one spot to the other in the assembly line—and unsafe production process—due to the presence of soft chalk powders, painting and sawing dust in the air. Second, they all share the same Italian economic context and organisation size (medium).

Concerning the data analysis, we maintain a methodological rigour following the guideline of Corbin and Strauss [28]. We considered all the data sources as a single corpus coded with first- and second-level codes by one single coder. Both authors discussed the coding in three iterations before reaching a final agreement on the coding. Table 2 presents the most salient interview excerpts.

4 Case Study

The three cases analysed here are a sanitary ceramic manufacturer (Case 1), a kitchen furniture manufacturer (Case 2) and a prosthesis device manufacturer (Case 3).

The traditional production processes used in the three cases are similar: the workers employ traditional utensils and technologies to produce the goods, manually move the goods along the assembly line, and inside and outside the warehouse.

In the traditional processes, the environment is not healthy due to the presence of chalks (Cases 1 and 3), painting and enamel (Case 1) and sawdust (Case 2). The unhealthy environment causes threats to worker health in terms of lungs and cancer diseases. Adding to this, in Case 3, the organisation lacked timely and accurate information on the production process since data collection was performed manually by workers, and they frequently mismanaged paper base forms or lose them.

To address these concerns, the adoption of I40 technologies seeks increased automation of the production process. The organisation in Case 1 adopted mechanical arms and automated forklifts in a semi-autonomous assembly line with machinery connected in a CPS. The organisation in Case 2 adopted automated cutting machines, mechanical arms and a fully automated warehouse integrated into a CPS. Finally, the organisation in Case 3 adopted mechanical arms in the assembly line, a more

Table 2 Interview excerpts

Topic	Exemplary interview excerpt
Improved workflow	This FM application is the first in the ceramic industry. We increased control over the processes, and we also produce high-quality products (Case 1, CEO)
	The innovative production system is positively impacting economic performance, reducing the time spent on each product production (Case 2, Web article)
	The mechanical arm is in charge of the first part of prosthesis production improved productivity and reduces time spent on production (Case 3, CIO)
Workers with higher competencies	The worker is requalified through vocational training, and now they are technology experts (Case 1, CPO)
	Now workers enriched their duties, and we provide courses that increased their informatics competencies (Case 2, CPO)
	We gave vocational courses for workers to teach the right competencies to deal with technologies (Case 3, CIO)
New business unit	We settled a new laboratory for materials research. We are the first in the ceramics industry (Case A, CEO)
	Did you see the new production unit? It is in a different plant since it required more space. We adopted new cutting machines and an automated warehouse (Case B, CIO)
	Digital administration unit became important. We hired two workers to move in digital all the admirative bills (Case 3, CTO)
Job enrichment: workers act as I40 machine supervisor	I40 technologies perform hard muscular tasks and move automatically finished products to the warehouse; workers now supervise operation (Case 1, CEO)
	Now the I40 technologies perform all the production and logistics activities; workers oversee the entire process (Case 2, CPO)
	The workers now supervise the mechanical arm, which performs the first part of the production (Case 3, CIO)
Better work condition	Now workers only supervise, and they do not have to raise heavy load products and move them (Case 1, CEO)

(continued)

Table 2 (continued)

Topic	Exemplary interview excerpt
	The manual sawing activities are reduced in the process, and workers mostly supervise machines operations (Case 2, CIO)
	There are fewer powders in the production line (Case 3, CIO)
Job enrichment: workers provide feedback for improving the I40 production process	Workers daily work with technologies; they give us feedback to improve the process (Case 1, CPO) We take workers' feedback which we send to the developers to improve the technologies (Case 2, CPO)
Less coordination problem among units	Now, we integrate the entire organisation. When prosthesis production concludes, the system automatically creates the bill (Case 3, CIO)
Reduction of repetitive activities	The mechanical arm does the first repetitive part of the prosthesis, and workers conclude the production (Case 3, CIO)

thorough traceability system based on automatic data collection and an advanced digital billing system integrated with the production system.

Table 3 summarises in detail the features of I40 adoption.

The organisations adopted I40 technologies with similar processes. They signed a contract with a technology provider which acted as a facilitator for the implementation of technologies [29]. The adoption was incremental. Each organisation gradually implemented one technology at a time seeking continuous improvement on the assembly line, and they eventually interconnected them. The management of the organisations anticipated the innovation to the workers who—not anonymously—showed a positive reaction. Finally, the technology provider offered vocational courses to train each worker to manage the new pieces of machinery.

The technology provider of Case 2 also proposed tailor-made vocational courses for workers offered by the producer of the machinery, a third subject located in Germany. Table 4 lists detailed data on the pieces of technologies adopted and on the changes in the number of staff prior and post-adoption.

After the adoption of I40 technologies, the production processes of Cases 1 and 2 are semi-automated: I40 technologies perform most of the production and logistic activities, while workers supervise the correct functioning of the technologies. They also provide feedback to the technology providers to optimise the settings of the machinery. In Case 3, the automation is limited to the first stage of the production process. Workers finalise unfinished products manually since the necessary customisation phase contains far too many exceptions for being automated.

All three workplaces resulted safer and cleaner and with well-established workflows at the end of the I40 technology adoption.

Table 3 Features of I40 technologies

I40 technology	Features
Mechanical arm	Facilitates the creating or products of various shapes from a solid block Handles components that move automatically along the production process
Traceability system	Set of integrated systems that make use of mobile devices, barcode scanners, QR code scanners and image recognition to trace work and materials flow on the assembly line. The system can be both automatic and manually operated by workers using manual barcode scanners
Advanced billing system	Administrative system integrated with the production traceability system used to automatically generate digital bills for the customer at the end of the production process
Automated forklift	Handles the movement of finished goods from the assembly line into the warehouse automatically
CPS	An autonomous system created by the interconnection of a different digitally enhanced machinery that can take decisions on the production process usually taken by workers
Automated cutting machine	An automated cutting machine that can cut large wood panels into small pieces optimising the number of components obtainable from one standard wooden panel, and minimising the amount of waste
Automated warehouse	Set of automated machinery that finished store products tracing their locations in real time and optimising handling and pickup for the subsequent shipping to customer phase

Table 4 Organisation facts

Case	Adopted I40 technologies	Staff before I40 adoption	Staff after I40 adoption
Case 1	Mechanical arm Automated forklifts CPS	223	224
Case 2	Automated cutting machine Mechanical arm Automated warehouse CPS	187	203
Case 3	Mechanical arm Digital bill system Traceability system	97	99

Each organisation set up new units strictly related to the I40 production process: the R&D unit in Case 1, the product unit in Case 2 and the digital administration unit in Case 3.

5 Findings

Table 5 summarises in detail the consequences of I40 adoption on the workplace, which we present in three main groups: a *safer workplace,* the *transition to a knowledge-intensive organisation* and the *development of new organisational units.*

Development of new organisational units. The adoption of I40 technologies allowed the organisation to improve workflow and internal coordination. To take advantage of the technology features, the organisation settled new organisational units hiring specialised workers. The newly employed personnel units contributed to maintaining the staff levels after the I40 adoption, as illustrated in Table 4.

In Case 1, the adoption of mechanical arms allowed replacing chalks with other materials on the assembly line. Consequently, Case 1 created an R&D unit to test new mixtures for more sustainable, enduring and efficient ceramics products.

In Case 2, the employment of the automated cutting machine and mechanical arms allowed to insource one previously external activity through the creation of a new production unit. The new unit produces higher-quality products and helps to increase the gamut of the products. In Case 3, the adoption of the digital billing system, together with the tracking system, afforded the organisation better internal coordination among units that now provide real-time information regarding the production process. Furthermore, the management created a new digital administration unit in charge of issuing dematerialised bills to customers.

Transition to a knowledge-intensive organisation. For an effective I40 adoption, the workers in all cases attended vocational courses to acquire the needed competencies to manage I40 technologies. In all the cases, workers act as machine supervisors, whereas in the traditional production systems, they produced the goods manually. Workers also check the respect of production schedules. They are also in charge of providing feedback on the performance of machinery to fine-tune the settings and to improve the process continuously.

The nature of the work turned from manual activities to knowledge-intensive activities. Also consequent to the established of the new organisational units, in all cases, we observed the introduction of knowledge-intensive positions within the

Table 5 Consequences on workplace after I40 adoption

Case(s)	Consequences
All	Improved workflow
All	Workers with higher competencies
All	New business unit
All	Job enrichment: workers act as I40 machine supervisor
All	Better work condition
1 and 2	Job enrichment: workers provide feedback for improving the I40 production process
3	Less coordination problem among units
3	Reduction of repetitive activities

organisation. The I40 adoption allowed the organisations to shift from a traditional manufacturing organisation into a knowledge-intensive organisation where the tasks require high skilled roles.

Safer Workplace. Following the I40 adoption, the workplace is safer and with better working conditions in all cases. The automation reduces hard muscular tasks previously performed by workers: the I40 autonomous pieces of machinery handle by-products and finished products. Case 1 adopted a mechanical arm to produce the good and an automated forklift to move the finished good to the warehouse. Case 2 employs an automated cutting machine to produce the wood layer, which will compose the finished good. After that, the mechanical arm moves the wood layer to a cart manually moved by a worker to the automated warehouse. This automated warehouse stores automatically the right tracking product positions. Case 3 settled the mechanical arms in a separate room, thus eliminating dangerous powders along with the production phase.

In all cases, acting the workers as supervisors, they now sit farther from the pieces of machinery and have less chance of inhaling soft powers. Moreover, in some cases, the new pieces of machinery afforded the use of less dangerous materials. In general, the adoption of I40 technologies reduced the likelihood for workers to suffer from lung diseases.

6 Discussion

According to the literature, how I40 adoption delivers positive consequences on the workplace is not well explored. Au contraire, the literature supports the hypotheses of work disruption consequent to the adoption of autonomous—including self-decision-making—pieces of machinery which would eventually lead to staff reduction on the production process [10, 11]. The top management commitment to a sustainable innovation for the workforce is crucial for avoiding potential staff reductions.

Our cases showed three top managements which are receptive to innovation to facilitate workforce activities. The I40 adoption automatised activities detrimental to the workforce. However, it maintained the staff in charge of those activities which are crucial to accomplish the production process, and it assigned the staff the task of providing feedback to technology experts to improve the production process.

Top management also has a strong commitment to supporting innovation during the adoption stage. Indeed, being the organisations we studied pioneers in the I40 adoption, the management decided to take on the risk of the I40 adoption and of the development of a new production process compatible and coherent with the traditional way of producing products. The cases showed the I40 adoptions are a means to address issues of the workplace which also have a positive effect on the improvements in quantity and quality production.

Furthermore, the cases showed how the management developed an I40 production process in a worker-centric manner since the workers' activities guide the deployment of the technologies. Even though I40 technologies supplanted workers in the most substantial part of the production process, human labour does not disappear. Workers remain as supervisors of pieces of machinery and as agents of continuous improvements providing feedback on how to fine-tune machinery operations. Even if they lost the manual tasks, the workers would maintain a prominent role within the I40 production process.

Finally, the organisations adopting I40 moved from traditional manufacturers into knowledge-intensive organisations, also contributing to preserving staff. The workforce composition changed both into the I40 production process and within the organisation where several knowledge-intensive positions entered the organisation. The workers' daily activities embed a higher level of knowledge, either to control the way the pieces of machinery work or to build over the digital data produced by the machines.

Vocational training supported the knowledge-intensive transition developing the needed competencies in workers to work with I40 technologies.

To conclude, we answer the research question explaining that positive consequences of I40 adoption in the workplace depend on the supporting role of top management towards innovation to develop a worker-centric deployment of I40 technologies on the production process. The transition to a knowledge-intensive organisation also increased the worker likelihood of I40 technology acceptance, since resistance connected to the potential job disruption if overpassed from the benefits of working in a less tiring, more healthy and highly professionalised job environment.

6.1 Implications for Researchers

Our study raises implications for future researchers. First of all, we suggest that researchers consider I40 adoption as a broader socio-technical system. I40 adoption does not automatically lead to reduced staff if observed from a broader perspective [11].

Our cases illustrate how I40 technology adoption improved worker conditions and intensified the degree of competence which the workers possessed. I40 technologies potentially widen the organisational socio-technical system as the socio-technical relationship is no longer limited to the interaction between the task and the tool needed to complete the task. It instead also involves other organisational units outside the assembly line—i.e. R&D units or administrative units—that are affected by the production process innovation, even though they do not take direct actions on the latter.

The implication for researchers studying the I40 adoption would then be of widening the perspective over the socio-technical dimension of the process beyond the mere interaction between the worker and the machine on the assembly line to study the more complex dynamic.

This work is based on the investigation of three Italian manufacturing organisations. Although this is a limitation of the paper, it is also a signification of its relevance, as Italy is the second-largest manufacturing company in Europe. The results of our study are mostly generalisable in the European context and for firm size, industry type. Therefore, we encourage researchers to investigate the consequences of I40 adoption in a different context from the Italian one, including developing countries, Asian and American nations.

6.2   Implications for Managers

The experience of the cases presented in this study represents a champion for similar organisations aiming at adopting I40 technologies, and scared by potential resistance from workers. Based on the case results, the role of the workforce within the processes of innovation is central for effective adoption of I40 technologies. The management shall set up a working system through I40 application which is compatible and coherent with the previous one in terms of roles and values within the organisations.

Vocational training plays a crucial role in I40 adoption and shall be targeted to each worker employed in the I40 production process. The continuous improvement of the I40 production process is pursued by the interplay of I40 technologies and workers with higher competence in managing I40 technologies and knowledge of the artisan process. Thus, the transition to I40 production process does not automatically imply the reduction of employment level.

The study is also useful for policymakers aiming at developing incentives to strengthen innovation, competitiveness, workers' conditions and employment levels in the manufacturing industry.

7   Conclusion

We began our study noticed that the way with which I40 adoption delivers positive consequences in the literature is poorly developed in the literature. The increasing automation delivered by I40 technologies raised concerns among scholars regarding the reduction of the workforce and the impoverishment of tasks. To address this gap, we proposed a multiple case study analysis of three Italian manufacturing organisations which effectively adopted I40 technologies delivering positive impacts on the workplace. We explained how top management support to I40 adoption plays a crucial role to address workplace issues and develop a worker-centric I40 production process which is mainly based on work tasks and coherent with the previous traditional production process. The transition to a knowledge-intensive organisation increased the worker likelihood of I40 technology acceptance since I40 technologies are in charge to perform repetitive activities of the production process. In contrast, workers are in charge to supervise pieces of machinery and propose feedback to continuous improvements in the production process.

The study has limitations. We acknowledge that the findings are limited to the pieces of evidence of cases selected from one context—the Italian manufacturing industry—though relevant internationally. We hence encourage further researchers to engage with similar studies, including units from different countries.

References

1. Lee, J., Bagheri, B.,& Kao, H. A. (2015). A cyber-physical systems architecture for industry 4.0-based manufacturing systems. *Manufacturing Letters 3.*
2. Kiel, D., Muller, J. M., Arnold, C., & Voigt, K. (2017). Sustainable industrial value creation: Benefits and challenges of industry 4.0.
3. Ardanza, A., Moreno, A., Segura, Á., de la Cruz, M., & Aguinaga, D. (2019). Sustainable and flexible industrial human machine interfaces to support adaptable applications in the industry 4.0 paradigm. *International Journal of Production Research.*
4. Lee, J., Lapira, E., Bagheri, B., & Kao, H. (2013). Recent advances and trend in predictive manufacturing systems in big data environment. *Manufacturing Letter, 1,* 38–41.
5. Sayar, D., & Er, Ö. (2018). The Antecedents of successful IoT service and system design: Cases from the manufacturing industry. *International Journal of Design, 12,* 67–78.
6. Shin, S., Woo, J., & Rachuri, S. (2014). Predictive analytics model for power consumption in manufacturing predictive analytics model for power consumption in manufacturing. *Procedia CIRP, 15,* 153–158.
7. Liang, Y. C., Lu, X., Li, W. D., & Wang, S. (2018). Cyber physical system and big data enabled energy efficient machining optimisation. *Journal of Cleaner Production, 187,* 46–62.
8. Schulze, C., Thiede, S., Thiede, B., Kurle, D., Blume, S., & Herrmann, C. (2018). Cooling tower management in manufacturing companies: A cyber-physical system approach. *Journal of Cleaner Production.*
9. Thiede, S. (2018). Environmental Sustainability of Cyber Physical Production Systems. *69,* 644–649.
10. Liao, Y., Deschamps, F., Loures, E. de F.R., & Ramos, L. F. P. (2017). Past, present and future of industry 4.0—a systematic literature review and research agenda proposal. *International Journal of Production Research 55,* 3609–3629.
11. Kang, H. S., Lee, J. Y., Choi, S., Kim, H., Park, J. H., Son, J. Y., Kim, B. H., & Noh, S. (2016). Do: Smart manufacturing: Past research, present findings, and future directions. *International Journal of Precision Engineering and Manufacturing-Green Technology 3,* 111–128.
12. Fatorachian, H., & Kazemi, H. (2018). A critical investigation of Industry 4.0 in manufacturing: theoretical operationalisation framework. *Production Planning & Control 7287,* 1–12.
13. Kagermann, H., Wolfgang, W., & Helbig, J. (2013). Recommendations for implementing the strategic initiative INDUSTRIE 4.0. Work. Group. Acatech, Frankfurt am Main, Ger. 82 (2013).
14. Yadav, A., & Jayswal, S. C. (2018). Modelling of flexible manufacturing system: A review. *International Journal of Production Research, 56,* 2464–2487.
15. Thoben, K.-D., Wiesner, S., & Wuest, T. (2017). "Industrie 4.0" and smart manufacturing—A review of research issues and application examples. *The International Journal of Automotive Technology 11,* 4–19.
16. Margherita, E.G., & Braccini, A.M. (2020). IS in the cloud and organizational benefits: An exploratory study. In Lazazzara A., Ricciardi F., Za S. (Eds.), *Exploring Digital Ecosystems. Lecture Notes in Information Systems and Organisation,* Vol. 33.
17. de Sousa Jabbour, A. B. L., Jabbour, C. J. C., Foropon, C., & Filho, M. G. (2018). When titans meet—Can industry 4.0 revolutionise the environmentally-sustainable manufacturing wave? The role of critical success factors. *Technological Forecasting and Social Change 132,* 18–25.
18. Ben-Daya, M., Hassini, E., & Bahroun, Z. (2017). Internet of things and supply chain management: A literature review. *International Journal of Production Research, 7543,* 1–24.
19. Lasi, H., Fettke, P., Feld, T., & Hoffman, M. (2014). Industry 4.0. *Business & Information Systems Engineering.*

20. Bonekamp, L., & Sure, M. (2015). Consequences of Industry 4.0 on human labour and work organisation. *Journal of business and media psychology 6*, 33–40.
21. Nurazwa, A., Seman, N. A., & Shamsuddin, A. (2019).Industry 4.0 implications on human capital : A review. *Journal for Studies in Management and Planning 4*, 221–235.
22. Braccini, A., & Margherita, E. (2019). Exploring Organizational sustainability of industry 4.0 under the triple bottom line: The case of a manufacturing company. *Sustainability 11*, 36.
23. Yuan, Z., Qin, W., & Zhao, J. (2017). Smart manufacturing for the oil refining and petrochemical industry. *3*, 1–4.
24. Lee, C. K. M., Lv, Y., Ng, K. K. H., Ho, W., & Choy, K. L. (2018). Design and application of internet of things-based warehouse management system for smart logistics. *International Journal of Production Research, 56*, 2753–2768.
25. Kembro, J. H., Danielsson, V., & Smajli, G. (2017). Network video technology: Exploring an innovative approach to improving warehouse operations. *International Journal of Physical Distribution and Logistics Management, 47*, 623–645.
26. Eisenhardt, K. M. (1989). Building theories from case study research. *Academy of Management Review, 14*, 532–550.
27. Yin, R. K. (2018). *Case Study Research and Applications*. Design and Methods. SAGE Publications Inc.
28. Corbin, J., & Strauss, A. (2015). *Basics of Qualitative Research*. Techniques and Procedures for Developing Grounded Theory. SAGE Publications Inc.
29. Mumford, E. (2003). *Redesigning human systems*. IGI Global.

Remote Locations Are not All the Same: Determinants of Work Well-Being Among Home-Based and Mobile e-Workers

Ylenia Curzi⬤, Tommaso Fabbri⬤, and Barbara Pistoresi⬤

Abstract This chapter analyses the impact of remote e-work on workers' well-being by exploring whether their perception of work-related stress and job satisfaction vary as a function of the type of remote location. It also explores whether organizational autonomy and discretion as well as work intensification have a differential impact on home-based and mobile e-workers' job satisfaction and work-related stress. The main results suggest that compared to home-based e-workers, mobile ones perceive a greater number of work intensification dimensions as drivers of work-related stress, some of which (i.e. frequent work interruptions, working during one's free time and time pressure) also have a significant negative impact on job satisfaction. Moreover, although several organizational autonomy and discretion variables positively affect mobile e-workers' job satisfaction, only discretion over work pace is also significant to reduce their work-related stress. Our findings contribute to advance the understanding of current trajectories of the micro-level organizational transformations associated with the use of new digital technologies, offering insights into the ability of today's European organizations to leverage the opportunity they open up to shape novel work practices that meet their organizational members' needs.

Keywords Work-related stress · Job satisfaction · Remote location

*This chapter is the result of a common undertaking. Ylenia Curzi, Tommaso Fabbri and Barbara Pistoresi contributed design and conception of the study. Barbara Pistoresi organized the database and performed the statistical analysis. The sections of the manuscript were authored as follows. Section 1 by Tommaso Fabbri. Section 2 by Ylenia Curzi. Section 3 by Barbara Pistoresi. Section 4 by Ylenia Curzi and Barbara Pistoresi. Section 5 by Ylenia Curzi, Tommaso Fabbri, and Barbara Pistoresi. Corresponding author: Ylenia Curzi, ylenia.curzi@unimore.it.

Y. Curzi (✉) · T. Fabbri · B. Pistoresi
Marco Biagi Department of Economics, University of Modena and Reggio Emilia, Via Berengario 51, 41121 Modena, Italy
e-mail: ylenia.curzi@unimore.it

1   Introduction

In a digitally transformed organization, work may be performed within digital work-places, which are accessible anytime and anywhere via digital mobile devices, freeing people from the need to be physically present at the conventional workplace, in conventional working time [12]. Fostered by these opportunities, remote e-work is rapidly spreading throughout Europe [10] with the promise of clear benefits for organizations and individuals alike.

At the firm level, research indeed suggests that remote e-work may be key to increase an organization's innovative potential, enabling management to capitalize on individual autonomy and innovative work behavior in complex work processes [1]. At the individual level, remote e-work allows workers to choose where, when and how to work and this may positively affect work well-being [15]. However, some scholars point to the negative consequences of remote e-work for individuals, mainly driven by increased work intensification [6, 23]. Thus, despite the growing popularity of this work mode, evidence regarding the nature of its impact on work well-being is still mixed. One explanation for the inconclusive research results may be that the majority of prior research does not distinguish between home-based and mobile e-work (i.e. work performed remotely from any other location than the office/factory and home such as customer sites, hotels, airports and cafes) [5].

Accordingly, this chapter seeks to get a more nuanced understanding of the impact of remote e-work on workers' well-being, by exploring whether perception of work-related stress and job satisfaction vary as a function of the type of remote location. It also analyses whether organizational autonomy and discretion as well as work intensification have a differential impact on home-based and mobile e-workers' job satisfaction and work-related stress. For this purpose, we use OLS multiple regression analysis and data from the 2015 European Working Conditions Survey [11].

The remainder of the chapter is organized as follows. Section 2 reviews the liter-ature on the impact of remote e-work on work-related stress and job satisfaction and presents research hypotheses. Section 3 describes the data and the empirical method. Section 4 presents the results, and Sect. 5 discusses the findings, implications and future research directions.

2   Background Literature and Hypotheses Development

In the past three decades, an extensive body of research has explored the impact of remote e-work on work well-being, focusing in particular on such cognitive dimen-sions as work-related stress and job satisfaction [2, 3, 5]. In the cognitive perspective on work well-being, work-related stress is the result of how an individual assesses his/her working conditions, and specifically the demands as well as the resources and capabilities at his/her disposal to cope with them. Job satisfaction is an evaluative attitude developed as workers make judgments about their overall work experience and/or specific aspects of their jobs. Since Karasek's seminal work [22], work-related stress and job satisfaction have been considered two central and tightly related variables, reflecting an individual's relationship with his/her work and his/her well-being at work.

Moreover, past research primarily focuses on the role of remote e-work intensity (i.e. the amount of scheduled working days an individual spends working outside the conventional workplace) to disentangle the implications of this work mode on work-related stress and job satisfaction. Notwithstanding, the evidence does not show a consistent pattern. For instance, Gajendran and Harrison [15], Fonner and Roloff [14] and Suh and Lee [29] suggest that job satisfaction increases with the intensity of remote e-work, while work-related stress decreases. In contrast, Golden and Veiga [19] and Golden [17] find an inverted-U shaped relationship between the intensity of remote e-work and job satisfaction, while Konradt, Hertel and Schmook [24] report no significant difference in levels of work-related stress between high- and low-intensity remote e-workers.

The overemphasis on remote e-work intensity has led scholars to neglect another variable that may affect working conditions and their implications on work well-being—the type of remote location where individuals work (home versus the field, the customer's premises, mobile locations such as cars and planes, public spaces like airports and cafes). One notable exception is Vartiainen and Hyrkkänen's [34] qualitative study which suggests that the higher the mobility, the higher the individual's perception of work-related stress and the lower their job satisfaction. Accordingly, we hypothesize that:

H1: Mobile e-workers are likely to experience higher levels of work-related stress and lower levels of job satisfaction than home-based e-workers and office-based ones.

The last above-mentioned study also suggests that the working conditions affecting work-related stress and job satisfaction are likely to differ depending on the type of remote location. However, with only a few exceptions (e.g. [9], quantitative research investigating the issue is quite rare. Therefore, in order to provide further evidence, we develop hypotheses on the specific working conditions that may explain work-related stress and job satisfaction of home-based and mobile e-workers drawing on the existing literature on remote e-work. Paying no attention to the remote location question, this literature implicitly suggests that the determinants of work-related stress and job satisfaction are uniform across the two types of remote e-workers. On the contrary, if our hypothesis is correct, it could be expected that not all the hypotheses confirmed by existing research on remote e-work would hold on when tested separately for home-based and mobile e-workers or that at least some differences between the most significant working conditions of the two groups would emerge.

Much of the literature points to job autonomy and work intensification as the major determinants of work well-being in the context of remote e-work.

More specifically, research confirms that compared to traditional workers, remote e-workers have greater organizational discretion in the choice of their work location, working schedules and pace, as well as working methods [15, 16]. Several authors argue that this may have positive effects reducing work-related stress and simultaneously increasing job satisfaction [19, 21, 26, 27, 28, 31, 33].

Remote e-workers also enjoy organizational autonomy in the choice regarding their work goals, colleagues and the organization of their department or company [1], and some scholars suggest that remote e-workers direct participation in setting their work goals reduces their experience of stress at work, simultaneously increasing job satisfaction [24].

Moreover, some evidence points to the beneficial effects of involvement in autonomous work groups, promoted by the most advanced information and communication technologies (hereinafter, ICTs), which allow remote e-workers to exchange high-quality and timely information regardless of their physical work location [14, 30, 31, 32].

Drawing on the above arguments, we test the following:

H2a: Organizational discretion and autonomy negatively relate to perception of work-related stress among home-based and mobile e-workers.
H2b: Organizational discretion and autonomy positively relate to job satisfaction of home-based and mobile e-workers.

On the other hand, research indicates that remote e-work is also characterized by increased work intensification. Frequent work interruptions are a key source of work intensification, driven by ease of connectivity increased by new digital technologies, which convey unexpected incoming e-mails and messages requiring the worker to interrupt the tasks he is working on to take on other urgent ones [2, 6 , 31, 36]. Ease of connectivity can also rise the expectation of permanent availability among co-workers, bosses and clients [4, 25, 29]. This blurs the boundaries between work and private life, leading remote e-workers to work longer hours, during free time and not have time to recover from work [18, 20, 13]. Working to tight deadlines is another source of work intensification frequently reported by remote e-workers [35]. Combined with others' expectation of constant accessibility and increased responsiveness, this may produce an environment where setting one's pace of work to adapt to a greater number of external demands (i.e. time pressure) and working at very high speed become the rule for remote e-workers. All the above aspects are likely to increase work-related stress among remote e-workers, thereby simultaneously reducing their job satisfaction as well [14, 29].

Drawing on these considerations, we hypothesize the following:

H3a: Work intensification positively relates to perception of work-related stress among home-based and mobile e-workers.
H3b: Work intensification negatively relates to home-based and mobile e-workers' job satisfaction.

3   Method

3.1   Data and Sample

This study draws on data from the 6th wave of the European Working Conditions Survey (EWCS) [11] carried out in 2015 in a random sample of 44,000 workers (employees and self-employed) in 35 European countries. In this study, the sample is restricted to 1,380 home-based e-workers and 2,574 mobile e-workers, who represent 3.15 and 5.87% of the whole sample, respectively.

The first group includes workers who work with ICTs "all of the time" or "almost all of the time" and work at home several times per month, and almost never at other remote locations (i.e. clients' premises, cars, an outside site and public spaces such as airports). Contrarily, the second group includes workers who usually work with ICTs and work at one or more other locations than the conventional workplace several times a month and almost never at home.

The 58% of home-based e-workers and 53% of mobile ones are in the 35–54 age group. More than 80% in both groups work as employees with a full-time contract and mainly in the tertiary sector (around 66%). Only 12% of workers in both groups are managers.

The 54% of home-based e-workers are women. The 21% of them are from UK, the 17% from France, the 8% from Germany, the 8% from Spain and the 2% from Italy. The 63% of workers in this group have a level of education higher than the bachelor's degree and the 41% of them work in large enterprises with more than 250 employees, mainly as professionals (56%).

Contrarily, the 63% of mobile e-workers are men. The 16% of them are from UK, the 15% from France, the 12% from Germany, the 8% from Spain and the 5% from Italy. The 42% of workers in this group have a level of education higher than the bachelor's degree. Moreover, the 40% of them work in medium-large businesses with 10 to 249 employees. The 28% of mobile e-workers are professionals and 25% are technicians and associate professionals.

Compared to office-based e-workers (i.e. workers who work daily at the company's premises and almost never at other remote locations, including home, using ICTs "all of the time" or "almost all of the time"), home-based and mobile e-workers have greater discretion over several aspects of their work. Specifically, the 70% of home-based e-workers and 68% of mobile ones have discretion over work pace against the 45% of office-based e-workers. They also more frequently declare to have discretion in the choice of their work methods (the 82% of home-based e-workers and 64% of mobile ones versus the 49% of office-based e-workers). However, both groups of remote e-workers suffer from greater work intensification than office-based e-workers, especially due to frequent work interruptions (around 45% versus 40%) and the demand to work in their free time (more than 30% versus 15%).

Within the remote e-workers' group, the 63% of home-based e-workers have autonomy over work goals (versus 55% of mobile ones), and the 82% of them have discretion over work methods (versus 64% of mobile e-workers). However, home-based e-workers more frequently work in their free time than mobile ones (59% versus 30%). On the other hand, the 50% of mobile e-workers enjoy greater discretion over work schedule (versus 30% of home-based e-workers), but they are also subject to a greater number of time pressures (42% of mobile e-workers versus 30% of home-based ones), and more frequently report to work at high speed and to tight deadlines (51 versus 45%).

Work-related stress seems to increase as mobility increases. The 75% of home-based e-workers and mobile e-workers experience stress at work at least sometimes compared to the 70% of office-based e-workers. Moreover, 31% of home-based e-workers and 36% of mobile ones feel stressed most of the time or always compared to the 29% of office-based e-workers. In contrast, there are only slight differences in the levels of job satisfaction between the three groups: around 50% of mobile e-workers are satisfied with their working conditions compared to the 51% of home-based e-workers and the 50% of office-based e-workers.

3.2 Measures

Work-related stress. It is measured by an item assessing how often the worker experiences stress during work (1 = Never; 5 = Always).

Job satisfaction. It is the mean of the z-scores of five items assessing the worker's perception that work is distributed fairly (1 = Strongly disagree to 5 = Strongly agree); the overall satisfaction with the working conditions in the main paid job (1 = Not at all satisfied to 4 = Very satisfied); the worker's perception that he gets paid appropriately (1 = Strongly disagree to 5 = Strongly agree); he receives the recognition he deserves for his work (1 = Strongly disagree to 5 = Strongly agree); the job offers good prospects for career advancement (1 = Strongly disagree to 5 = Strongly agree).

Involvement in autonomous work groups. It is measured by a binary item assessing whether the worker works in a team that has common tasks and can plan its work.

Autonomy over work goals. It is measured by an item assessing how often the worker participates in goal setting (1 = Never; 5 = Always).

Autonomy in the choice of work colleagues. It is measured by an item assessing how often the worker can choose his own colleagues (1 = Never; 5 = Always).

Autonomy in the organizational choices of one's department/company. It is measured by an item assessing how often the worker is involved in the choices regarding the organization of his department/company ((1 = Never; 5 = Always).

Discretion over work methods. It is the mean of the z-scores of four binary items assessing whether the worker can (1) assess himself the quality of his work; (2) solve unforeseen problems on his own; (3) choose/change the order of tasks and (4) the methods of work, as well as of a variable assessing how often the worker can apply his ideas into his work (1 = Never; 5 = Always).

Discretion over work pace. It is the mean of the z-scores of a dummy variable assessing if the worker can change/choose the speed/rate of work, as well as of a variable assessing how often he can take a break when he wishes (1 = Never; 5 = Always).

Discretion over work schedule. It is measured by a dummy variable with 1 = the worker can choose his work schedule within certain limits.

Working at very high speed/to tight deadlines. It is the mean of the z-scores of three items assessing if the worker's job involves 1) working at high speed or 2) to tight deadlines (1 = Never; 7 = all of the time) and 3) if the worker has enough time to do his job (1 = Always; 5 = Never).

Time pressure. It is the mean of five dummy variables assessing whether the worker's pace of work depends on (1) demands from customers, (2) from colleagues, (3) from the superior, (4) performance or productivity targets, (5) the speed of a machine/movement of a product.

Frequent work interruptions. It is measured by an item assessing how often the worker has to deal with work interruptions (1 = Never; 4 = Very often).

Long working hours. It is measured by a continuous variable assessing how many times a month the worker works more than 10 hours per day.

Working in one's free time. It is measured by an item assessing how often the individual works in his free time to meet work demands (1 = Never; 5 = Daily).

Lack of recovery time. A binary item assessing if the worker has had less than 11 hours to recovery after work at least once in the last month.

Controls. Several demographic and employment variables (i.e. age, gender, education, employment contract and occupation, sector), as well as other organizational variables (i.e. supervisor and co-workers' support, having undergone some forms of training, on the job learning, being subject to variable pay schemes, perceived skill match and task complexity) are included in the analysis based on their potential link to the study variables (e.g. see [2, 5, 8, 15, 26, 33]).

3.3 Analytic Approach

We compute OLS regressions for work-related stress and job satisfaction including in each model dummy variables representing different groups of e-workers: office-based e-workers, the home-based and the mobile e-workers. On the one hand, this allows us to assess if being a member of these groups is significantly related to the levels of work-related stress and job satisfaction, and on the other hand if the last two vary as a function of the type of remote location. Finally, it permits to test if these e-workers' groups are significantly different with respect to the other types of workers in the EWCS whole sample.

To determine if the influence of organizational autonomy and discretion as well as of work intensification on work-related stress and job satisfaction vary depending on the type of remote location, we also estimate multiple OLS regressions for home-based and mobile e-workers separately, following a general to specific strategy to

Table 1 Work-related stress and job satisfaction of office-based workers, home-based e-workers and mobile e-workers compared to the EWCS whole sample of workers. OLS regressions

Regressors	Work-related stress	Job satisfaction
Constant	2.81***	−0,04***
	(0,008)	(0.005)
Office-based e-workers	0.17***	0.14***
	(0.016)	(0.01)
Home-based e-workers	0.28***	0.19***
	(0.032)	(0.02)
Mobile e-workers	0.38***	0.15***
	(0.024)	(0.016)
Number of observations	44,000	44,000

Notes Office-based e-workers is a dummy = 1 when workers use ICTs intensively and work daily at the company's premises and almost never in other remote locations, including home, and = 0 otherwise; $N = 6,710$. Home-based e-workers is a dummy = 1 when workers use ICTs intensively and work several times a month at home and almost never in other remote locations, and = 0 otherwise; $N = 1,380$. Mobile e-workers is a dummy = 1 when workers use ICTs intensively and work in one or more other locations than the conventional workplace several times a month and almost never at home, and = 0 otherwise, $N = 2,574$. ***, **, * denote 1, 5 and 10% significance level, respectively. Robust standard errors in parenthesis. Standardized coefficients are reported

obtain parsimonious models explaining work-related stress and job satisfactions, respectively. These final models are optimal in terms of explained variance (adjusted R square) and they have no multi-collinearity problems among regressors (VIF factor < 10) [7].[1] We use SPSS to perform the above analyses.

4 Results

Hypothesis 1 suggests that mobile e-workers are likely to experience higher levels of stress at work and to be less satisfied with their working conditions than home-based e-workers and office-based ones. Note that descriptive statistics show that work-related stress increases linearly as the degree of mobility increases whereas there are only slight differences in the levels of job satisfaction of office-based, home-based and mobile e-workers. Therefore, to test the hypothesis that the type of work location affects work-related stress and job satisfaction, we compute OLS regressions to assess whether work-related stress and job satisfaction levels of mobile, home-based and office-based e-workers are significantly different from those reported by the other workers in the EWCS whole sample. Table 1 outlines that all the three groups are statically different compared to the whole sample (at 1% significance level) with respect to work-related stress. The magnitude of the coefficients suggests

---

[1] The outcome of this reduction strategy is available on request. In the following section, we only report the findings for the optimal specifications.

that greater mobility corresponds to higher levels of stress: office-based workers have the lower level of work-related stress while mobile e-workers are the most stressed. The findings for job satisfaction are also all significant (at 1% significance level), indicating that the three groups are statistically different from the workers of the whole sample also in terms of job satisfaction. The magnitude of the coefficients indicates that the level of job satisfaction is greater for the group of home-based e-workers and lower for mobile e-workers. Hence, satisfaction increases non-linearly as the level of mobility increases.

The above results suggest that perception of work-related stress increases as the level of mobility increases, while satisfaction does not grow in the same linear way. This finding provides support for the hypothesis that work-related stress and job satisfaction vary as a function of the type of remote location. The above findings also highlight that home-based e-workers are more stressed as well as more satisfied than office-based ones, suggesting that higher levels of work-related stress do not necessarily correspond to lower levels of job satisfaction.

Tables 2 and 3 show the optimal models explaining work-related stress and job satisfaction for home-based and mobile e-workers, respectively. All the coefficients are also standardized. In this way, we compare the magnitude of the coefficients and their capacity to explain the dependent variable: a high value of a coefficient describes a high impact on the dependent variable considered. The variance inflation factor (VIF) of each regressor in all models suggests no multi-collinearity problem.

Gender, education, age and other employment variables explain less than 1% of the work-related stress and less than 2% of the job satisfaction perceived by home-based and mobile e-workers. For this reason, we do not report the estimated coefficients for these controls.

Regarding the organizational control variables, the supervisor's support reduces work-related stress and increases job satisfaction among both home-based e-workers (for stress $stand\beta = -0.079, p \leq 0.05$ and for satisfaction $stand\beta = 0.42, p \leq 0.01$) and mobile e-workers (for stress $stand\beta = -0.095, p \leq 0.01$ and for satisfaction $stand\beta = 0.39, p \leq 0.01$). For home-based e-workers, the colleagues' support only increases job satisfaction ($stand\beta = 0.089, p \leq 0.01$), while for mobile e-workers, it has beneficial effects on both work-related stress ($stand\beta = -0.08, p \leq 0.01$) and job satisfaction ($stand\beta = 0.172, p \leq 0.01$). Task complexity increases the level of work-related stress of both groups (for home-based e-workers, $stand\beta = 0.09, p \leq 0.01$, and for mobile e-workers, $stand\beta = 0.076, p \leq 0.01$) and reduces the job satisfaction of home-based e-workers ($stand\beta = -0.043, p \leq 0.10$). On the job, learning increases the job satisfaction of home-based e-workers ($stand\beta = 0.039, p \leq 0.10$), while the perceived skill match reduces work-related stress among mobile e-workers ($stand\beta = -0.056, p \leq 0.05$). Variable pay schemes is also relevant to increase the job satisfaction of mobile e-workers ($stand\beta = 0.054, p \leq 0.01$).

H2a states that organizational discretion and autonomy negatively relate to perception of work-related stress among home-based and mobile e-workers. Table 2 shows that discretion over work pace ($stand\beta = -0.14, p \leq 0.01$), discretion over work schedule ($stand\beta = -0.085, p \leq 0.05$) and autonomy over work goals ($stand\beta = -0.073, p \leq 0.10$) have statistically significant effects, reducing work-related

Table 2 Determinants of work-related stress and job satisfaction among home-based e-workers

Regressors	Work-related stress		Job satisfaction	
	β	Stand.β	B	Stand.β
Autonomy over work goals	− 0.057* (0.029)	−0.073	0.078*** (0.016)	0.151
Discretion over work methods	0.112 (0.087)	0.046	0.008 (0.046)	0.007
Discretion over work pace	− 0.196*** (0.051)	-0.140	0.094*** (0.028)	0.100
Autonomy in the choice of work colleagues	0.016 (0.024)	0.022	0.028** (0.012)	0.059
Involvement in autonomous work groups	0.15** (0.069)	0.066	− 0.099*** (0.036)	−0.062
Autonomy in the organizational choices of one's department/company	0.034 (0.032)	0.041	0.016 (0.018)	0.026
Discretion over work schedule	−0.181** (0.072)	−0.085	0.143*** (0.039)	0.101
Working at high speed/to tight deadlines	0.214*** (0.062)	0.113	0.072** (0.032)	0.056
Time pressure	0.200 (0.131)	0.047	− 0.15** (0.074)	-0.050
Frequent work interruptions	0.182*** (0.036)	0.163	− 0.067*** (0.021)	-0.092
Long working hours	− 0.002 (0.0025)	−0.024	0.002 (0.001)	0.033
Working during free time	0.150*** (0.03)	0.167	− 0.035** (0.017)	-0.059
Lack of recovery time	0.114 (0.070)	0.051	− 0.089** (0.039)	-0.060
Supervisor's support	− 0.09** (0.04)	-0.079	0.339*** (0.025)	0.421
Colleagues' support	− 0.085 (0.057)	−0.050	0.102*** (0.032)	0.089
Complex tasks	0.260*** (0.087)	0.090	− 0.082* (0.044)	-0.043
On the job learning	− 0.147 (0.157)	−0.033	0.117* (0.069)	0.039
Skill match	− 0.068 (0.055)	-0.040	0.002 (0.024)	0.001
Training	− 0.039 (0.071)	−0.016	− 0.021 (0.038)	-0.013
Variable pay	0.016 (0.064)	0.007	0.047 (0.035)	0.032
Adjusted R^2	0.20		0.45	

(continued)

Table 2 (continued)

Regressors	Work-related stress		Job satisfaction	
	β	Stand.β	B	Stand.β
F-test (p-value)	0.24		0.71	

Notes Standβ: standardized coefficients. ***$p \leq 0.01$; **$p \leq 0.05$; *$p \leq 0.1$. Robust standard errors in parenthesis. F test for the null that all single non-significant coefficients are also jointly not relevant. Demographic and employment controls are also included. VIF always < 1.49

stress among home-based e-workers. Unexpectedly, involvement in autonomous work teams positively relates to home-based e-workers' experienced level of stress at work (stand$\beta = 0.066$, $p \leq 0.05$). This result is consistent with prior research, which suggests that working as part of an autonomous team may be frustrating for remote e-workers as they heavily rely on standardized communication to interact with others, which is unsuitable for the ongoing dynamic interaction and exchange of tacit knowledge that typically characterize autonomous teamwork [19]. For mobile e-workers, Table 3 indicates that discretion over work pace (stand$\beta = -0.129$, $p \leq 0.01$) is the only dimension that significantly reduces work-related stress. Thus, hypothesis 2a is only partially supported for this group.

H2b suggests that organizational discretion and autonomy positively relate to job satisfaction of home-based and mobile e-workers. As shown in Table 2 and 3, except for involvement in autonomous work teams, which significantly reduces job satisfaction of both groups (stand$\beta = -0.062$, $p \leq 0.01$ among home-based e-workers; stand$\beta = -0.035$, $p \leq 0.05$ among mobile ones), there are several dimensions of organizational autonomy and discretion that positively and significantly affect job satisfaction in both groups. For home-based e-workers, the most relevant variables are autonomy over work goals (stand$\beta = 0.151$, $p \leq 0.01$), discretion over work pace (stand$\beta = 0.10$, $p \leq 0.01$), discretion over work schedule (stand$\beta = 0.10$, $p \leq 0.01$) and autonomy in the choice of work colleagues (stand$\beta = 0.059$, $p \leq 0.05$). For mobile e-workers, besides autonomy over work goals (stand$\beta = 0.10$, $p \leq 0.01$), autonomy in the choice of work colleagues (stand$\beta = 0.096$, $p \leq 0.01$), and discretion over work pace (stand$\beta = 0.064$, $p \leq 0.01$), autonomy in the choices regarding the organization of one's department/company (stand$\beta = 0.075$, $p \leq 0.01$) and discretion over work methods (stand$\beta = 0.048$, $p \leq 0.05$) also have statistically significant effects. In contrast, discretion over work schedule is not statistically significant.

H3a proposes a positive relationship between work intensification and work-related stress for both home-based and mobile e-workers. Table 2 shows that working in one's free time (stand$\beta = 0.167$, $p \leq 0.01$), frequent work interruptions (stand$\beta = 0.163$, $p \leq 0.01$), and working at high speed and to tight deadlines (stand$\beta = 0.113$, $p \leq 0.01$) are the work intensification dimensions with the most significant influence on home-based e-workers' perception of work-related stress. For mobile e-workers (Table 3), besides working at high speed and to tight deadlines (stand$\beta = 0.128$, $p \leq 0.01$), frequent work interruptions (stand$\beta = 0.165$, $p \leq 0.01$), and working in one's free time (stand$\beta = 0.09$, $p \leq 0.01$), time pressure (stand$\beta = 0.075$, $p \leq 0.01$) and

Table 3 Determinants of work-related stress and job satisfaction among mobile e-workers

Regressors	Work-related stress		Job satisfaction	
	β	Stand.β	β	Stand.β
Autonomy over work goals	− 0.016 (0.021)	−0.020	0.054*** (0.011)	0.101
Discretion over work methods	0.006 (0.058)	0.003	0.068** (0.032)	0.048
Discretion over work pace	− 0.187*** (0.036)	−0.129	0.062*** (0.020)	0.064
Autonomy in the choice of work colleagues	0.01 (0.018)	0.014	0.047*** (0.01)	0.096
Involvement in autonomous work groups	− 0.055 (0.053)	−0.023	− 0.057** (0.028)	−0.035
Autonomy in the organizational choices of one's department/company	0.023 (0.023)	0.027	0.043*** (0.013)	0.075
Discretion over work schedule	−0.075 (0.049)	−0.034	0.042 (0.026)	0.027
Working at high speed/to tight deadlines	0.240*** (0.042)	0.128	−0.008 (0.022)	−0.006
Time pressure	0.320*** (0.095)	0.075	−0.139*** (0.051)	−0.048
Frequent work interruptions	0.195*** (0.028)	0.165	−0.112*** (0.015)	−0.139
Long working hours	0.001 (0.002)	0.013	−0.001 (0.001)	−0.021
Working during free time	0.096*** (0.024)	0.090	−0.040*** (0.014)	−0.055
Lack of recovery time	0.148*** (0.054)	0.059	−0.005 (0.029)	−0.003
Supervisor's support	− 0.113*** (0.031)	−0.095	0.32*** (0.020)	0.393
Colleagues' support	− 0.138*** (0.043)	−0.080	0.201*** (0.024)	0.172
Complex tasks	0.208*** (0.063)	0.076	0.021 (0.032)	0.011
On the job learning	− 0.103 (0.083)	−0.030	− 0.060 (0.043)	−0.026
Skill match	− 0.090** (0.035)	−0.056	0.012 (0.020)	0.012
Training	− 0.012 (0.054)	−0.005	0.034 (0.027)	0.020
Variable pay	− 0.061 (0.047)	−0.027	0.083*** (0.025)	0.054
Adjusted R^2	0.16		0.47	

(continued)

Table 3 (continued)

	Work-related stress		Job satisfaction	
Regressors	β	Stand.β	β	Stand.β
F-test (p-value)	0.55		0.48	

Notes Standβ: standardized coefficients. ***$p \leq 0.01$; **$p \leq 0.05$; *$p \leq 0.1$. Robust standard errors in parenthesis. F test for the null that all single non-significant coefficients are also jointly not relevant. Demographic and employment controls are also included. VIF always < 1.7

lack of recovery time (stand$\beta = 0.059$, $p \leq 0.01$) also have an influence on work-related stress. Thus, the detrimental effects of work intensification on work-related stress appear stronger among mobile e-workers than among home-based e-workers.

Finally, H3b points to the negative influence of work intensification on job satisfaction in both groups. Table 2 reports the results for home-based e-workers, showing that frequent work interruptions (stand$\beta = -0.092$, $p \leq 0.01$), lack of recovery time (stand$\beta = -0.060$, $p \leq 0.05$), working in one's free time (stand$\beta = -0.059$, $p \leq 0.05$), and time pressure (stand$\beta = -0.050$, $p \leq 0.05$) are the most significant work intensification variables reducing job satisfaction in this group. Unexpectedly, we also find that working at high speed and to tight deadlines have a beneficial influence, increasing job satisfaction among home-based e-workers (stand$\beta = 0.056$, $p \leq 0.05$). For mobile e-workers, three dimensions have a significant negative effect. Namely, frequent work interruptions (stand$\beta = -0.139$, $p \leq 0.01$), followed by working in one's free time (stand$\beta = -0.055$, $p \leq 0.01$), and time pressure (stand$\beta = -0.048$, $p \leq 0.01$) (Table 3).

5 Discussion, Implications and Future Research Directions

This study contributes to the debate on the current trajectories of the micro-level organizational transformations associated with the use of new digital technologies, offering a more nuanced understanding of the implications of remote e-work on work well-being, and specifically on work-related stress and job satisfaction. Overall, this research adds to existing knowledge in three ways.

Firstly, it supports the hypothesis that the type of remote location is a key variable to understand the way remote e-work affects work-related stress and job satisfaction. With only a few exceptions, extant research devotes no attention to the remote location question, implicitly suggesting that work well-being and its determinants are uniform across home-based and mobile e-workers. In contrast, our findings show that work-related stress increases and job satisfaction slightly decreases as mobility of remote e-workers increases. Thus, among remote e-workers, mobile ones are those who suffer most from the detrimental effects of working away from the company premises, especially in terms of work-related stress. Our study also highlights that the role played by organizational autonomy and discretion as well as work intensification differs as a function of the remote location. More specifically, compared to home-based e-workers, mobile ones perceive a greater number of work intensification dimensions as drivers of work-related stress, some of which (i.e. frequent work interruptions, working during one's free time and time pressure) also have a significant negative impact on job satisfaction. Moreover, we find that several dimensions of autonomy and discretions have beneficial effects on home-based e-workers (i.e. autonomy over work goals and discretion in the choice of their work pace and work schedule), simultaneously increasing job satisfaction and reducing work-related stress. In contrast, except for discretion over work pace, the other autonomy and discretion variables that significantly increase job satisfaction among mobile e-workers (i.e. autonomy over work goals, in the choice of work colleagues and in the organizational choices of ones' department/company, as well as discretion over work methods) have no significant beneficial effects on their levels of work-related stress.

A second contribution of this study has to do with the conceptualization of work well-being prevalent in the literature on remote e-work. More specifically, this study shows that home-based e-workers feel more stressed but also more satisfied than office-based e-workers. Moreover, we find that a key dimension of work intensification, i.e. working at high speed and to tight deadlines, simultaneously increases work-related stress and job satisfaction of home-based e-workers. Finally, our results underline that there are several organizational discretion and autonomy variables, which increase job satisfaction of mobile e-workers but have no beneficial effect on their work-related stress. Overall, these results might question the not problematized hypothesis in the literature on remote e-work that work-related stress and job satisfaction are two tightly related dimensions consistently reflecting the individual's well-being at work, suggesting the need to explore alternative conceptualizations to analyse work well-being in digital workplaces.

Thirdly, using representative data at European level, this contribution offers insights into the European organizations' ability to leverage the opportunity opened up by new digital technologies to shape novel work practices that not only benefit organizational performance but also meet their organizational members' needs. It seems that organizations across Europe have been able to adopt remote e-work practices that increase the job satisfaction of their employees, but they are lagging behind in terms of the prevention of work-related stress risks associated with this work mode, especially among mobile e-workers. Our results suggest to organizations that want to fill this gap to focus primarily on work intensification. Rather than a blanket approach, however, organizations should develop strategies considering the differences between the sources of work intensification in the two groups of home-based and mobile e-workers. Consistently, eliminating or reducing work interruptions and the demand to work at high speed and to tight deadlines should be a top priority to reduce work intensification among mobile e-workers, while for home-based ones, it could also be important to eliminate or reduce the demand of working in one's free time.

The contributions of this study should be viewed in light of some limitations, which represent avenues for future research. First, we used self-reported data collected from a single respondent at a single moment in time. Consequently, reverse causality and common-method bias might be issues. Future research could address these points by adopting a longitudinal research design and gathering additional data on the dependent and independent variables from other sources. Another limitation is that we used a single item to measure work-related stress. Therefore, it could be interesting to replicate this study using multiple-items to assess home-based and mobile e-workers experience of stress at work. We also encourage future studies to test whether the institutional settings of different European countries may influence the way in which organizations shape remote e-work practices, thereby affecting working conditions of home-based and mobile e-workers and their implications on work well-being.

Acknowledgements The authors gratefully acknowledge financial support from the grant FAR2019 (awarded by the University of Modena and Reggio Emilia, Italy).

References

1. Albano, R., Curzi, Y., Parisi, T., & Tirabeni, L. (2018). Perceived autonomy and discretion of mobile workers. *Studi Organizzativi, 2,* 31–61.
2. Allen, T. D., Golden, T. D., & Shockley, K. M. (2015). How effective is telecommuting? Assessing the status of our scientific findings. *Psychological Science in the Public Interest, 16*(2), 40–68.
3. Bailey, D. E., & Kurland, N. B. (2002). A review of telework research: Findings, new directions, and lessons for the study of modern work. *Journal of Organizational Behavior, 23,* 383–400.
4. Cavazotte, F., Lemos, A. H., & Villadsen, K. (2014). Corporate smart phones: Professionals' conscious engagement in escalating work connectivity. *New Technology, Work and Employment, 29*(1), 72–87.
5. Charalampous, M., Grant, C. A., Tramontano, C., & Michailidis, E. (2018). Systematically reviewing remote e-workers' well-being at work: A multidimensional approach. *European Journal of Work and Organizational Psychology.* https://doi.org/10.1080/1359432X.2018.154 1886,lastaccessed2020/06/14
6. Chesley, N. (2014). Information and communication technology use, work intensification and employee strain and distress. *Work, Employment and Society, 28*(4), 589–610.
7. Cohen, J., Cohen, P., West, S. G., & Aiken, L. S. (2003). *Applied multiple regression/correlation analysis for the behavioral sciences* (3rd ed.). Lawrence Erlbaum Associates.
8. Curzi, Y., Fabbri, T., & Pistoresi, B. (2020). Performance appraisal criteria and innovative work behaviour: the mediating role of employees' appraisal satisfaction. In T. Addabbo, E. Ales, Y. Curzi, T. Fabbri, O. Rymkevich, I. Senatori (Eds.), *Performance appraisal in modern employment relations:An interdisciplinary approach* (pp. 11–34). Palgrave Macmillan.
9. Curzi, Y., Fabbri, T., & Pistoresi, B. (2020). The stressful implications of remote e-working: Evidence from Europe. *International Journal of Business and Management, 15*(7), 108–119.
10. Eurofound, & The International Labour Office. (2017). Working anytime, anywhere: The effects on the world of work. Publications Office of the European Union, Luxembourg, and the International Labour Office, Geneva.
11. European Foundation for the Improvement of Living and Working Conditions. (2017). *European working conditions survey, 2015.* (3rd ed.). UK Data Archive, Colchester, Essex, SN: 8098.

12. Fabbri, T. (2018). Digital work: An organizational perspective. In E. Ales, Y. Curzi, T. Fabbri, O. Rymkevich, I. Senatori, & G. Solinas (Eds.), *Working in digital and smart organizations: Legal, economic and organizational perspectives on the digitalization of labour relations* (pp. 29–38). Palgrave Macmillan.

13. Felstead, A., & Henseke, G. (2017). Assessing the growth of remote working and its consequences for effort, well-being and work-life balance. *New Technology, Work and Employment, 32*(3), 195–212.

14. Fonner, K. L., & Roloff, M. E. (2010). Why teleworkers are more satisfied with their jobs than are office-based workers: When less contact is beneficial. *Journal of Applied Communication Research, 38*(4), 336–361.

15. Gajendran, R. S., & Harrison, D. A. (2007). The good, the bad, and the unknown about telecommuting: Meta-analysis of psychological mediators and individual consequences. *Journal of Applied Psychology, 92*(6), 1524–1541.

16. Gajendran, R. S., Harrison, D. A., & Delaney-Klinger, K. (2015). Are telecommuters remotely good citizens? Unpacking telecommuting's effects on performance via i-deals and job resources. *Personnel Psychology, 68*, 353–393.

17. Golden, T. D. (2006). The role of relationships in understanding telecommuter satisfaction. *Journal of Organizational Behavior, 27*, 319–340.

18. Golden, T. D. (2012). Altering the effects of work and family conflict on exhaustion: Telework during traditional and nontraditional work hours. *Journal of Business and Psychology, 27*, 255–269.

19. Golden, T. D., & Veiga, J. F. (2005). The impact of extent of telecommuting on job satisfaction: Resolving inconsistent findings. *Journal of Management, 31*(2), 301–318.

20. Grant, C. A., Wallace, L. M., & Spurgeon, P. C. (2013). An exploration of the psychological factors affecting remote e-worker's job effectiveness, well-being and work-life balance. *Employee Relations, 35*(5), 527–546.

21. Hornung, S., & Glaser, J. (2009). Home-based telecommuting and quality of life: Further evidence on an employee-oriented human resource practice. *Psychological Reports, 104*(2), 395–402.

22. Karasek, R. (1979). Job demands, job decision latitude, and mental strain: Implications for job redesign. *Administrative Science Quarterly, 24*(2), 285–308.

23. Kelliher, C., & Anderson, D. (2010). Doing more with less? Flexible working practices and the intensification of work. *Human Relations, 63*(1), 83–106.

24. Konradt, U., Hertel, G., & Schmook, R. (2003). Quality of management by objectives, task-related stressors, and non-task-related stressors as predictors of stress and job satisfaction among teleworkers. *European Journal of Work and Organizational Psychology, 12*(1), 61–79.

25. Mazmanian, M., Orlikowski, W. J., & Yates, J. (2013). The autonomy paradox. The implications of mobile devices for knowledge professionals. *Organization Science 24*(5), 1337–1357.

26. Nijp, H. H., Beckers, D. G. J., van de Voorde, K., Geurts, S. A. E., & Kompier, M. A. J. (2016). Effects of new ways of working on work hours and work location, health and job-related outcomes. *Chronobiology International, 33*(6), 604–618.

27. O'Neill, T. A., Hambley, L. A., Greidanus, N. S., MacDonnell, R., & Kline, T. J. (2009). Predicting teleworker success: An exploration of personality, motivational, situational, and job characteristics. *New Technology, Work and Employment, 24*(2), 144–162.

28. Sardeshmukh, S. R., Sharma, D., & Golden, T. D. (2012). Impact of telework on exhaustion and job engagement: A job demands and job resources model. *New Technology, Work and Employment, 27*(3), 193–207.

29. Suh, A., & Lee, J. (2017). Understanding teleworkers' technostress and its influence on job satisfaction. *Internet Research, 27*(1), 140–159.

30. Ten Brummelhuis, L. L., Bakker, A. B., Hetland, J., & Keulemans, L. (2012). Do new ways of working foster work engagement? *Psicothema, 24*(1), 113–120.

31. Ter Hoeven, C. L., & van Zoonen, W. (2015). Flexible work designs and employee well-being: Examining the effects of resources and demands. *New Technology, Work and Employment, 30*(3), 237–255.

32. Ter Hoeven, C. L., van Zoonen, W., & Fonner, K. L. (2016). The practical paradox of technology: The influence of communication technology use on employee burnout and engagement. *Communication Monographs, 83*(2), 239–263.
33. Van Steenbergen, E. F., van der Ven, C., Peeters, M. C. W., & Taris, T. W. (2018). Transitioning towards new ways of working: Do job demands, job resources, burnout, and engagement change? *Psychological Reports, 121*(4), 736–766.
34. Vartiainen, M., & Hyrkkänen, U. (2010). Changing requirements and mental workload factors in mobile multi-locational work. *New Technology, Work and Employment, 25*(2), 117–135.
35. Vendramin, P. (2007). Les métiers des TIC: Un nomadisme coopératif. In A. F. Saint Laurent-Kogan & J. L. Metzger (Eds.), *Où va le travail à l'ère du numérique?* (pp. 89–104). Presses Des Mines.
36. Vendramin, P., & Valenduc G. (2016). Le travail virtuel. Nouvelles formes d'emploi et de travail dans l'économie digitale, working paper. http://hdl.handle.net/2078.1/174224. Last Accessed 14 June 2020.

Work Datafication and Digital Work Behavior Analysis as a Source of HRM Insights

Tommaso Fabbri, Anna Chiara Scapolan, Fabiola Bertolotti, Federica Mandreoli, and Riccardo Martoglia

Abstract The digital transformation of organizations is boosting workplace networking and collaboration while making it "observable" with unprecedented timeliness and detail. However, the informational and managerial potential of work datafication is still largely unutilized in human resource management (HRM) and its benefits, both at the individual and the organizational level, remain largely unexplored. Our research focuses on the relationship between digitally tracked work behaviors and employee attitudes and, in so doing, it explores work datafication as a source of data-driven HRM policies and practices. As a chapter of a wider research program, this paper presents some data analysis we performed on a collection of enterprise collaboration software (ECS) data, in search for promising correlations between behavioral and relational (digital) work patterns and employee attitudes. To this end, the digital actions performed by 106 employees in one year are transformed into a graph representation in order to analyze data under two different points of view: the individual (behavioral) perspective, according to the user who performed the action and the performed action, and the social (relational) perspective, making explicit the interactions between users and the objects of their actions. Different employees' rankings are thus derived and correlated with their attitudes. Finally, we discuss the obtained results and their implications in terms of people analytics and data-driven HRM.

T. Fabbri · A. C. Scapolan (✉) · F. Bertolotti · F. Mandreoli · R. Martoglia
University of Modena and Reggio Emilia, Modena, Italy
e-mail: annachiara.scapolan@unimore.it

T. Fabbri
e-mail: tommaso.fabbri@unimore.it

F. Bertolotti
e-mail: fabiola.bertolotti@unimore.it

F. Mandreoli
e-mail: federica.mandreoli@unimore.it

R. Martoglia
e-mail: riccardo.martoglia@unimore.it

© The Author(s), under exclusive license to Springer Nature Switzerland AG 2022
L. Solari et al. (eds.), *Do Machines Dream of Electric Workers?*, Lecture Notes in Information Systems and Organisation 49,
https://doi.org/10.1007/978-3-030-83321-3_4

Keywords Work datafication · HRM data driven · People Analytics

1 Introduction

The digital transformation of organizations is boosting workplace networking and collaboration while making it "observable" with unprecedented timeliness and detail. However, the informational potential of work datafication is still largely under-utilized in human resource management (HRM) and its benefits, both at the individual and the organizational level, remain largely unexplored. Indeed, researchers till now focused prevalently on how digital technology can help address traditional HRM issues (for instance related to performance appraisal processes), still overlooking how new digital work scenarios can trigger new key research questions [21]. In addition, even if the digitalization of work makes available a greater array of data, the current theoretical and managerial understanding is lacking with respect to how to take advantage of this new data [2]. Recent contributions propose to overcome the tendency to apply analytics mainly to analyze data on demographic attributes and to favor the adoption of a "relational analytics" approach, more focused on how people interact and influence each other [11]. Despite this call, the same authors lament that people analytics has made only modest progress over the past decade. What is needed to fill this gap seems to be a combination of organizational competences, analytical skills, and data modeling abilities that could be achieved only through interdisciplinary approaches [3, 20].

As a part of a wider research program[1] involving organization scholars, business and information engineers, and computer scientists, this paper presents some data analysis that we performed on a collection of digital actions extracted from an enterprise collaboration software (ECS), in search for promising correlations between behavioral and relational digital work patterns and employee attitudes. To this end, we transformed the digital actions performed by 106 employees during a one-year period into a graph representation to analyze data under two different points of view: the individual (behavioral) perspective, according to the user who performed the action and the performed action undertaken, and the organizational (relational) perspective, making explicit the interactions between users and the objects of their actions. Different employees' rankings are thus derived and correlated with the employees' attitudes (namely organizational embeddedness) that we collected by means of two rounds of survey handed out at one-year distance.

We discuss the obtained results and their implications in terms of human resource management. We suggest that, on the one hand, employee attitudes can be efficiently monitored and better analyzed on an on-going basis (film-like) out of digital work behaviors, instead of relying on traditional periodical expensive surveys (picture-like). On the other hand, digital work behaviors expressive of specific employee

---

[1] The research program "Framing employee attitudes and digital work behaviors to support data-driven human resource management" is supported by UniMoRe FAR [7].

attitudes can be fruitfully exploited to predict other workers' decisions and behaviors (e.g., retention, attrition) that could potentially affect performance at different levels.

2 Theoretical Framework

The digital transformation of organizations, that is the embedding of ICTs, networking, and Web technologies in particular, into work processes, has at least two relevant consequences on the management of organizations [6]. First, it is making workplace collaboration more and more powerful, in line with [12] statement that "[W]here media are primitive, coordination system is primitive" […] and "[T]he more the efficiency of the communication in the organization, the higher the "tolerance for interdependence." Second, and along with the progressive adoption of enterprise collaborative software (ECS), either as stand-alone solutions (for example the platforms Jive, Slack, Yammer, Prism, Stride) or as part of fully-fledged "digital workplaces" (for example Microsoft 365, Google Suite, Facebook Workplace), it is making work—both execution and collaboration behaviors—always "observable" in the digital traces it leaves. In other words, as work processes become increasingly digitalized, work behaviors produce an asset of digital traces that provides unprecedented information that can potentially inform organization and HRM theory and research and also transform HRM into an evidence-based, data-driven practice [7, 13]. However, the informational and managerial potential of data point "exhausts" generated by collaborative platforms or digital workplaces still lack a theoretical framework; therefore, data are still largely unutilized and consequently the potential benefits deriving from work datafication remains unexplored.

To the best of our knowledge, the few existing studies in HRM limit their scope to the social network behavior (see e.g., Recker et al. [20]) and only few large companies are now starting to address the issue with the help of some newly hired HR data scientist. In this respect, we envision two modes of social value extraction from "digital work behaviors," defined as those actions performed on corporate digital platforms/workplaces (e.g., ECSs, intranets…) in the execution of employees' job that are traced and stored in digital formats.

The first mode consists of correlating digital "behavioral" (i.e., at the individual level) and "relational" (i.e., at the organizational level) patterns with performance (for an example on sales representatives see Fuller [8]).

The second mode consists in correlating the same patterns with employee attitudes (i.e., job satisfaction, commitment, organizational embeddedness, and the like), given that, according to well-established research in organization and HRM, attitudes are deemed relevant predictors of organizational behaviors. For instance, the more satisfied employees are with their job, the better they perform (e.g., Petty et al. [19]); the more committed they are, the more they adopt behaviors that exceed task prescriptions (e.g., Meyer et al. [14]), the more organizationally embedded they are, the less they leave the organization [15, 10].

Our present research adopts this second mode, and it builds on some previous preliminary analysis and evidence [5] to answer the following exploratory research question:

Does a correlation exist between digital work behaviors and employee attitudes?

3   Data and Methods

To answer our research question, we collected data in an Italian business unit of a large-sized global retail company which employs approximately 1500 people. To support employees' collaboration, the business unit recently introduced "Jive,"[2] which is an ECS platform and knowledge management tool where users can provide personal contribution in different sections (forums, blogs, wikis, communities) and in relation to different types of contents (post, subscription, document). All the content is managed in a uniform way and can be accessed through a common search interface. At the time of our study, all the employees had a user profile and started to perform some activities on the collaborative platform, even though none of them had switched completely their work to a digital mode.

3.1   Data Collection

To collect data on employee attitudes, we surveyed in two rounds, at a distance of one year, the entire population of the business unit, including both store employees and employees in the headquarters. More specifically, we administered the same online structured questionnaire at the beginning of 2016 and at the beginning of 2017.

Through the questionnaire, we first collected information on personal characteristics of employees, specifically age, gender, education, organizational position, organizational tenure, and previous work experience. In addition, we surveyed the following attitudes: job satisfaction, organizational identification, and organizational embeddedness. However, the attitudes that we consider in this paper's analysis are the following two organizational embeddedness' components: (1) fit, i.e., the extent to which an individual perceives that her abilities and values match organizational requirements and culture and (2) sacrifice, i.e., the perceived economic and psychological costs associated with leaving the current organization [10]. We measured fit and sacrifice using the scale of organizational embeddedness developed by Mitchell and colleagues [15] and Ng and Feldman [17]. The scale consists of eight items for fit dimension (e.g., "I feel like I am a good match for this company" and "My company utilizes my skills and talent well") and seven items for sacrifice dimension (such as "I am well compensated for my level of performance" and "The perks on this

---

[2] http://www.jivesoftware.com.

Table 1 Statistics about survey data over all the 106 employees

	Mean	std	Min	25%	50%	75%	Max
2016							
Job Embeddedness: Fit	5.679	0.907	2.625	5.25	5.75	6.25	7
Job Embeddedness: Sacrifice	5.458	0.998	2.714	4.857	5.714	6.286	7
2017							
Job Embeddedness: Fit	5.718	0.867	1.75	5.375	5.875	6.25	7
Job Embeddedness: Sacrifice	5.438	1.016	2	4.857	5.571	6.143	7

organization are outstanding"). We used a Likert-type scale ranging from 1 (strongly disagree) to 7 (strongly agree).

As far as the collection of digital behaviors is concerned, by means of the Jive Data Export Service, we extracted in CSV format the raw data corresponding to the employees' actions performed on and tracked by the collaborative platform in the time between the two surveys and in the 12 months after the second survey.

Compliance to data privacy imposed the request for permission on each and every employee involved in the surveys, to connect their data, i.e., their responses to surveys 1 and 2 and their digital behaviors on the collaborative platform (identified by a LDAP). The result is a dataset made up of attitudes of 106 employees, surveyed at two distinct moments in time, and about 600.000 digital work behaviors (such as sharing documents, blog post, likes/dislikes, following/unfollowing, tagging/untagging, voting, uploading/downloading, etc., plus the associated metadata about time of execution and "place" of execution, to be intended as one of the sections of the collaborative platform), associated with the 106 respondents and distributed over a 24 month period.

3.2 Data Analysis

For the analysis of employees' attitudes, we followed the procedure adopted by Mitchell and colleagues [15], and we calculated the variables fit and sacrifice averaging, respectively, their eight and seven items. Table 1 shows the main descriptive statistics of fit and sacrifice over all the 106 employees for both the 2016 (upper part) and 2017 (lower part) surveys.

To analyze the employees' digital behaviors, we adopted the Neo4j graph database management software[3], and we transformed the data extracted from the Jive platform into an EC network graph, constituted by nodes and relationships, each having a series of properties modeling the details (e.g., the ID of an employee, the title of a document, and so on). The node types of our graph are the following: actor nodes, i.e., the users of the ECS; content nodes, i.e., content objects (sub-types are documents,

---

[3] http://neo4j.com.

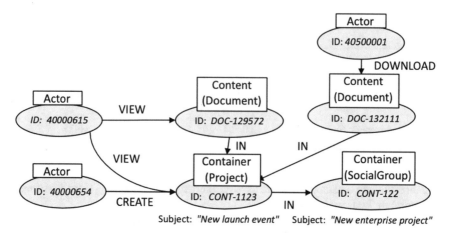

Fig. 1 A portion of the resulting final graph

videos, etc.); container nodes, i.e., container objects (sub-types are social groups, communities, projects, etc.); keyword nodes, i.e., keyword strings searched by users (e.g., "Launch event"). Graph relationships include both action and containment relationships. Action relationships connect users (actor nodes) with the targets of their action (content, container, keyword nodes). Containment relationships connect content to their containers. In particular, the graph models four "groups" of actions: "content actions," i.e., actions performed on a content object (e.g., view or create); "container actions," i.e., actions performed on a container object; "user actions," i.e., actions performed on a user (e.g., view or update user profile); "search actions," i.e., actions looking for specific keywords. The final graph contains a total of 31,711 nodes (11,996 content nodes, 1549 container nodes, 106 user nodes and 18,060 keyword nodes) and 324,121 relationships (306,463 action relationships and 17,658 containment relationships).

As an example, Fig. 1 shows a (very small) portion of the complete graph: user 40,000,654 created the "New launch event" project, which was viewed by user 40,000,615. Moreover, user 40,000,615 viewed document DOC-129572 and user 40,500,001 downloaded document DOC-132111, both related to the project.

We followed an approach that exploits both the usage data (broadly capturing the level of individual activity on the platform) and the structural data available in our EC graph (broadly capturing how people relate to each other). More specifically, we looked for specific patterns characterizing the employee digital actions from different points of view that we labeled as behavioral patterns and relational patterns.

Behavioral patterns focus on the isolated behavioral component of employee actions, i.e., they represent the action of a specific employee, independently from the impact/reactions of the other employees. Based on the target (content and container types) of the action, we introduce two types of behavioral patterns:

- task-oriented behavioral patterns, describing actions performed on documents inside communities and projects;
- people-oriented behavioral patterns, describing actions performed on events, blog posts and videos inside social groups.

Both types include very active (A+), active (A-), and passive (P) patterns, depending on the extent to which the performed action is related to the creation or addition of new contents as opposed to a simple view or download. In practice, the different "content actions" are grouped in three classes, A+ , A-, and P.

Relational patterns focus on the relational component of employee actions, expressing what kind of impact/reaction is generated by the digital actions of an employee. More specifically, we represented a relational pattern as the very active (A+) action (e.g., CREATE) performed by an employee on an object (e.g., a project) on which another employee worked on through an active (A-, e.g., LIKE) or passive (P, e.g., VIEW) action. Thus, a relational pattern represents the indirect relation between the two employees or, put differently, the action of a user and the reaction of other users to it. For instance, it might be useful to analyze the reactions to the documents that users create in projects (i.e., task-oriented pattern A+) in terms of views and likes by other users (i.e., task-oriented patterns A- and P). In fact, even if the creation of a project is certainly not a very frequent activity, all the activities that are performed around it can give us a measure of "influence" of the user who created it (as in the case of user 40,000,654 which created a seemingly popular project). Thus, the interesting aspect about relational patterns is that they enable us to define views of the data graph through which we can deeply analyze the inter-employee connections by means of SNA techniques. During our work, we tested different views by considering possible variations of relational patterns. In this paper, we focus on the following views, which are among the most representatives (also because they include all the behavioral patterns we defined):

- (P, A-)- > A + task-oriented (composed by 106 nodes and 54,128,369 links);
- (P, A-)- > A + people-oriented (composed by 106 nodes and 4064 links).

Then, we adopted different techniques, ranging from the simple counting of the behavioral patterns to well-established centrality algorithms applied on relational patterns views of the graph to test if and how the attitudes of employees are correlated to their digital actions. More specifically, we computed different employees' rankings based on the behavioral patterns counts and on employees' attitudes and we measured the correlations between these rankings through the Spearman rank-order correlation coefficient. Moreover, we ranked employees according to the impact/reaction generated by their digital actions, applying the following two centrality measures on the above-mentioned relational patterns:

- degree centrality: It measures the number of incoming relationships into a node; it has been found useful in many application scenarios (e.g., [9]). For example, in the case of our task-oriented views, employees performing very active actions (e.g., creation) on objects (e.g., documents) on which a large number of other employees' work will be "rewarded" with a high score;

– Eigenvector centrality: It is an algorithm that measures the transitive connectivity of nodes so that relationships to high-scoring nodes will contribute more to the score of a node than connections to low-scoring nodes [1]. In our case, this means that employees who created, for instance, many "popular" documents will contribute more to the centrality of coworkers when working, in turn, on the latter's contents. This is especially true if they worked exclusively on documents created by few other employees (the ones they possibly consider more "reliable").

Finally, we computed the Spearman correlation between the employees' rankings based on these centrality measures and the rankings based on employees' attitudes.

4 Findings

As we mentioned above, we computed the correlation between the rankings induced by the behavioral patterns counts and the ones based on the employee attitude measures through the Spearman rank-order correlation coefficient. The obtained results, together with the corresponding p-values, are shown in Table 2. The significant values (shown in boldface) assess that a correlation exists between the number of

Table 2 Spearman rank-order correlation coefficients and p-values for behavioral patterns

	Fit			Sacrifice		
	rho	p-value	Significant ($\alpha = 0.05$)	rho	p-value	Significant ($\alpha = 0.05$)
2016						
Count task oriented A+	0.107	0.276		0.132	0.177	
Count task oriented A-	**0.198**	**0.042**	*	**0.255**	**0.008**	*
Count task oriented P	**0.203**	**0.037**	*	**0.293**	**0.002**	*
Count people oriented A+	0.04	0.68		0.07	0.479	
Count people oriented A-	0.152	0.119		0.083	0.396	
Count people oriented P	0.037	0.709		0.027	0.784	
Count any action	**0.216**	**0.026**	*	**0.286**	**0.003**	*
2017						
Count task oriented A+	**0.241**	**0.013**	*	**0.198**	**0.042**	*
Count task oriented A-	**0.196**	**0.044**	*	0.155	0.113	
Count task oriented P	0.179	0.066		0.081	0.408	
Count people oriented A+	**0.237**	**0.014**	*	**0.238**	**0.014**	*
Count people oriented A-	**0.251**	**0.009**	*	**0.211**	**0.03**	*
Count people oriented P	**0.235**	**0.015**	*	**0.308**	**0.001**	*
Count any action	**0.221**	**0.023**	*	0.171	0.079	

Table 3 Spearman rank–order correlation coefficients and p-values for relational patterns (2017 survey)

	Fit 2017			Sacrifice 2017		
	rho	p-value	Significant (α =0.05)	rho	p-value	Significant (α =0.05)
Degree task oriented (P,A-) -> A+	**0.253**	**0.009**	*	0.134	0.172	
Degree people oriented (P,A-) -> A-	**0.206**	**0.034**	*	**0.201**	**0.039**	*
Eigen task oriented (P,A-) -> A+	**0.322**	**0.001**	*	**0.244**	**0.012**	*
Eigen people oriented (P,A-) -> A+	0.166	0.088		**0.225**	**0.02**	*

actions performed and the fit and sacrifice measures of the surveys preceding (2016) and following (2017) the monitored activity period.

More specifically, results show that the higher the perceived level of fit and sacrifice at the beginning of 2016, the higher the level of (active and passive) task-oriented actions on the Jive platform during the year 2016. In addition, our results show also that those employees who performed during 2016 a higher number of very active or active task-oriented digital actions, experienced higher fit and sacrifice at the beginning of the following year (2017). The same happens for those employees who performed a higher number of people-oriented digital actions (very active, active, or passive) on the ECS platform.

We computed the Spearman correlations also between the centrality scores, obtained for each of the considered relational patterns and centrality measures, and the employees' attitudes. Results are reported in Table 3 (significant values are shown in boldface). We show in particular the correlations with the 2017 survey; in this case, we have several significant values, assessing that a correlation exists between the digital relational patterns and the employees' attitudes (fit and sacrifice) measured after the period in which the digital actions were monitored.

More specifically, results show that the degree centrality in task-oriented relational patterns (performed during the 2016) correlates to fit (surveyed at the beginning of 2017), while the degree centrality in people-oriented relational patterns (performed during the 2016) correlates to both fit and sacrifice (surveyed at the beginning of 2017). The eigenvector centrality in task-oriented relational patterns (performed during the 2016) correlates to both fit and sacrifice (surveyed at the beginning of 2017), while the eigenvector centrality in 2016 people-oriented relational patterns correlates to 2017 sacrifice only. Taken together, these findings suggest that the impact generated by employees' digital actions on ECS platform affect employees' attitudes so that the more the employee is central in digital relational patterns the more he/she will perceive fit and sacrifice. This relationship seems to be stronger between, respectively:

– degree centrality and fit;
– eigenvector centrality and sacrifice.

That is the higher the employee's degree centrality in relational patterns is, the more he/she will perceive fit to the organization. This suggests that performing digital behaviors that generate impact in terms of many reactions by other affects positively the perception of match between those employees and their job, work group and the company. Similarly, the more the employee's eigenvector centrality in relational patterns is, the more he/she will perceive sacrifice associated with leaving the organization. This suggests that when influential actors react to digital behaviors, thus increasing the transitive centrality of employees who performed these behaviors, these latter will feel highly respected at work and will perceive to have excellent opportunities for promotion. Indeed, in many organizations such opportunities depend on links to influential people and on decisions made by central actors.

5   Discussion and Conclusion

As part of a process of digital transformation, ECSs have the potential to change what firms do, the way firms organize what they do, and the way employees work, coordinate and cross boundaries to accomplish their tasks, with likely consequences on the way they perceived the overall work experience. However, many theories and methodologies currently adopted in organization and HRM studies may not be able to exploit the potentialities offered by work datafication, enhancing the so-called theory–practice divide (e.g., Ungureanu and Bertolotti [4]). In fact, empirical research on how ECSs affect the employees' work experience is paradoxically scant as compared to the increasing frequency of adoption in practice of such platforms.

In this paper, we argue that to capture the impact of these changes at multiple levels (individuals, teamwork, and organizations) it may be necessary to leverage on different knowledge fields. In particular, we propose a novel pattern analysis and SNA approach to digital work behaviors and showed how it can positively improve individual and organizational information processing and decision-making. The revealed existence of correlations between employees' attitudes and digital work behaviors (that are currently detectable on a continuous basis) suggest that algorithmic models could be developed and implemented to detect and represent employee attitudes from digital work behaviors on an on-going basis, in a film-like mode. For instance, the counting of (active) behavioral patterns seems suitable to model employees' job embeddedness (i.e., fit and sacrifice).

Moreover, data on the degree centrality in digital relational patterns might provide information on employees' fit to their job, work group and organization, and data on the eigenvector centrality (transitive influence) may offer useful insights on the sense of sacrifice experienced by employees. Such information, insights, models can be exploited by companies to improve decisions and policies about human resources in terms of efficiency (for example, avoiding expensive employee surveys) and accuracy (for example, timely spotting employees' discomfort). Also, such information, insights and models might be used to improve employees' working experience, leveraging on appropriate HRM practices which may increase employees' positive attitudes. Indeed and moreover, since employee attitudes (and specifically job embeddedness) are identified as predictors of employees' in-role and extra-role performance, including innovative behaviors [16], they could be much better understood, managed and predicted relying on the digital work behaviors data extracted from collaborative platforms or digital workplaces. Similarly, drawing on extant research which suggests that individual creativity is affected by social relationships [18], data on employees' centrality derived by the graph analysis on relational patterns might help to better understand, predict, and manage creative and innovation processes inside organizations.

5.1   Limitations and Future Directions

The aim of our research was to provide one of the first empirical evidence on the (possible) relationships between the digital actions of employees on ECSs and their work attitudes. In a previous preliminary analysis [5], we had already found support for this prediction, demonstrating that both the "quantity" (i.e., the amount) and the "quality" (i.e., the intensity and the orientation) of these digital action relate to employees' attitudes. However, at that time, we concluded that while the relationship between quantity of digital behaviors and attitudes of employees was quite straightforward, more complex was the relationship between the quality of digital behaviors and such attitudes. This is because the possible relation between the two relies on the behavioral meaning of digital actions, and specifically on the question if there are single meaningful digital actions or rather sets of digital behaviors, whose underlying intentions can be associated to the attitudes.

In this paper, we draw on our previous work but also extends it by first introducing and using the idea of behavioral patterns. They are interpreted as a combination of a specific digital action performed on a particular object of the work (i.e., content) and in a particular section (i.e., container) of ECSs, thus distinguishing between task-oriented vs people-oriented digital behaviors. In doing so, we assumed, first, that the architecture of the digital environment maybe somehow related to individuals' intentions and, second, that compared to a single behavior, a behavioral pattern is definitely more expressive of any possible intentionality. In addition, since we assumed that there would not be a universal meaning associated to the different sections (or containers) of ECSs, we investigated relational patterns too, in search for possible correlations between the type and structure of digital interactions in which the actor/individual is immersed and his/her attitudes. We believe that the concept of relational patterns can open the way to several interesting avenues of research because they could be fruitfully related to issue of team conflict, inclusion, diversity to name just a few. At the same time, even though we found some interesting correlations, we are aware that ours represents only the first, however, promising, attempt of systematization of digital behaviors. Future research should further address the understanding of how individuals interpret and give meaning of digital behaviors.

Another relevant point to discuss refers to the entity of the dataset, i.e., the limited number of employees that we were finally able to track. Only 106 individuals agreed to complete both surveys and decided to disclose their names to match survey responses to behaviors on the collaborative platform defining our final sample size. To this regard, our study faces the recognized issue of being characterized by a large amount of data coming from a relatively small sample of respondents. On one hand, we show how the application of novel graph analyses and social network techniques can partially overcome this issue. On the other hand, we acknowledge that future research should inevitably consider issues related to the data privacy and transparency, which appear still largely unsolved. In fact, even if the availability of a large amount of data allowed by the digitalization of workplace pushes toward the use of these data and can promote the perception of an increased democracy in the workplace, it can also trigger perception that such data could promote micro-managed forms of control. Thus, employees and management could develop ambivalent feelings potentially limiting not only future research but above all the future development of data-driven (HR) management.

Finally, our dataset is also narrow because only a limited portion of overall work behaviors are really performed on the ECS since in our setting, people keeps on working largely in a traditional way, i.e., on site/offline. This limits the representativeness of available digital behaviors as thorough indicators of employees' attitudes. Thus, we believe that it would be interesting to investigate the relationship between digital actions and behaviors and performance outside the ECS.

References

1. Al-garadi, M. A., Varathan, K. D., Ravana, S. D., Ahmed, E., Shaikh, G. M., Khan, M. U. S., & Khan, S. U. (2018). Analysis of online social network connections for identification of influential users: Survey and open research issues. *ACM Computing Surveys (CSUR), 51*(1), 1–37.
2. Angrave, D., Charlwood, A., Kirkpatrick, I., Lawrence, M., & Stuart, M. (2016). HR and analytics: Why HR is set to fail the big data challenge. *Human Resource Management Journal, 26*(1), 1–11.
3. Bersin, J. (2015). HR's role in the digital workplace: A time for reinvention. In D. Ulrich, W.A. Schiemann, & L. Sartain (Eds.), The rise of HR. Wisdom from 73 Thought leaders, (pp. 19–24). HR Certification Institute.
4. Ungureanu, P., & Bertolotti, F. (2020). From gaps to tangles: A relational framework for the future of the theory-practice debate. *Futures, 118*, 102532.
5. Fabbri, T., Scapolan A. C., Bertolotti F., & Canali, C. (2019). HR Analytics in the digital workplace: Exploring the relationship between attitudes and tracked work behaviors. In R. Bissola, & B. Imperatori (Eds.), *HRM 4.0 for human-centered organizations. Advanced series in management* (Vol. 23, pp. 161–175). Emerald, Bingley.
6. Fabbri, T. (2018). Digital work: An organizational perspective. In I. Senatori, & Ales, E. (Eds.), *Working in digital and smart organizations—Legal, economic and organizational perspectives on the digitalization of labour relations* (pp. 29–38). Palgrave, MacMillan.

7. Fabbri, T., & Scapolan A. C. (2018). Digitalization and HR analytics: A big game for an HR manager. In F. Cantoni & G. Mangia (Eds.), *Human resource management and digitalization. Routledge-Giappichelli Studies in Business and Management* (pp. 243–254). Routledge, London.
8. Fuller, R. (2015). *What makes great salespeople.* Harvard Business Review, July 08, 2015. https://hbr.org/2015/07/what-makes-great-salespeople
9. Kim, J., & Hastak, M. (2018). Social network analysis: Characteristics of online social networks after a disaster. *International Journal of Information Management, 38*(1), 86–96.
10. Lee, T. W., Mitchell, T. R., Sablynski, C. J., Burton, J. P., & Holtom, B. C. (2004). The effects of job embeddedness on organizational citizenship, job performance, volitional absences and voluntary turnover. *Academy of Management Journal, 47*(5), 711–722.
11. Leonardi, P., & Contractor, N. (2018). Better people analytics. *Harvard Business Review, 96*(6), 70–81.
12. March, J. G., & Simon H. A. (1958). *Organizations.* Wiley.
13. McAbee, S. T., Landis, R. S., & Burke, M. I. (2017). (2017): Inductive reasoning: The promise of big data. *Human Resource Management Review, 27*(2), 277–290.
14. Meyer, J. P., Stanley, D. J., Herscovitch, L., & Topolnytsky, L. (2002). Affective, continuance, and normative commitment to the organization: A meta-analysis of antecedents, correlates, and consequences. *Journal of vocational behavior, 61*(1), 20–52.
15. Mitchell, T. R., Holtom, B. C., Lee, T.W., Sablynski, C. J., & Erez, M. (2001). Why people stay: Using job embeddedness to predict voluntary turnover. *Academy of Management Journa,l 44*(6), 1102–1121.
16. Ng, T. W. H., & Feldman, D. C. (2010). The impact of job embeddedness on innovation-related behaviors. *Human Resource Management, 49*(6), 1067–1087.
17. Ng, T. W., & Feldman, D. C. (2009). Occupational embeddedness and job performance. *Journal of Organizational Behavior, 30*(7), 863–891.
18. Perry-Smith, J. E. (2006). Social yet creative: The role of social relationships in facilitating individual creativity. *Academy of Management Journal, 49*, 85–101.
19. Petty, M. M., McGee, G. W., & Cavender, J. W. (1984). A meta-analysis of the relationships between individual job satisfaction and individual performance. *Academy of management Review, 9*(4), 712–721.
20. Recker, J., Malsbender, A., & Kohlborn, T. (2016). Using enterprise social networks as innovation platforms. *IT Professional, 18*(2), 42–49.
21. Thite, M. (2018). *Digital HRM: Nirvana or Nemesis? Symposium organized at the 78th annual academy of management meeting*, Chicago.

Shaping the Future of Work

Martina Gianecchini⊙**, Sara Dotto, and Paolo Gubitta**⊙

Abstract The fast pace of the technological evolution forces workers to update their competencies in order to remain attractive in the labor market. Those changes suggest that in order to remain employable, workers need to add new skills (either soft or digital) to their "traditional" competencies, demonstrating the ability to work in an interdisciplinary agile fashion. We argue that this professional evolution resembles the characteristics of the T-shaped professionals, and that it is possible to interpret the changes of jobs that are caused by the technological revolution drawing on job design literature. Hence, analyzing the data of a survey administered to a sample of 238 workers employed in Veneto Region, we explore the skill shapes of jobs that are present in the labor market and we assess their relationship with the workers' and organizational characteristics.

Keywords Job design · Technology · T-shaped professionals

1 Introduction

The fast pace of the technological evolution forces workers to update their competencies in order to remain attractive in the labor market: in this instance, the World Economic Forum [1] identified upskilling and re-skilling as two of the main challenges for reducing the risk of job loss. Interestingly, proficiency in new technologies is only one part of the future skills requirement, as other "human" skills (e.g., analytical thinking, active learning, and creativity) are growing in prominence.

Those changes suggest that in order to remain employable, workers need to add new skills (either soft or digital) to their "traditional" competencies. Indeed, as recently suggested by research reports [1, 2], new hybrid jobs [3] or superjobs stem

M. Gianecchini (✉) · P. Gubitta
Department of Economics and Management "M. Fanno", University of Padova, 35123 Padova, Italy
e-mail: martina.gianecchini@unipd.it

S. Dotto
IAE de Paris, Paris 1 Panthéon Sorbonne University, Paris, France

© The Author(s), under exclusive license to Springer Nature Switzerland AG 2022
L. Solari et al. (eds.), *Do Machines Dream of Electric Workers?*, Lecture Notes in Information Systems and Organisation 49,
https://doi.org/10.1007/978-3-030-83321-3_5

from "traditional" jobs because of the blending of several types of competences: soft skills, professional competences, and digital competences. The professional trajectory leading to these new jobs resembles the characteristics of the T-shaped professionals. The term was initially adopted to describe the evolution of the professionals in the R&D field [4]. It was then extended to define professionals who have the ability to work in an interdisciplinary agile fashion as they combine deep expertise in one professional area with a breadth of skills (e.g., communication, problem solving, and project management) enabling faster adaptation to role changes and better collaboration in multifunctional contexts [5]. T-shaped professionals do not represent the entire panorama of professional "shapes" [6], as we can have experts in just one area (I-shaped), professionals who have deep knowledge in two connected areas (H-shaped); professionals who are experts in two areas and possesses a superficial knowledge of other areas (Pi-shaped). Drawing on the literature on work design [7, 8], we can assert that the new jobs require both higher skill variety, i.e., the ability to use different skills to perform the job, and higher skill specialization, i.e., the depth of knowledge in a particular area.

We argue that the professional evolution suggested by the studies about the T-shaped professionals, that is possible to describe using the concepts provided by the literature about job design, is particularly suitable to interpret the changes of jobs that are caused by the technological revolution. However, the extent of these changes and what are the characteristics of the skill shapes of jobs remains unexplored. Analyzing the data of a survey administered to a sample of 238 workers employed in Veneto Region, we aim at exploring the skill shapes of jobs that are present in the labor market and at assessing their relationship with the workers' and organizational characteristics.

The contribution of our study is twofold. First, we contribute to the studies about T-shaped professional that have analyzed few professions and industries, focusing their attention on the development of the jobs but neglecting the diffusion of different professional shapes. Second, we contribute to the research about the effect of the technological changes on the jobs that have mainly adopted a descriptive approach overlooking the adoption theoretical concepts (e.g., the ones provided by the literature about work design) in order to illustrate what are the job characteristics that are affected by those changes.

Finally, our study provides useful insights to employers and policy makers to design effective training programs and to employees in order to manage their professional development.

2 Theoretical Framework

2.1 The T-shaped Professionals

In the new competitive environment, workers and professionals need to cope with tasks and jobs that are continuously changing. And, as team working is spreading in flat and agile organizations, they are required to collaborate in multifunctional groups [9].

The need for workers to leave a logic of specialism favoring instead the development of interfunctional competencies was first suggested by David Guest [10] in an editorial on The Independent, where he coined the term "T-shaped" person. The T-shaped person is, according to the author, "a variation on Renaissance Man, equally comfortable with information systems, modern management techniques and the 12-tone scale".

Few years later, the term was adopted by Iansiti [11] for describing the combination of skills needed by professionals operating in research and development teams, as "on the one hand, they have a deep knowledge of a discipline [...], represented by the vertical stroke of the T. On the other hand, these [...] specialists also know how their discipline interacts with others—the T's horizontal top stroke" [p. 139]. Leonard–Barton [12] explored the roles of T-shaped professionals as drivers of innovation in companies. According to the author, those professionals are especially valuable anywhere problem solving is required across different deep functional knowledge bases. On the same tone, Barile, Saviano, and Simone [13] emphasize the fact that such individuals have the ability to deal with different problematic contexts effectively addressing change; in fact, they have both "disciplinary knowledge in at least one area, and understanding of systems" that allow them to be "adaptive innovators" [p. 1179]. Donofrio, Spohrer, and Zadeh [14] remind that the breadth of knowledge of T-shaped people makes them fast in adapting to job changes, able to communicate and to collaborate in heterogeneous teams, hence being capable of "interacting with and understanding specialists from a wide range of disciplines and functional areas" [4, p. 11]. Gardner [5] argues that the peculiarity of the T-shaped individual consists in the ability to cross the boundaries of a single discipline, being able to collaborate, understanding roles, motives, and responsibilities from different areas.

As suggested by Demirkan and Spohrer [15], the digital transformation paves the way for the development of other "shapes" of professions, identified by the broadness and depth of their expertise: H-shaped, Pi-shaped, and Dash-shaped. H-shaped professionals, instead, have deep knowledge in two areas, and are able to connect them; the Pi-shaped professional is an expert in two areas, but she possesses a broad—though more superficial—knowledge other areas as well. Finally, the Dash-shaped professional is a proper generalist: she possesses general knowledge in several areas, with a good breadth and she's able to apply knowledge in different situations.

Notwithstanding the value of workers having multiple domains of knowledge, their professional development is not usually planned by companies as incentives are usually directed to the development of I-shaped individuals who are experts in just one area [12]. And then, T-shaped competences emerged from the willingness of some individuals to pursue another possible career. On the contrary, as suggested by Hansen and Von Oetinger [16], the attitude to combine knowledge from different areas should be encouraged by organizations as T-shaped professionals can create value both by achieving strong results in their business unit and by sharing knowledge across different units.

2.2 Hybrid Jobs and Work Design

A framework which is helpful in investigating the professional shapes of jobs and in the evolution of job contents; it is the stream of literature related to the work design. Studies about job design are situated at "the intersection of industrial and organizational psychology" [7, p. 423], has important impacts both on organizational success and individual well-being, since it focuses on the requirements of jobs in terms of outcomes, efficiency and effectiveness, but at the same time it takes into account motivational theories aimed at the satisfaction of workers—or, in other words, it looks for the best possible allocation of limited resources (time, skills, investments in human capital) to maximize the outcome of a job. Due to the increasing attention to the "hybrid" nature of jobs [3], as well as the different shapes jobs are assuming [6, 15], such kind of reflections are of particular interest: jobs are changing, and so should their design.

According to Morgeson and Humphrey [8], the works characteristics—that is, the "attributes of the task, job and social and organizational environment" (p. 1322)— can be classified in three main categories: motivational, social and contextual. The motivational characteristics, argue the authors, are a reflection of the complexity of the job and of its enrichment, and therefore could lead to a higher satisfaction coming from its accomplishment. Motivational characteristics are then subdivided by Morgeson and Humphrey [8] in two groups: the first is constituted by "Task characteristics," which are "concerned with how the work itself is accomplished and the range and nature of tasks associated with a particular job" (p. 1323) and include autonomy, task variety, task significance, task identity, and feedback from the job. Then, there are knowledge characteristics, which "reflect the kind of knowledge, skill and ability demand" (p. 1323) that are required to a worker occupying a determined job position. Knowledge characteristics are composed of job complexity, information processing, problem solving, skills variety, and specialization. All of these items are positively related to an increase in the motivation and satisfaction of the worker since a higher degree of commitment is required to successfully complete harder tasks [17].

In particular, Morgeson and Humphrey [8] define skill specialization as "the extent to which a job involves performing specialized tasks or possessing specialized knowledge or skills": it "reflects a depth of knowledge and skill in a particular area" (p. 1323). On the other hand, skill variety "reflects the extent to which a job requires an individual to use a variety of different skills to complete the work" (p. 1323). An important distinction is the one between skill variety and task variety: while skills refer to the competences a person possesses (which can be used or not in carrying out the job), the variety of tasks is referred to the breadth of activities a job includes [8]. As it emerges, such a point of view is helpful in the design of T-shaped jobs, as the two characteristics of skill specialization and skill variety mirror the vertical stroke and the horizontal top stroke, respectively.

However, the historical view of the theories of job design dates back to Taylor's division of labor, and it was contrasting with the main concept of mixing competences suggested by the theories emerging from the insights about T-shaped professionals.

According to this view, the division of labor in simple tasks favors mastering the job thanks to their repetition over time: this would guarantee the maximum of efficiency and specialization [18]. In addition, the costs related to variety, which requires to invest time and energy in the acquisition of different skills to accomplish various tasks, were lowered. Finally, as suggested by Rosen [19], since the required investment in the acquisition of any set of skills by a worker constituted a fixed cost, in order to maximize the rate of return it was "advantageous" to "specialize investment resources to a narrow band of skills and employ them as intensely as possible" [19, p. 44]. Campion [20] defines this approach to job design as "mechanistic," recalling the "classic industrial engineering" origins (p. 4)—in contrast with other approaches, such as the motivational, the biological and the perceptual/motor ones. The author highlights that the focus on repetition of simple tasks allowed a high specialization, efficiency, staffing ease, and low training times. At the same time, such an approach is linked to "lower mental ability requirements" (p. 17).

On the other hand, Staats and Gino [18] underline that such an approach turned out not to be as effective as desired: the continuous repetition of a task leads workers to be disengaged, to lack motivation and therefore to perform worse than expected. In fact, as reminded by Herzberg [21] and Oldham, Hackman and Pearce [22], allocating a variety of activities in a job content would be a better option, due to the higher "motivation and engagement" [18, p. 1141] experienced by the worker, which could improve her performance as well as gaining knowledge that could "be applied to other tasks," thus favoring learning and "the opportunity for knowledge transfer between tasks" [18, p. 1143].

O'Brien [23], moreover, highlights that the satisfaction in jobs is related to five attributes: skill variety, task identity, task significance, autonomy, and feedback [p. 461] and underlines the importance of adding to these elements the skill utilization, defined as "the degree of match or congruence between an individual's skills and the level of skills required by his or her job" [23, p. 462]—such concept is similar to the one of skill variety, which is, according to Oldham, Hackman and Pearce [22, p. 395] "the degree to which a job requires a variety of different activities in carrying out the work, which involve the use of a number of skills and talents of the person". However, argues O'Brien, "even if the skills are meaningful to the employee, the level of skills required by the job may not be similar to the level of skills possessed by the employee": the problem many jobs face is that emphasis is put on increasing the variety of skill used, but it is the utilization of skills that turns out to be a better predictor of jobs satisfaction. Hence, according to O'Brien [23], to better motivate people, it is necessary to find a better match between the skills to be utilized to carry out the job and those of the worker.

In support to the motivational approach to job design [20], which is oriented to "outcomes such as satisfaction, intrinsic motivation, and involvement, as well as performance and attendance" [20, p. 4], Campion and McClelland [24] argue that not only task enlargement is effective, but that an even more effective way to reach a higher satisfaction for the worker is the knowledge enlargement of the job. In fact, job enlargement consists of expanding the variety of tasks required to the worker, but it can be done either by adding tasks on the same level of responsibility, or by increasing the requirements for activities which need an "understanding of procedures and rules relating to different products sold by the organization" [24, p. 1]; hence, knowledge enlargement is seen as more enriching due to the fact that enhancing "mental processes may […] be more psychologically meaningful" [p. 2], and it is "likely to have a greater influence on mental ability requirements […] and compensable factors […] than is task enlargement" [p. 2], thus linking it to the positive effects of motivation. Also, positive effects of knowledge enlargement are linked to the enrichment of the professional identity of the worker and on the compensation [24].

Hence, the literature on job design and the debate around the trade-offs between specialization and variety, together with the new shapes of jobs, seem to suggest that the requirements for any kind of job are switching to higher requirements for flexibility, a wider range of competence managed at a deeper level, a higher proactivity and willingness to learn in order to enrich the areas of competence mastered. The importance of proactivity of adopting an attitude directed to the lifelong learning and the continual gaining of new capabilities is strongly sustained also by authors focusing on the theme of employability, defined by Hillage and Pollard [25], as "having the capability to gain initial employment, maintain employment and obtain new employment if required" [25, p. 1]. The employability of the individuals is related to various factors: the assets in terms of "knowledge, skills or attitude" they possesses, together with their ways of using them and their ability to present them to potential employers. However, the individual's employability is also strongly dependent on the context they works in [25]. Therefore, developing more skills and expertise in various areas is an investment that can guarantee individuals with a higher amount of employability—which is more and more necessary to face the uncertainty and unpredictability of the world of work [26, 27].

2.3 Technological Change and Work Design

The recent literature about the evolution of jobs and the requirements of skills and competences of workers brings evidence that different ad new areas of expertise are demanded to employees, also as a consequence of the technological innovations. In fact, not only technical and soft competences are demanded to employees, but digital competences and IT skills are increasingly needed in the workplace [1, 2, 28].

The importance of the digital competences as a relevant area of expertise is underlined by Murawski and Bick [29], who highlight the attention and relevance given by employers and institutions to the development of such skills to cope well with the tasks required by the jobs. According to Vieru [30], digital competences are defined as "the ability to adopt and use new or existing information technology to analyze, select, and critically evaluate digital information in order to investigate and solve work-related problems and develop a collaborative knowledge body while engaging in organizational practices in a particular organizational context" [p. 6718]. This type of competence includes a technological dimension, a cognitive dimension, a dimension related to the organizational culture, and the integration among the three dimensions is relevant as well. Such considerations are coherent with the evidences brought by a report by the World Economic Forum [1], emphasizing that many of the "21st century skills" are being developed in a cross-curricular way, thus fostering the contamination across different areas of knowledge; and by Deloitte [2] as well, who underlines that the evolution of jobs is integrating more and more digital competences in their content. For example, "superjobs" [2] require a blending of several types of competences to be carried out effectively: soft skills, professional competences—that is, the area of expertise which is related to the function of the job, and digital competences—those implying the usage of new technology.

According to Di Maglio and colleagues, jobs require an enlarged portfolio of competences, due to the fact that "complexity imposes a return to capacity (breadth) to deal with decisional contexts in which the skills possessed (depth) are inadequate" [31, p. 425]. The authors underline the fact that people—and therefore jobs—do not require simply general competences, but instead "generalizable" ones [31, p. 425] that is, "a general level of knowledge that can be usefully applied to in different contexts to face the variety and variability of phenomena, that also allows learning to be deep in multiple areas more rapidly than before." Therefore, job contents are requiring the integration of competences from various domains; workers need to adapt to such trends and constantly update their abilities.

Therefore, as it emerges, various types of competences are blending in the new, emergent types of jobs: soft skills, functional-relates (professional) skills, computer-related skills, and digital skills. The first aim of our research is to get insights about whether different job profiles exist that assume different shapes with respect to the number and the type of skills for whom a higher level of skill specialization is required.

The reason why such an analysis turns out to be relevant is fourfold: first, as suggested by the literature on work design [e.g., 22–24] the higher the skills variety required to perform a job, the more likely it is that such job is motivating for the worker, thus increasing her satisfaction and employability. Second, as the stream of literature on the T-shape jobs and professionals reminds, the greater the amount of areas of expertise a worker can gain, the more easily she could understand the needs and issues of the other functions, she could solve more complex problems, related not only to a specific domain, but situated at the intersection of two or more of them. Consequently, when the skills acquired are more varied, this process of blending is increased and enriched further [13]. Third, due to the transformations the world of work is facing, many authors acknowledge the relevance and the prominent importance of the informatic and digital skills; since a growing body of literature is studying their development and is trying to provide a more organized theoretical framework for their analysis [29], it is interesting to understand to which extent such competences are required in terms of depth of knowledge and mastery by the actual jobs and which the main trends are for the future. Fourth, the changing and growing instability in the world of work—that has led to more and more uncertain career paths [27] has underlined the importance—in order to enhance the individual's employability and therefore her probability to maintain or find another job in an equivalent or better position [32]—to develop different sets of skills, together with the adoption of proactive behavior and the investment in the personal and professional development.

A second purpose of our analysis is directed at understanding whether some characteristics—both at the individual and at the organizational level—exist that make it more likely for an individual to occupy a job that requires a certain variety and specialization of skills: in other words, we aim at identifying which can be the variables influencing the probability that an individual could be required to gain a higher specialization and to utilize a higher variety of skills in her job.

3   Research Methods

3.1   Research Setting and Sample

In order to explore the shapes of the jobs that are developing in the labor market and to assess their relationship with the workers' characteristics, we administered a survey (October 2018) to a sample of 300 workers employed in Veneto Region. The survey is part of the Osservatorio Professioni Digitali activities, a joint research project between Veneto Region and the University of Padova. The sample was extracted from a larger population of 2864 workers, who signed an employment contract in November 2017 and that were still employed after eleven months (data were provided by VenetoLavoro). The survey was administered using a computer-assisted telephone interviewing technique. For the purpose of this paper, after controlling for missing values and outliers, 62 respondents were excluded from the original sample.

The analyzed sample is therefore composed of 238 workers (Table 1): the average age is 37.8 years (with a labor market seniority of 15.5 years), 51.7% are female, 47.5% have a high school diploma, and 38.1% a bachelor degree or above. The majority of the respondents (59.2%) are employed with a temporary contract, in small companies (49.2% less than 50 employees), and operating in different industries (39.1% manufacturing, 29.8% commerce, 31.1% services).

Table 1 Characteristics of the sample

Individual characteristics	N	%
Gender Male Female	238	48.3 51.7
Age ≤ 30 years old 31–40 years old 41–50 years old >50 years old	238	26.1 35.2 26.2 12.5
Education Elementary or middle school High school Bachelor's degree Master's degree or PhD	232	12.1 48.7 15.9 24.3
Contractual arrangement Permanent contract Temp contract or self-employed	238	40.8 59.2
Organizational functions Operations Marketing and sales Staff	238	38.2 31.5 30.3
Company characteristics	N	%
Industry Manufacturing Commerce Business and personal services	235	39.1 29.8 31.1
Size < 10 employees 10–49 employees 50–249 employees 250–999 employees ≥ 1000 employees	237	24.1 25.7 16.9 12.6 20.7

3.2 Variables

In order to explore the professional shapes of the jobs, we asked the respondents to provide information about the skills required to perform their job. We identified four areas of skill specialization:

- soft skills, such as helping and influencing others, leadership, and problem solving;
- functional-related skills that are a different set according to the functional area in which the worker is employed. For instance, the functional-related skills for workers employed in the area Accounting and Finance (one the staff functions) include: analyzing financial data, check financial statements, prepare forecasts, and evaluating the financial feasibility of business investments;

- computer-related skills such as using a spreadsheet or an online communication tool;
- digital skills such as big data analysis, cloud computing, robotics, and artificial intelligence.

Each one of the four areas of skill specialization represents one possible vertical stem of the professional shape. The level of skill specialization for each area was measured multiplying the skill level (from 1 = basic to 5 = expert) and the frequency of utilization of the skill (from 0 = never to 4 = always) required to perform the job. As suggested by the mechanistic approach to job design [20], which is derived from classic industrial engineering and reflects recommendations from scientific management, skill specialization is increased by having the workers repeatedly executing the task. Specialization benefits individual workers' learning, and hence productivity, because work on the same task over time imparts knowledge related to the task that is likely to improve a worker's ability. Together with the knowledge of the core skills, the workers may get familiar with topics as the specific set of steps to follow, the specialized tools used, and the customer being served [18]. The horizontal stem of the professional shape (breadth) is represented by the number of areas that requires a higher level of skills specialization.

As predictors of different skill shapes of jobs, we considered a set of workers' and organizational characteristics. The workers' characteristics included in the analysis are: age, education level (considered as a continuous variable ranging from 1 = elementary or middle school to 6 = PhD), gender (1 = woman; 0 = man), and employment contract (1 = permanent; 0 = temporary contract or self-employed). The organizational characteristics included in the analysis are: company size (number of employees), industry (1 = manufacturing; 2 = distribution and sales; 3 = business and personal services); the functional area where the worker is employed (1 = Operations; 2 = Marketing and sales; 3 = Staff activities).

3.3 Data Analysis

To map the professional shapes of the jobs and to analyze their relationships with workers' and organizational characteristics, we applied a two-step analytical strategy that involves cluster analysis and multinomial logistic regression.

Cluster analysis is an exploratory data analysis technique aimed at identifying and organizing the observed data into relatively homogeneous and meaningful groups on the basis of proximity, namely specific similar characteristics. We apply cluster analysis to the four areas of skill specialization. Among the different existing clustering procedures, the one that fits best both the data gathered and the aim of this research is the agglomerative hierarchical procedure because it is suitable when the number of clusters is not known a priori [33]. The agglomerative hierarchical procedure begins from the single observations, considered clusters themselves and moves toward larger groups by merging the clusters two-by-two on the basis of a measure of similarity or distance between the clusters. More specifically, we used Ward's method, which uses the Euclidean distance to obtain the distance from the cluster's mean. After clustering the skill areas, we used post-hoc analysis (the Bonferroni method) to test the differences between the means of the single variables in different clusters.

The second step of the analysis involved identifying workers' and organizational characteristics related with the likelihood that a person work in a job with a professional shape identified by the cluster analysis. We applied a multinomial logistic regression, a technique that is usually considered an extension of a binary model as we predict a nominal-dependent variable that contains four categories with no natural order, given one or more independent variables [34]. In our case, the clusters are the dependent variable, whereas the workers' and organizational characteristics are the independent variables.

4 Findings

The results of the cluster analysis suggest the existence of four clusters of jobs, representing four professional shapes (see Fig. 1 and Table 2). Cluster 1 resembles the characteristics of an I-shaped job, where the only skills with a higher level of specialization are the soft skills. Cluster 2 represents an example of Dash-shaped as all the four areas of expertise are requested and adopted on the job. Cluster 3 resembles the characteristics of an H-shaped job as two skills (computer-related and soft) are particularly developed. Finally, Cluster 4 can be associated with a Pi-shaped job, as it has two areas of skill specialization (functional-related and soft skills), but it possesses a broad—though more superficial—knowledge the other two areas as well.

The results of the multinomial logistic regression (Table 3) suggest that both individual characteristics (namely gender and education level) and organizational characteristics (namely the size and the industry of the company and the function

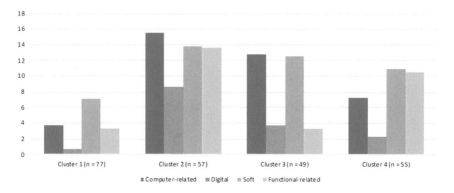

Fig. 1 The skill shapes of the jobs ($N = 238$)

Table 2 Results of the cluster analysis ($N = 238$)

	Cluster 1 ($n = 77$)		Cluster 2 ($n = 57$)		Cluster 3 ($n = 49$)		Cluster 4 ($n = 55$)		ANOVA	Cluster significantly different at 0.05 level*
	Mean	St. Dev	Mean	St. Dev	Mean	St. Dev	Mean	St. Dev		
Computer-related	3.76	4.29	15.56	3.52	12.80	3.36	7.28	3.58	$F = 127.058$	[1, 2] [1, 3] [1, 4] [2, 3] [3, 4]
Digital	0.75	1.39	8.59	4.57	3.73	2.93	2.34	2.48	$F = 80.842$	[1, 2] [1, 3] [1, 4] [2, 3]
Soft	7.15	3.46	13.86	3.00	12.56	2.12	10.94	2.76	$F = 65.480$	[1, 2] [1, 3] [1, 4] [3, 4]
Functional-related	3.39	2.40	13.65	4.73	3.31	2.90	10.55	2.77	$F = 150.183$	[1, 2] [1, 4] [2, 3] [3,4]

*Square brackets include (two-by-two) clusters significantly different at 0.05 level

Table 3 Parameter estimates: reference group Cluster 2 (Dash-shaped) ($N = 238$)

		b(SE)	Odds ratio
Cluster 1 I-shaped	Age	0.013 (0.025)	1.013
	Education level	−0.576 (0.217)**	0.562
	Gender	−0.958 (0.454)*	0.384
	Employment contract	0.161 (0.445)	1.174
	Company size	0.000 (0.000)*	1.000
	Organizational function (Operations)	1.445 (0.676)*	4.242
	Organizational function (Marketing and Sales)	−1.441 (0.605)*	0.237
	Industry (Manufacturing)	1.356 (0.628)*	3.88
	Industry (Distribution and Sales)	2.099 (0.669)**	8.16
Cluster 3 H-shaped	Age	0.049 (0.028)	1.05
	Education level	−0.087 (0.203)	0.917
	Gender	−1.637 (0.476)**	0.195
	Employment contract	0.007 (0.473)	1.007
	Company size	0.000 (0.000)	1.000
	Organizational function (Operations)	1.323 (0.671)*	3.754
	Organizational function (Marketing and Sales)	−2 (0.616)**	0.135
	Industry (Manufacturing)	−0.381 (0.601)	0.683
	Industry (Distribution and Sales)	0.641 (0.668)	1.899
Cluster 4 P-shaped	Age	0.002 (0.025)	1.002
	Education level	−0.153 (0.186)	0.859
	Gender	−0.898 (0.434)*	0.408
	Employment contract	0.021 (0.433)	1.022
	Company size	0.000 (0.000)	1.000
	Organizational function (Operations)	1.705 (0.69)*	5.499
	Organizational function (Marketing and Sales)	−0.038 (0.562)	0.962
	Industry (Manufacturing)	0.718 (0.585)	2.051
	Industry (Distribution and Sales)	1.498 (0.584)**	4.474

(continued)

Table 3 (continued)

		b(SE)	Odds ratio
Overall Model Evaluation—Likelihood Ratio Test, $\chi^2 = 104.714$, $p < 0.000$			
Goodness of fit—Pearson, $\chi^2 = 649.935$, p $= 0.471$; Deviance, $\chi^2 = 518.665$, $p = 1.000$			
Pseudo-R^2 statistics—Cox and Snell $= 0.367$; Nagelkerke $= 0.392$			

Notes Standard errors are in parentheses; *$p < 0.05$, **$p < 0.01$. Reference groups for the dichotomous and categorical independent variables: Gender, 1 = Woman; Employment contract, 1 = Permanent; Organizational function, 3 = Staff; Industry, 3 = Business and personal services. The odds ratios for continuous variables represent the change in odds of belonging to the respective groups given a change of one unit in the model variable. Odds ratios for dichotomous and categorical variables represent the change in odds of belonging to the respective groups given a change in the model variable from 0 to 1

where the person is employed) are significantly related with the professional shape of the job.

In particular, the I-shaped jobs (that are the more traditional ones in terms of professional development) are more likely to be occupied by workers with a relatively lower level of education (20.8% of the individuals belonging to this cluster has only an elementary or middle school diploma) employed in smaller companies operating in the manufacturing industry. The Dash-shaped jobs (Cluster 2) are more likely to be hold by higher educated male workers, operating in the marketing and sales functions of service companies. The H-shaped jobs (Cluster 3) are more likely to be occupied by female workers operating in staff functions, such as human resources or accounting. Finally, individuals occupying a job that is represented as P-shaped (Cluster 4), are more likely to be occupied in the logistic departments of distribution companies. According to our analysis, neither the age of the person nor the type of employment contract (permanent or temporary) plays a role in predicting the shape of the job the person will occupy.

5 Discussions and Conclusions

The present research aimed at understanding how new jobs are developing, in terms of skill variety and skill specialization. Drawing on the literature on work design and on the T-shaped professionals, we found that different shapes coexist in the labor market: I-shaped, Dash-shaped, H-shaped, and Pi-shaped. The likelihood that a worker is employed in a job with a specific skill shape is related with his/her personal and professional characteristics.

Our findings contribute to the studies on T-shaped professional showing the diffusion of different skill shapes in a sample of workers recently employed in an Italian region. Differently from the traditional settings of the studies about T-shaped professionals, those workers are not operating in innovative companies, but they are employed in traditional activities and functions. As a consequence, our findings show that the majority of jobs regularly offered in the labor market still have a traditional

I-shape (Cluster 1). Those jobs are occupied by less educated workers operating in smaller firms in manufacturing industry. As a consequence of these characteristics, those workers appear to have the higher likelihood of being substitute by machines, as the predictable physical tasks are highly susceptible to rapid automation. Together with those jobs, our findings demonstrate that other skill shapes are emerging. In particular, jobs requiring a relationship with customers in service businesses are the ones requiring the higher level of skill specialization in all the areas of expertise analyzed. These jobs require the higher application of both computer-related and digital skills, confirming that the digital transformation has strong repercussions on marketing and sales jobs even though such effects are twofold, whereas some aspect of the relationship with the customer can be completely automatized (e.g., payment and reservation systems, systems creating customized product offers), still the establishment of a personal contact with the clients, requiring the possess of functional-related and soft skills, can increase the economic value of the "commercial" relationship. Together with the Dash-shaped jobs, other skill shapes are present in the labor market. Both the H-shaped and the Pi-shaped jobs are characterized by skill variety, and in both cases, the computer-related skills are required with a high level of specialization, confirming that the predicted hybridization of the jobs [3] is already happening for many employed individuals.

Finally, our findings are useful to employers and policy makers to design effective training programs and to employees to manage their professional development. For instance, in the case of dash jobs with a high level of depth, individuals can gain knowledge through formal education (such as high schools, university degrees, and continuing education programs) and through dedicated company training programs. Instead, the case of Pi-shaped jobs shows a progressive hybridization, requiring the ability to use, with a medium level of expertise, both computer-related and traditional (either soft or functional-related) skills. In these cases, a formal learning process might not be necessary, whereas relevant skills can be acquired on the jobs and/or through short training courses.

References

1. World Economic Forum (2018). *The future of jobs report*. https://www.weforum.org/reports/the-future-of-jobs-report-2018
2. Deloitte Insights (2019). Leading the social enterprise: Reinvent with a Human focus, deloitte global human capital trends
3. Gubitta, P. (2018). I lavori ibridi e la gestione del lavoro. *Economia e Società Regionale XXXVI, 1*, 70–82.
4. IfM and IBM. (2008). *Succeeding through service innovation: A service perspective for education, research, business, and government*. University of Cambridge Institute for Manufacturing.
5. Gardner, P. (2017). Flourishing in the face of constant disruption: Cultivating the T-professional or adaptive innovator through WIL. In T. Bowen & M. T. B. Drysdale (Eds.), *International perspectives on education and society* (pp. 69–81). Emerald Publishing Limited

6. Barile, S., Franco, G., Nota, G., & Saviano, M. (2012). Structure and dynamics of a T-shaped knowledge: From individuals to cooperating communities of practice. *Service Science, 4*, 161–180.
7. Morgeson, F., & Campion, S. (2003). Work Design. In W. C. Borman, D. R. Ilgen & R. J. Klimosky (Eds.), *Handbook of psychology: Vol 12* (pp. 423–452). New York: Wiley
8. Morgeson, F. P., & Humphrey, S. E. (2006). The work design questionnaire (WDQ): Developing and validating a comprehensive measure for assessing job design and the nature of work. *Journal of Applied Psychology, 91*, 1321–1339.
9. Piciocchi, P., Bassano, C., Pietronudo, M. C., & Spohrer, J. C. (2019). Digital workers in service systems: challenges and opportunities (pp. 409–432). In P. P. Maglio, C. A. Kieliszewski, J. C. Spohrer, K. Lyons, L. Patrício & Y. Sawatani (Eds.), *Handbook of service science, Vol. II*. Springer
10. Guest, D (1991). The hunt is on for the Renaissance Man of computing. Independent (London)
11. Iansiti, M. (1993). Real-world R&D: jumping the product gap generation. *Harvard Business Review*, 138–147
12. Leonard-Barton, D. (1995). *Wellsprings of knowledge: Building and sustaining the sources of innovation*. Harvard Business Press.
13. Barile, S., Saviano, M., & Simone, C. (2015). Service economy, knowledge, and the need for T-shaped innovators. *World Wide Web, 18*, 1177–1197.
14. Donofrio, N., Spohrer, J., & Zadeh, H. S. (2010). Driven medical education and practice: A case for T-shaped professionals. MJA Viewpoint. http://www.ceri.msu.edu/wp-content/upl oads/2010/06/A-Case-for-T-Shaped-Professionals-20090907-Hossein.pdf
15. Demirkan, H., & Spohrer, J. C. (2018). Commentary—cultivating T-shaped professionals in the era of digital transformation. *Service Science, 10*, 98–109.
16. Hansen, M. T., & Von Oetinger, B. (2001). Knowledge management's next generation. *Harvard Business Review, 79*(3), 106–117.
17. Steers, R. M., Mowday, R. T., & Shapiro, D. L. (2004). Introduction to special topic forum: The future of work motivation theory. *The Academy of Management Review, 29*, 379–387.
18. Staats, B. R., & Gino, F. (2012). Specialization and variety in repetitive tasks: Evidence from a Japanese bank. *Management Science, 58*, 1141–1159.
19. Rosen, S. (1983). Specialization and human capital. *Journal of Labor Economics, 1*, 43–49.
20. Campion, M. A. (1989). Ability Requirement Implications of job design: An Interdisciplinary perspective. *Personnel Psychology, 42*, 1–24.
21. Herzberg, F. (1968) One more time: how do you motivate employees? *Harvard Business Review*, 52–62
22. Oldham, G. R., Hackman, J. R., & Pearce, J. L. (1976). Conditions under which employees respond positively to enriched work. *Journal of Applied Psychology, 61*, 395–403.
23. O'Brien, G. E. (1983). Skill-utilization, skill-variety and the job characteristics model. *Australian Journal of Psychology, 35*, 461–468.
24. Campion, M. A., & McClelland, C. L. (1993). Follow up and extension. *Journal of Applied Psychology, 78*(3), 339–351.
25. Hillage, J., Pollard, E. (1999). Great Britain, department for education and employment. Employability: Developing a framework for policy analysis. Dept. for Education and Employment, London
26. De Grip, A., Van Loo, J., & Sanders, J. (2004). The industry employability index: Taking account of supply and demand characteristics. *International Labour Review, 143*(3), 211–233.
27. Forrier, A., & Sels, L. (2003). The concept employability: A complex mosaic. *International Journal of Human Resource Development, 3*(2), 102–124.
28. Accenture: People First: the Primacy of People in a Digital Age (2016). https://www.accent ure.com/t20160314t114937__w__/us-en/_acnmedia/accenture/omobono/technologyvision/ pdf/technology-trends-technology-vision-2016.pdf
29. Murawski, M., & Bick, M. (2017). Digital competences of the workforce—a research topic? *Business Process Mgmt Journal, 23*, 721–734.

30. Vieru, D. (2015). Towards a multi-dimensional model of digital competence in small and medium-sized enterprises. In *Encyclopedia of information science and technology* (3rd ed.). Information Science Reference

31. Maglio, P. P., Kieliszewski, C. A., Spohrer, J. C., Lyons, K., Patrício, L., Sawatani, Y. (Eds.) (2019). *Handbook of service science, Vol. II*. Service science: Research and innovations in the service economy. Cham: Springer.

32. Rothwell, A., & Arnold, J. (2007). Self-perceived employability development and validation of a scale. *Personnel Review, 36*(1), 23–41.

33. Kaufman, L., Rousseeuw, P. J. (2005). *Finding groups in data: An introduction to cluster analysis.* Wiley series in probability and mathematical statistics. Hoboken, N.J.: Wiley.

34. Hosmer, D. W., Lemeshow, S., Sturdivant, R. X. (2013). *Applied logistic regression* (3rd ed.). Wiley series in probability and statistics. Hoboken, New Jersey: Wiley.

Blue Ocean or Dry Desert? Blockchain and Bitcoin Impact on Tourism Industry

Chiara Acciarini⬤, **Francesco Bolici**⬤, **Gabriele Diana**⬤,
Lucia Marchegiani⬤, **and Luca Pirolo**⬤

Abstract The technological innovation has yielded great opportunities to expand and innovate the scope of services offered. This is particularly true for tourism, which has always been characterized by extensive innovativeness. The pace at which technological innovations diffuse within a specific sector depends on a variety of factors, including the influence of peers and relevant actors. The present study explores the level of interest about these new technologies on social media with the aim to explore the dynamics of reciprocal networking influence in technological diffusion. To capture the attitudes expressed in the industry, the study analyzes the ongoing discussions on Twitter as a proxy for the actors' interest. Through a social network analysis of the flow of tweets, the analysis maps the current online discourse about new technologies diffusion. Moreover, the sentiment analysis draws the current perceptions toward the diffusion of new technologies. While previous research is focused on the users' perception toward the development of new technologies in tourism, the aim of this study is to investigate the dynamics underneath the level of diffusion of information and awareness about these new technologies, which still represents an unexplored area of research. Thus, the paper contributes to the literature on new technology diffusion by intercepting current social media debate and literature studies focused on the diffusion of new technologies in tourism. The paper also highlights the role of knowledge broker in influencing this public debate.

Keywords Social network analysis · Tourism · Blockchain · Bitcoin · Artificial · Intelligence · Booking · Technology adoption · Technology diffusion · Perception · Social media

C. Acciarini · L. Pirolo
Department of Business and Management, Luiss University, Rome, Italy

F. Bolici · G. Diana
Department of Economics and Law, OrgLab-UniCLAM, University of Cassino, Cassino, Italy

L. Marchegiani (✉)
Department of Business Studies, Roma Tre University, Rome, Italy
e-mail: lucia.marchegiani@uniroma3.it

1 Introduction

Tourism is a global driver of economic and social growth. A recent research conducted by the World Travel and Tourism Council in conjunction with Oxford Economics reported that 5 billion international tourist arrivals were recorded in 2019. Furthermore, the sector contributes to almost 9 $ trillion to the world's GDP.

Nowadays, with the advent of unexpected events like the COVID-19 outbreak and the digitalization, tourism is undergoing significant changes and new business models are emerging within the sector. For instance, according to the World Economic Forum (2017), digitalization will enable an additional value of $305 billion for the sector and $700 billion for the society by 2025. Moreover, the online travel service bookings increased rapidly by 230% from 2015 to 2016 with the higher amount of revenue generated in the USA with $93.7 billion in 2018, followed by Europe with $92.3 billion of revenue in the same year; by 2023, it is expected that China will surpass the US market (Statista, 2019).

The main transformations of the sector are enabled by the digitalization phenomenon and are largely linked to the diffusion of big data, to the rise of platform economy and artificial intelligence, and to the improvement of the customer experience. On the one hand, improvement of online presence, enhancement of interactions, and development of networking structures and digital collaborations represents the principal reasons for digitalizing the business. On the other hand, the major obstacles in implementing digital technologies within the tourism industry are the lack of finance, the presence of high training costs, and the rapid technological change [1]. At the European level, the Digital Tourism Network has been established with the aim to involve either tourism operators and relevant stakeholders into an informal forum to strengthen the skills, to raise the awareness of developments in the smart use of technologies, and to support the integration of tourism businesses.

The evolution of new technologies, like cloud computing, wearable devices, and mobile tools, creates many opportunities but also several challenges. First and foremost, the digitalization of the industry supports the growth of online transactions and service activities; in addition, the interconnectedness between physical and digital worlds facilitates data exchanges and improves the communication between the parties. It is needed to consider that more than 4.5 billion people are now using the Internet, and the social media users are more than 3.8 billion today [2]. One of the main trends that will reshape the future of tourism is represented by the development of blockchain technology and its practices related to the use of digital currencies (e.g., bitcoin), the creation of smart contracts, the adoption for public services, the management of digital contents and sales, the tracking of records, the automation of supply systems, and the development of apps [3].

Although a wealth of reports shows this promising trend of technological innovation adoption in the tourism industry, to the best of our knowledge, no systematic study has been devoted so far to understand the dynamics underneath this trend. Nonetheless, diffusion of innovation has been considered a very interesting phenomenon for decades. With the increasing rate of technological innovations and the uprising of digital technologies, capturing how certain innovations diffuse has become of primary importance not only to understand the socioeconomic trends but also to leverage opportunities for service innovations. This is particularly true for specific industries like tourism where digital technologies can impact the communication, the user experiences, or even the definition of completely new business models. Diffusion of innovation theories show that within a social system, the influence of peers impacts the diffusion of certain innovation (e.g., Rogers, 1995). While a large number of previous studies focus on the influence of perceived value on the users' attitudes (Tzeng, 2011), the aim of the present research is to investigate the dynamics underneath the level of diffusion of information and awareness about new technologies in tourism. In particular, since social media analysis has been used to assess public opinion on a wide array of topics (Bian et al., 2016), the paper analyzes the social media debate around these new technologies (such as blockchain and bitcoin) as a proxy to measure how the information exchange could impact on their level of diffusion. In fact, numerous scholars have underlined how this aspect still remains an unexplored area of research (Grover et al., 2019; Min et al., 2019). Thus, our main assumption is that users who are at least informed by the existence of specific products' features and potentialities represent the basis for technology diffusion. In this sense, the degree of knowledge related to technologies represents a sort of antecedent of innovation diffusion and, consequently, adoption. To summarize, the paper attempts to answer to the following research question: *Which are the dynamics of information exchange on social media that could influence the attitude toward the diffusion of new technologies in tourism?*

2 Theoretical Background

2.1 Virtual Currency Definition

As already reported by Beccalli et al. [4], the European Central Bank defined virtual currency as "a type of unregulated, digital money, which is issued and usually controlled by its developers, and used and accepted among the members of a specific virtual community" (ECB 2012). The European Bank Authority narrowed this description as "a digital representation of value that is neither issued by a central bank or a public authority, nor necessarily attached to a fiat currency, but is accepted by natural or legal persons as a means of payment and can be transferred, stored or traded electronically" (EBA 2014). US Department of Treasury preferred a wider delineation: "a medium of exchange that operates like a currency in some environments but does not have all the attributes of real currency" [5].

The use of virtual currency has become so pervasive that major financial institutions and multinational companies have invested in their own start-up. The last recent example is the announcement of Libra, the digital currency launched by Facebook and a consortium of other companies like Vodafone, Uber, Visa, Mastercard, etc.

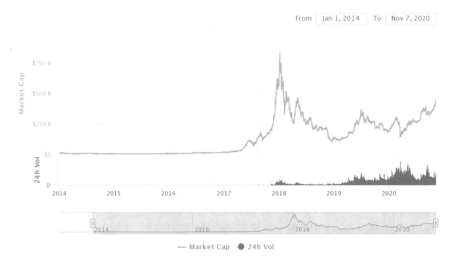

Fig. 1 Cryptocurrencies market capitalization *Source* Statista.com

The first transactions through bitcoin, in 2009, can be considered the founding moment for the cryptocurrency domain. In time, several different types of cryptocurrencies have been created, and of those, a consistent number is already forgotten. Figure 1 displays the percentage of total market capitalization evolved in the last six years.

Even with strong differences, bitcoin has always been the dominant cryptocurrency. Nowadays, bitcoin market capitalization represents around 60% of all the cryptocurrency market. This privileged position of primus inter pares is the reason for which we will include bitcoin in our analysis, as it is the best proxy to represent the whole cryptocurrency domain.

2.2 Blockchain Definition

Blockchain has recently become a "hot topic" across a broad range of sectors: from finance to healthcare, to tourism and public administration. The main appeal of blockchain is the possibility to conclude transactions without the need for a central authority, thus to operate along a decentralized model without increasing the risks of the transaction.

Blockchain is the technology behind bitcoin [1]. Satoshi Nakamoto released it publicly in 2008 when she/he/they published her/his/their paper "Bitcoin: a peer-to-peer electronic cash system." Blockchain could be defined as the first public peer-to-peer decentralized ledger being distributed to every user among the network. Blockchain relies on seven design principles: networked integrity, distributed power, value as incentive, security, privacy, rights preserved, and inclusion [6].

As synthesized by Bolici [7], its specific design (a mix of cryptography, governance model, distributed computer network, and individual economic incentives) defines blockchain as an enabler for trustless transactions: every actor does not need to trust anyone else (the other part of the transaction or a central authority) to conclude her/his arrangement. The absence of intermediaries and a strong anti-tempering system makes possible a transaction system without central authority.

This scenario was simply not possible before blockchain: a distributed database shared and replicated among all the nodes of a distributed network. It was developed as basis for bitcoin and its double-spending problem, but it does not necessarily require a cryptocurrency to work.

2.3 Technology Perception and the Adoption of Emerging Technologies

According to the definitions provided by Omar et al. (2007) and McDougall and Levesque (2000), the perceived value is considered as an overall assessment of the desirability of a product based on the trade-off between the related costs and benefits. There are several features associated with such trade-offs (Porter, 1990; Sweeney and Soutar, 2001), and one of the most common is represented by the comparison between quality and price (Cravens et al., 1988, Monroe, 1990). Furthermore, the study conducted by Sheth, Newman, and Gross (1991) classifies the perceived value into functional value, epistemic value, conditional value, social value, and emotional value; for instance, the epistemic value has a "stronger influence on intention if mediated by attitude" (p.162). More in general, the way in which users determine how valuable a product (or service) is also form their perceptions about that product (or service).

The increasing adoption of emerging technologies enables businesses, customers, and stakeholders to create value and to take advantage from innovation. Whether these technologies can be considered radical innovation, that represent a dramatic shift from the previous paradigm, is still unclear. Radical innovation would create new businesses and transform or destroy existing ones. The present stage resembles the era of ferment [8, 9], when alternative technologies have been introduced to the market, and a dominant design has not yet emerged, that is the basic architecture of product or process accepted as market standard. In general, the digitalization of the travel and tourism industry provides several benefits in terms of (i) reduction of administrative and personnel costs for flight booking processes [10]; (ii) higher customer satisfaction [11–14]; (iii) clearer and more dynamic communication of information and interactions [14, 15]; (iv) efficiency improvement; (v) maximization of profitability and services' development; (vi) long-term prosperity of tourism enterprises [16]. Moreover, according to Min (2008), new technologies increase the development of innovative service produced at minimal cost. Then, while Staab et al. [17] and Neuhofer et al. [18] emphasized the overall improvement of tourists' travel experience, together with the provision of more intelligent platform and better tourism resources allocation. Stamboulis and Skayannis [19] underlined that the attractive nature of the technology adoption enables feedback from customers, sense of involvement and belonging of the users, customer loyalty and interactive learning. To summarize, cost reduction, data and processes integration, cooperation between tourism production and distribution partners (Buhalis and O'Connor, 2005) [20, 21] as well as services specialization, flexible network's configurations, combination between consumers, processes and stakeholders [22] are some of the main advantages that arise from the use of technology. Thus, the adoption of intelligent and smart systems within the travel and tourism industry allows to create a more personalized tourism experience [23] and a "more convenient, safe, exciting, and sustainable living spaces for both residents and tourists" ([24], p. 185).

Focusing on the increasing adoption of blockchain technologies, they are generating better opportunities for action in the social media space (Wang et al., 2014). According to Statista (2020), the number of blockchain wallets has been growing with over 54 millions of users reached at the end of September 2020.[1] The usage of blockchain allows to save time and to locate travel data in one token, facilitating the management of tickets, rationalizing operations and saving transaction costs [20, 25]. In addition, recorded benefits have been investigated in other sectors like the healthcare one with lower medical costs, improvement of electronic health record and development of smarter medical devices [26]. More in general, the higher customer engagement and interaction, the provision of integrated set of experiences, and the higher the growing adoption of mobile devices and apps that generate positive returns [10–12, 21, 27]. Blockchain is a recent technology associated with the use of smart contracts and digital currencies that ensures high level of anonymity due to the use of wallets not directly connected to the identity of the owners [28, 29]. The complex and fascinating world of cryptocurrencies is evolving with new challenges and competences that should be considered and developed. According to the World Economic Forum [30], the application of cryptocurrencies creates social impact thanks to the investments in habitat restoration, species conservation, and also in public charging for electric vehicles. As an example of "cryptoconservation," Gainforest uses smart contracts to incentivize farmers to preserve the Amazon returning crowdfunded financial rewards. Furthermore, a recent report states that different central banks are interested in examining the different roles of blockchain and in experimenting central bank digital currencies. Nowadays, new currencies like Libra are emerging with a lower level of decentralization if compared with bitcoin or Ethereum, but more intense when compared with PayPal. In fact, in the digital age, in which new operators are entering the sectors, disintermediation of the activities becomes a key value driver. For instance, fintech innovations range from credit (crowdfunding and peer-to-peer lending) to payment services, from bitcoin to consulting services (e.g., robo-advisor) and blockchain. In this sense, the digital

---

[1] https://www.statista.com/statistics/647374/worldwide-blockchain-wallet-users/#:~:text=The%20number%20of%20Blockchain%20wallets,the%20end%20of%20September%202020.

channel tends to be integrated with traditional channels more and more decisively, favoring a whole redefinition of the processes.

2.4 The Level of Technology Diffusion: A Network-Based Approach

Diffusion of innovation can be defined as "the process by which an innovation is communicated through certain channels over time among the members of a social system" (Rogers, 1995). The four main elements of this concept are thus the (i) innovation, (ii) communication channels, (iii) time, (iv) social system. This study adopted the definition of innovation as "an idea, practice, or object that is perceived as new by an individual or other unit of adoption" (Rogers, 1995, p. 11). The newness of an innovation is thus a subjective concept that strongly depends on the perception of the individuals in the social systems where the innovation spreads. Generally, the diffusion of innovations over time can be represented by a S-shaped curve: at the beginning only few agents adopt a specific innovation, then a sensible increase in the number of adopting actors takes place after which a deceleration in the adoption rate follows and the curve grows at a decreasing rate (Bass, 1969). Economists explained the S-curve pattern in terms of balance between supply and demand: the upsurge in the diffusion would be caused by the decrease of innovation costs, which would increase demand and, therefore, diffusion. The probability that an initial adoption of a new service or product will be made at time t given no adoption has yet been made is a linear function of the proportion of the population that has already adopted the service or product. The model includes the coefficients p and q, where p is "the coefficient of innovation," as it captures the external influence and it refers to the probability of initial adoption independent of the influence of previous adopters, under the effects of mass media coverage or other external factors. On the other side, q is "the coefficient of imitation," as it captures the internal influence and it refers to the pressure on imitators from previous adopters, through for example the mechanism of word-of-mouth. Lyytinen and Damsgaard (2001) argue that it is necessary to adopt a network approach to understand the diffusion of complex and interactive innovations. Innovation is influenced by the perception of individuals belonging to the same social system and a network approach—that considers the relationships among actors—is deemed as the most appropriate in studying the diffusion of complex and interactive innovations.

In this context, the adoption of digital networks facilitates the sharing of ideas and the distribution of knowledge (Sproull and Kiesler 1991). In fact, several studies associate the role of specific actors' characteristics with their influence on the electronic word-of-mouth (eWOM) and so on the diffusion of information (Araujo et al., 2017) that can ultimately lead to innovation diffusion. Thus, it is interesting to investigate the communication dynamics on social media to capture the information exchange and the emergent behavior of knowledge brokers.

The present study aims to analyze both the individual actors' perception of blockchain in tourism, as well as the network of connections (and potential influences) among the actors. The assumption is that the network of tweets collected through a selected combination of keywords (e.g., #blockchain & #tourism) is a proxy of the interest toward the use of distributed solutions—as blockchain and bitcoin—in the tourism sector. Thus, the study builds on the consideration that technology and social aspects are not dichotomous, but rather inseparable [31]. Adopting this approach, the paper (i) identifies the characteristics and the dimensions of the public debate about distributed systems, in particular blockchain, in the tourism sector; (ii) qualitatively identifies the structure of the information networks and the relative positions of the individual nodes (profiles) to investigate the potentialities and limitations of the communication dynamics; (iii) conducts a sentiment analysis to have a general understanding of the positive or negative attitude of the actors toward the object of their discussion.

3   Research Approach and Methods

To perform this analysis, we followed the same sounded methodology we already used in other studies [32] crossing a set of domain specific keywords (#tourism, #travel, and #hotel) with those connected to distributed technological solutions (#bitcoin and #blockchain). Then, we have set up a specific script to automatically collect the 6 combinations of those hashtags (#tourism and #bitcoin; #tourism and blockchain; #travel and #bitcoin; #travel and blockchain; etc.) in real time. The data collection (during the period March15–June 24, 2019) amounts to 9304 tweets generated by over 3 thousand accounts.

First, we perform a descriptive analysis of frequencies (both of profiles and tweets) to identify the level of discussion around the six different networks on the social media. The first step of analysis allowed us to identify and select the two most dynamic networks (#travel associated with the two technological keywords). We then performed a social network analysis (SNA) on the two subnetworks in order to identify their key characteristics and eventually similarities and differences between them. Social network analysis is based on the assumption of the importance of relationship among actors [33, 34] and focuses on concepts like: (i) actors and their actions; (ii) flow, or links among actors; (iii) network models at the individual level (as set of opportunities and constraints); (iv) network models as structure.

4   Main Findings

The analysis of the six datasets has provided two main insights: i. Information about the characteristics of each network and ii. The possibility to identify similarities and differences in the networks interested in different technological aspects (bitcoin vs blockchain).

Figure 2 represents the number of Twitter profiles (nodes) that have tweeted or retweeted the selected combination of hashtags. It is clear that the number of profiles interested in the touristic domain associated to blockchain platform is much larger than those interested in bitcoin.

The very same insight is reinforced also by the number of tweets and retweets (Fig. 3) that in around 66% of the cases concern #blockchain.

On the basis of this descriptive analysis, we selected the two combinations: i. #travel and #bitcoin, and ii. #travel and #blockchain as the richest from communication flow and public interest perspective. We selected these two networks to compare their characteristics and structure.

#Travel & #bitcoin. The network #travel & #bitcoin has 642 actors (twitter profiles) and a total of 2555 tweets. Five profiles have been identified as the most active in the whole network: three of them are travel agencies, one is a influencer e web marketing specialist, and the last one is a travel blog. Most of the tweets are focused on the possibility to buy touristic services (hotel, trips, travels packages) though cryptocurrencies (not only bitcoin).

The analysis of the modularity class [35] confirms the high centralization level of the network: out of the 126 communities detected by the algorithm, the five communities centered around the aforementioned nodes include the 64.3% of all nodes in the network (Fig. 4).

#Travel & #blockchain. This is the largest of the selected networks with 1639 actors (twitter profiles) and a total of 4515 tweets. The structure of this network is similar to the previous one, but the size is the double, both in the number of profiles and tweets.

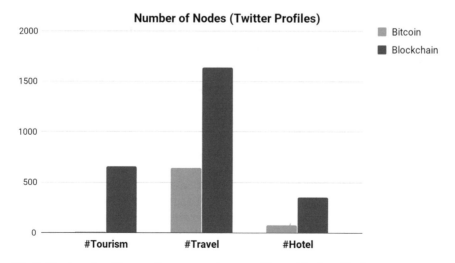

Fig. 2 Number of profiles tweeting or retweeting a specific combination of hashtags

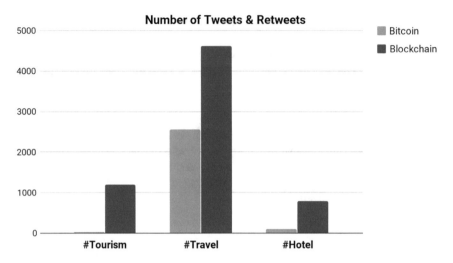

Fig. 3 Number of tweets mentioning a specific combination of #hashtags

Another insight is that the main profiles have a high engagement rate, showing that the interest of the general public toward this topic is potentially high.

Again, the analysis of the modularity confirms the high centralization of the network: not surprisingly, the number of identified communities is far larger compared to the first network (344) but at the same time, we can observe higher levels of centralization around a specific node: the community centered around the node TratokT includes the 19% of all relations and node in the network, highlighting the role of this node in the whole diffusion of information process on the social media (Fig. 5).

5 Discussion and Conclusions

Our study demonstrates a rising interest of the Twitter debate toward blockchain and cryptocurrencies in tourism. In particular, an increasing number of profiles is exchanging information about tourism, and the predominant number of tweets refers to blockchain and bitcoin although the discussion is fostered by few nodes brokering the discussion on the selected micro-blogging platform. Thus, our study shows that there is a growing interest toward blockchain and cryptocurrencies within the sector. Another interesting insight that we gained is referred to the characteristics of both structure and centralization level of the information networks. Indeed, through the analysis of the discourses posted on Twitter over a significant time span, this paper proposes an exploratory analysis of the information exchange that influence the diffusion of technology solutions in this specific industry. This growth in the level of interest by actors operating in the sector is furtherly confirmed by the constantly

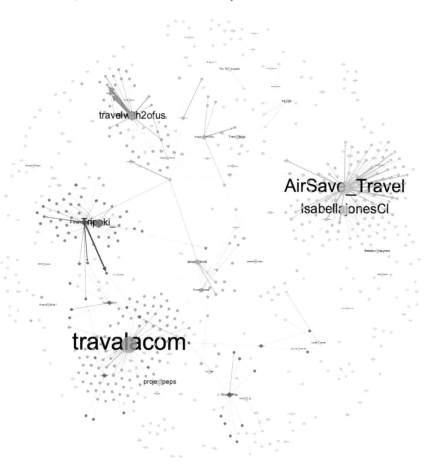

Fig. 4 Information network emerging combining #travel & #bitcoin hashtags

increasing number of tweets and profiles discussing and debating around this topic. We show that the main profiles have a high engagement rate, and that the interest of the general public toward this topic is potentially high. At a deeper level of analysis, the results of the SNA show that the #travel network is currently the largest one (with 73% of tweets dealing with blockchain) and has expanded more rapidly than the #tourism network. Both networks are highly centralized, and the central actors are associated with cryptocurrency and cryptocurrencies trade.

Notwithstanding the interesting results that were obtained through our study, this work has some limitations useful to trace future developments. Firstly, the statistical analysis has been conducted during a limited period of time. Even though social networks in general, and Twitter in particular, are digital platforms on which contents are constantly updated, a longer period of time can provide a deeper comprehension of the social interaction on these topics. Secondly, a specific content analysis can be performed with the aim to identify the most discussed topics and technologies

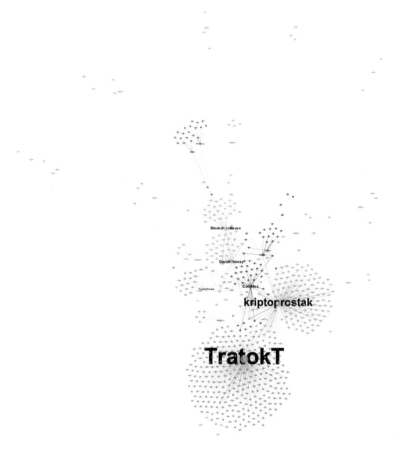

Fig. 5 Information network emerging combining #travel & #blockchain hashtags

within the sector. Further analysis might be focused on studying the role of brokers in fostering the information exchange on the platform by studying their social media strategies and highlighting which type of content maximizes people engagement.

References

1. Cai, Y., Zhu, D. (2016) Fraud detections for online businesses: A perspective from blockchain technology. *Financial Innovation, 2*(1), 20. https://doi.org/10.1186/s40854-016-0039-4
2. We Are Social (2020). Digital Around The World In April 2020
3. Nam, K., Dutt, C. S., Chathoth, P., & Khan, M. S. (2019). Blockchain technology for smart city and smart tourism: latest trends and challenges. *Asia Pacific Journal of Tourism Research*, 1–15
4. Beccalli E., Bolici F., Virili, F. (2015). Anonymity or Speculation? Risks and sources of legitimacy for virtual currencies, WOA2015

5. USDT2013 Application of FinCEN's regulations to persons administering, exchanging, or using virtual currencies. Financial Crimes Enforcement Network. 18 March 2013

6. Tapscott, D., Tapscott, A. (2016). Blockchain revolution: How the technology behind bitcoin is changing money, business, and the world. Penguin

7. Bolici, F. (2019). Blockchain as innovation model: A coordination framework for inter-organizational interactions, WOA2019

8. Abernathy, W., & Utterback, J. (1978). Patterns of industrial innovations. *Technology Review, 80*(7), 40–47.

9. Dosi, G. (2016). Technological paradigms and technological trajectories. *Research Policy, 1982*(11), 147–162.

10. Jeon, H. M., Ali, F., & Lee, S. W. (2019). Determinants of consumers' intentions to use smartphones apps for flight ticket bookings. *The Service Industries Journal, 39*(5–6), 385–402.

11. Buhalis, D., & Sinarta, Y. (2019). Real-time co-creation and nowness service: Lessons from tourism and hospitality. *Journal of Travel & Tourism Marketing, 36*(5), 563–582. https://doi.org/10.1080/10548408.2019.1592059

12. Presenza, A., Messeni Petruzzelli, A., & Sheehan, L. (2019). Innovation trough tradition in hospitality. *The Italian case of Albergo Diffuso, Tourism Management, 72*, 192–201.

13. Stankov, U., & Filimonau, V. (2019). Reviving calm technology in the e-tourism context. *The Service Industries Journal, 39*(5–6), 343–360.

14. Zhang, S. N., Li, Y. Q., Liu, C. H., & Ruan, W. Q. (2019). Critical factors in the identification of word-of-mouth enhanced with travel apps: The moderating roles of Confucian culture and the switching cost view. *Asia Pacific Journal of Tourism Research, 24*(5), 422–442.

15. Alvaro, E., Arenas, J. M. G., & Urueña, A. (2019). How does IT affect design centricity approaches: Evidence from Spain's smart tourism ecosystem. *International Journal of Information Management, 45*, 149–162.

16. Buhalis, D. (1998). Strategic use of information technologies in the tourism industry. *Tourism Management, 19*(5), 409–421, ISSN 0261-5177, https://doi.org/10.1016/S0261-5177(98)00038-7

17. Staab, S., Werthner, H., Ricci, F., Zipf, A., Gretzel, U., Fesenmaier, D. R., Paris, C., & Knoblock, C. (2002). Intelligent systems for tourism. *IEEE intelligent systems, 6*, 53–64.

18. Neuhofer, B., Buhalis, D., & Ladkin, A. (2013). A typology of technology-enhanced tourism experiences. *International Journal of Tourism Research, 16*(4), 340–350.

19. Stamboulis, Y., & Skayannis, P. (2003). Innovation strategies and technology for experience-based tourism. *Tourism management, 24*(1), 35–43.

20. Karinsalo, A., Halunen, K. (2018). Smart Contracts for a Mobility-as-a-Service Ecosystem. In 2018 IEEE International Conference on Software Quality, Reliability and Security Companion (QRS-C), Lisbon, pp. 135–138. https://doi.org/10.1109/QRS-C.2018.00036

21. Treiblmaier, H., & Önder, I. (2019). The impact of blockchain on the tourism industry: A theory-based research framework. In Business Transformation through Blockchain (pp. 3–21). Palgrave Macmillan: Cham

22. Werthner, H. (2002). Intelligent systems in travel and tourism. In IJCAI 2003: 18th International Joint Conference on Artificial Intelligence

23. Capriello, A., & Riboldazzi, S. (2019). How can a travel agency network survive in the wake of digitalization? Evidence from the Robintur case study. *Current Issues in Tourism.* https://doi.org/10.1080/13683500.2019.1590321

24. Gretzel, U., Sigala, M., & Xiang, Z. (2015). Smart tourism: Foundations and developments. *Electron Markets, 25*, 179. https://doi.org/10.1007/s12525-015-0196-8

25. Goldman Sachs (2014). All about Bitcoin, Goldman Sachs Global Marco Research

26. Pilkington, M. (2017). Can blockchain technology help promote new tourism destinations? The example of medical tourism in Moldova. Available at SSRN: https://ssrn.com/abstract=2984479 or https://doi.org/10.2139/ssrn.2984479

27. Qin, M., Tang, C. H. H., Jang, S. S., & Lehto, X. (2017). Mobile app introduction and shareholder returns. *Journal of Hospitality and Tourism Management, 31*, 173–180.

28. Leung D., Dickinger A. (2017). Use of Bitcoin in online travel product shopping: The European perspective. In R. Schegg & B. Stangl (Eds.) *Information and communication technologies in tourism 2017*. Springer: Cham

29. Polasik, M., Piotrowska, A., Wisniewski, T. P., Kotkowski, R., & Lightfoot, G. (2015). Price fluctuations and the use of bitcoin: An empirical inquiry. *International Journal of Electronic Commerce, 20*(1), 9–49.

30. World Economic Forum (2018). Building Block(chain)s a Better Planet

31. Bolici, F., Giustiniano, L. (2013). Design science and eTrust: Designing organizational artifacts as nexus of social and technical interactions. In organizational change and information systems (pp. 177–190). Berlin, Heidelberg: Springer

32. Bolici, F., Acciarini, C., Marchegiani, L. & Pirolo, L. (2020). Innovation diffusion in tourism: How information about blockchain is exchanged and characterized on twitter, The TQM Journal, Vol. ahead-of-print No. ahead-of-print. https://doi.org/10.1108/TQM-01-2020-0016

33. Scott, J. (1988). Social network analysis. *Sociology, 22*(1), 109–127.

34. Wasserman, S., & Faust, K. (1994). Social network analysis: Methods and applications, Vol. 8. Cambridge University Press

35. Blondel, V. D., Guillaume, J. L., Lambiotte, R., & Lefebvre, E. (2008). Fast unfolding of community hierarchies in large networks. *Journal of statistical mechanics: Theory and Experiment, 10*(10), 10008.

Ecosystems in Blockchain Competence Certification: An Explorative Multi-Perspective Analysis

Francesco Bolici, Roberta Cuel, Cristiano Ghiringhelli, and Francesco Virili

Abstract The need for specific skills and competencies evolves in response to environmental, social and organizational conditions. However, the model for certifying competence levels has remained almost unchanged for centuries: universities (and other institutions) verify and certify that a person has reached a certain level of knowledge and through a standalone solution. The output is often a signed and stamped document that undoubtedly contains limitations in the present international, multilingual and dynamic job market. Universities, educational institutions and consortiums are increasingly exploring how technologies enable and support innovative models of competence certification. In this paper, we investigate how blockchain technologies improve the certification system and generate added value for different involved actors: learners, educational institutions and businesses. An exploratory study is proposed to systematize the overall impacts of blockchain in the field of digital certification while focusing on university education as the main research field. We conducted a first set of interviews with key players of the two Italian universities that first adopted a blockchain certification system. The aim is to investigate, through different but complementary organizational theories, the value creation factors and conditions for the various actors in the blockchain-based competence certification ecosystem.

F. Bolici
University of Cassino and Southern Lazio, Loc. Folcara, 03043 Cassino, Italy
e-mail: f.bolici@unicas.it

R. Cuel
University of Trento, Via Inama 5, 38122 Trento, Italy
e-mail: roberta.cuel@unitn.it

C. Ghiringhelli
University of Milano-Bicocca, Piazza dell'Ateneo Nuovo 1, 20126 Milan, Italy
e-mail: cristiano.ghiringhelli@unimib.it

F. Virili (✉)
University of Sassari, DiSea, Via Muroni 25, 07100 Sassari, Italy
e-mail: fvirili@uniss.it

© The Author(s), under exclusive license to Springer Nature Switzerland AG 2022
L. Solari et al. (eds.), *Do Machines Dream of Electric Workers?*, Lecture Notes
in Information Systems and Organisation 49,
https://doi.org/10.1007/978-3-030-83321-3_7

Keywords Explorative analysis · Value generation · Blockchain · Organizational perspectives · Certification platforms

1 Purpose of the Research

Studies on skills and competencies have often taken for granted that universities and other educational institutions would continue to act as key certification bodies. This traditional certification routine is now under pressure. On the one hand, there are new actors (not necessarily universities or traditional educational institutions) in the education and training market. On the other, technological progress and globalization, to name but two factors, demand a radical innovation of the whole educational sector and thus introduce new competitive challenges for traditional institutions.

Universities are now at the centre of this challenging scenario where tension exists among legacy systems, European and national regulations, learner empowerment and an increasing number of students who complete their learning programs across different institutions utilizing different learning techniques. In this scenario, innovative forms of competence certification, enabled by digital platforms and in particular blockchain systems, are playing an increasingly relevant role.

Our aim is to explore value generation in competence certification ecosystems enabled by blockchain and digital platforms. Included in these ecosystems are universities, students and firms with diverse value perceptions and drivers. Organizational theories, as discussed in the following section, constitute a useful lens to analyse the ecosystem at different levels (individual, organizational and institutional) and to make sense of value generation drivers and conditions.

We propose an exploratory study to systematize the overall impacts of blockchain in the field of digital certification, focusing on university education as the main research field. We conducted a first set of interviews and a focus group with key players from the Italian universities that first adopted a blockchain certification system. The aim is to investigate through different theoretical lenses and organizational perspectives what the factors and conditions for value creation in the ecosystems of blockchain competence certification are perceived to be.

2 Theoretical Framework and Theories Applied

To make sense of the potential value generated by blockchain-based competence certification in complex organizational ecosystems, we use different organizational theories as analytical lenses [18].

In order to define the boundaries of our research and prepare a first version of interview agenda, we take advantage of consolidated streams of studies as the institutional perspective, and the digital ecosystem theories, grounded in the socio-technical perspective.

3 The Neo-Institutional Perspective

As stated in Hinings et al. [14, p. 53], "Institutional theory emphasizes that orga-nizations are [...] social and cultural systems that are embedded within an "insti-tutional" context of social expectations and prescriptions about what constitutes appropriate ("legitimate") behaviour. [...] Organizations are seriously constrained by social expectations and the social approval legitimacy of particular actions and ways of organizing [9, 16]".

The neo-institutional theory analyses complex patterns of technology adoption in the light of isomorphic processes of organizational convergence: normative, mimetic and coercive pressures [10]. "Adoption becomes a way of demonstrating organiza-tional legitimacy through copying other organizations (mimetic isomorphism), or is legislated because of that societal legitimacy (coercive legitimacy) or is diffused as the appropriate professional standard (normative legitimacy)" [13, p. 53].

Neo-institutional analysis, when applied to complex multi-level systems, contains limitations: its lack of an explicit account of agentic action, together with its vagueness on measures and operationalization at the different levels of analysis, makes it difficult to address circumstances of institutional complexity and to explain conflicting evidence of differing organizational responses [4, 19, 20].

Nevertheless, the neo-institutional perspective, supplemented by complementary views in the form of economic studies on network effects, is appropriate when accounting for the relational dimension of adoption choices in digital ecosystems and how isomorphic social forces are driving organizations towards convergent patterns.

3.1 The Socio-Technical Perspective and the Digital Ecosystems Theories

The socio-technical perspective [2, 3] enables us to analyse the complex compe-tence certification system by addressing the process of certification and the corre-sponding work design as a nexus of interactions between people and technology in the development of innovative solutions in and among organizations.

Research has shown the relationships between products and service characteristics and the traits of the organizations (e.g. communication, coordination, decision struc-ture) that create them [7, 13, 24]. This approach is an application of task contingency theory [11, 15, 25] to complex technical systems, useful when studying the design and development of a new process (and product) which requires the coordination of a wide range of actors.

The socio-technical perspective aids the analysis of the relationship between the characteristics of universities and the technological solutions adopted in the process of competence certification. This becomes even more interesting at a higher level of analysis where a network of universities collaborate to develop shared technical solutions through distributed technologies (as in the blockchain case—Blockcerts).

Thus, a socio-technical perspective can be utilized to analyse both the intra- and inter-organizational settings. Moreover, recent studies on digital ecosystems may be seen as an evolution of the socio-technical perspective. The term digital business ecosystem (DBE) initially referred to a collaborative organizational networked environment made up of different organizations and actors that co-create value through information and communication technologies [17, 23, p. 52]. In recent years, a systematic understanding was given by [8] through a convincing comparative analysis of digital platforms and digital ecosystems and by [12] when distinguishing different types of ecosystems (business, innovation and digital). The digital ecosystems theory explicitly considers the influence in the social system of the technically oriented, utility-based factors, according to the so-called mirroring hypothesis [7].

All in all, the socio-technical perspective on digital ecosystems is complemented by the neo-institutional perspective, discussed in the previous section, by explicitly addressing the organizational search of legitimacy and its isomorphic pressures. A unifying view is provided by the analysis of the value generated in the ecosystems by the composite effects of multiple-level choices: studies from different perspectives on value co-creation in ecosystems [1, 6, 22, 26, 27] are a useful reference point.

4 Research Methods

The study proposed here is aimed at a systematic exploration of the ongoing development process of digital academic credentials in the field of university education. We conducted a first set of interviews with key players that promote a blockchain certification system. The interviews were targeted as an initial interpretive investigation—through a set of organizational lens—on value creation factors and conditions for the different entities of the blockchain certification ecosystem.

We collected data through a three-step process:

1. desk analysis;
2. direct observation;
3. semi-structured interviews.

The desk analysis represents the initial collection of secondary data needed to frame our research work. We extensively searched and analysed the literature regarding:

- the most common stream of studies in organization and ICT identifying three main perspectives (see Sect. 2);
- past experiences aimed at developing an innovative framework of competence certification systems, regulations and ICT solutions (with a specific focus on blockchain).

Two of the authors are personally involved in the processes of developing a distributed digital system for competence certification in their own institutions. Thus, we were able to collect a set of direct observations on the motivations, gateways, triggers, obstacles and potentialities at different stages of the process. We recognize the potential bias of collecting data through participatory research [5, 21], and we smooth them out by integrating such data with semi-structured interviews with key actors.

We developed an interview protocol to facilitate and guide semi-structured open-ended interviews. We recorded the interviews and all the researchers listened to them for later discussion. All the collected data were analysed individually by each researcher, and then discussed and structured together. Significant episodes retold by the interviewer emerged and were then matched to organizational elements. In the following section, we highlight some key episodes and point out their organizational relevance.

5   Main and Expected Findings

In 2016, the University of Milan-Bicocca (hereafter UniMiB) started a pilot project to develop a digital academic credential system. The aim was to build an innovative model enabling universities to digitally certify learners' competences, skills and participation activities. Three key requirements lead the system development:

1. Self-verification: each certificate can be verified without the involvement of the issuer;
2. Incorruptibility: to ensure that the certificate is not counterfeit;
3. Autonomy: the digital certificate, once verified, remains valid even if the issuer ceases to exist.

The interoperability among all the interested universities is a key outcome of this digital academic credential system to facilitate student exchange, ECTS recognition and authentication, especially at European level. During the interviews, one of the experts mentioned estimations of around 60 million students moving from emerging countries to advanced economies university systems in the near future. If confirmed, this trend will dramatically challenge the existing structure and organization of the university system. As a consequence, the role of digital learning is becoming more and more important, both in providing a partial solution to the high number of students as well as sustaining "stackable" degree programs between academic institutions and learning platforms.

According to the process depicted in Fig. 1, the increasing effort on soft skill development recommended by several European institutions, including the European University Association, strongly triggered the project aimed at developing a digital academic credential system at UniMiB.

Indeed, UniMiB introduced the focus on soft skills development as a key issue in its three-year strategic plan. At the same time, the CINECA consortium, a major technology partner for Italian Universities, developed a digital certification management system called open digital badge platform. As a result, collaboration with CINECA

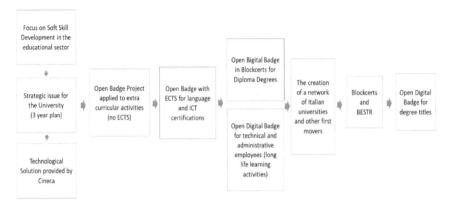

Fig. 1 The development of a digital academic credential system

occurred and the first main outcome was the open digital badge project. This represents the first stage of the process aimed at developing a digital academic credential system. Since it was possible to integrate it with the existent technical platform (e.g. esse3), the open digital badge project provided the inclusion of the "Diploma Supplement" in the formal certification process.

Other universities then started similar or parallel processes, e.g. the University of Padua started to collaborate with UniMiB and was involved in the network of Italian universities and now other universities are interested in the project; for instance, the University of Trento is currently evaluating the adoption of Blockcerts for certifying their degree titles.

5.1 A Neo-Institutional Interpretation

The interviews confirmed that the neo-institutional perspective provides significant insights in the study of the development of a digital academic certification system in that diverse forces, dynamics and pressures that influence actors and patterns become evident.

According to normative isomorphism, a constellation of various actors are investing extensive resources with the aim of introducing a new model of competence certification based on blockchain technologies. For example, Europass aims to assist citizens, employers education and training authorities to define, certify and effectively communicate the content of curricula (according to national and international standards). MIT coordinates a group of leading universities, and founded the digital academic credential consortium aimed at designing an infrastructure for digital academic credentials and a set of international standards. This initiative wants to avoid a "lock-in" effect which could be imposed by private leading companies. In Italy, the network of the first-movers is leading the development of specific standards which the main regulatory national institutions (i.e. CRUI, ANVUR and MIUR) can recommend as a good practice for the Italian university system. Moreover, a further normative effect could emerge from other European universities (especially in Scandinavia) that act as a valuable benchmark.

In the light of coercive isomorphism, European Commission has put forward recommendations which underline the alignment of national certification with:

- the European Qualifications Framework, which acts as a translation device to make national qualifications more readable across Europe, promoting workers' and learners' mobility between countries and facilitating their lifelong learning;
- European Skills, Competences, Qualifications and Occupations (ESCO), a multilingual classification of skills, competences, qualifications and occupations;
- the electronic IDentification, Authentication and trust Services (eIDAS), the unique identifier that enables a verified, legally recognized digital signature.

In terms of mimetic isomorphism, universities may mimic and other organizations adopting the digital academic certification system. Although resistance to change can be a crucial obstacle, the successful examples of other universities, perhaps those using the same information system (esse3), makes emulating others easier.

5.2 A Socio-Technical Interpretation: Digital Ecosystems Analysis

According to the socio-technical perspective, four common dimensions should be analysed:

- the issuing process, managing and using the open digital badge;
- the structure of educational organizations;
- "physical" systems such as legacy systems, software, third platforms and other facilities used in the process;
- people and how technicians, administrative staff, professors and learners interpret and use the open digital badges platform.

The process relies heavily on the technological layer, but some other significant aspects (e.g. tensions and resistance) may come to light. In the focus group, some actors expressed a resistance to the system because they do not see the potential advantages in reducing the costs of administrative procedures (physical system), and they also want to retain complete control of the data since traditionally universities are the sole recognized authority of certification (structure). Contrarily, an interviewee promoting the digital academic Credentials considers the system as very valuable, and explained that a decentralized system of certification would radically change the role played by universities and other organizations in the educational market (structure). The same divergent opinions can be found on the lack of regulations.

The interviewees have different expertise and attitudes toward technology and the foreseen certification systems.

The ecosystem lens provides a means of investigation that underline aspects of critical mass, network effects and mutual interdependencies that create value. This would lead to the adoption of a wider ecosystem perspective instead of the digital ecosystem view.

Leading organizations can promote a broader adoption, eventually sustained also by coercive and top-down rules introduced by regulators. The interviews confirmed that a key issue related to the development of such ecosystems is the value perceived by the involved actors. Universities represent an extremely good setting to observe, calculate and unlock the value that a digital academic credential system can generate. Not only is it crucial in terms of competitive advantage in a task environment that places each university in an international and "stackable" market but also provides key opportunities in terms of brand reputation, transforming into institutional value the direct and indirect endorsements. Moreover, important economic savings are introduced by the adoption of a digital academic credential since it facilitates the digitalization and simplification of administrative processes. From the employer's point of view, a digital academic credential can dramatically reduce the amount of risk taken during recruitment processes (it is possible to verify that the certificates provided by the candidate are not counterfeit), and also increase the efficacy and efficiency of the CV screening.

In Italy, the critical mass can be achieved quicker than in other countries because various services are centralized at national level. For instance, the national register of students (ANS) registers and monitors 1.5 million student careers, thus each student is uniquely identified, and the related information can be easily created and updated.

6 Conclusions

This paper has analysed the introduction of the digital academic credential system in the university sector. On the one hand, the adopted perspectives enabled the authors to identify the most critical threads in the progress of the digital academic credential system in all its phases of development (Fig. 1); on the other, they confirmed the need for a multi-perspective analysis.

We did not investigate additional perspectives that emerged during the interviews analysis. These will be taken into consideration in further studies and are:

- a more in depth understanding of the ecosystems perspective, a broader view of digital ecosystem than adopted in our study;
- trust and reputation issues, which are relevant at the beginning of the process and when the market is established. Trust is also influenced by multiple factors, the reputation of the issuers and regulatory rules which tend to identify and avoid opportunistic behaviours;

- value perception and generation for the entities involved in the digital academic credential system, such as universities, learners, companies and other newcomers.

The analysis might focus not only on the recruitment processes but also on career development and employee assessment and lifelong learning as sources for competitive advantages.

Finally, a systematic approach of analysis should be investigated in depth and an operationally actionable theoretical framework validated. In particular, as suggested in [16], integrating multiple theoretical lenses would require an explicit evaluation of the conceptual distance between theories and of their different underlying assumptions.

Acknowledgements This research was supported by the Italian Ministry of Education (MIUR): "Dipartimenti di Eccellenza" Program (2018–2022)—Department of Economics and Business—University of Sassari.

References

1. Beirão, G., Patrício, L., & Fisk, R. P. (2017). Value cocreation in service ecosystems: Investigating health care at the micro, meso, and macro levels. *Journal of Service Management, 28*, 227–249.
2. Bostrom, R. P., Heinen, J. S. (1977). MIS problems and failures: a socio-technical perspective. Part II: The application of socio-technical theory. *MIS quarterly*, 11–28
3. Bostrom, R. P., Heinen, J. S. (1977). MIS problems and failures: A socio-technical perspective. Part I: The causes. *MIS quarterly*, 17–32
4. Boxenbaum, E., & Jonsson, S. (2017). Isomorphism, diffusion and decoupling: Concept evolution and theoretical challenges. *The Sage handbook of organizational institutionalism, 2*, 79–104.
5. Campbell, J. (2002). A critical appraisal of participatory methods in development research. *International Journal of Social Research Methodology, 5*, 19–29.
6. Ceccagnoli, M., Forman, C., Huang, P., & Wu, D. J. (2012). Cocreation of value in a platform ecosystem! The case of enterprise software. *MIS quarterly*, 263–290
7. Colfer, L. J., & Baldwin, C. Y. (2016). The mirroring hypothesis: Theory, evidence, and exceptions. *Industrial and Corporate Change, 25*, 709–738.
8. de Reuver, M., Sørensen, C., & Basole, R. C. (2018). The digital platform: A research agenda. *Journal of Information Technology, 33*(2), 124–135.
9. Deephouse, D. L., & Suchman, M. (2008). Legitimacy in organizational institutionalism. *The Sage handbook of organizational institutionalism, 49*, 77.
10. DiMaggio, P. J., & Powell, W. W. (1983). The iron cage revisited: Institutional isomorphism and collective rationality in organizational fields. *American sociological review*, 147–160
11. Galbraith, J. R. (1974). Organization design: An Information processing view. *Interfaces*, 28–36
12. Gupta, R., Mejia, C., & Kajikawa, Y. (2019). Business, innovation and digital ecosystems landscape survey and knowledge cross sharing. *Technological Forecasting and Social Change, 147*, 100–109.
13. Henderson, R. M., & Clark, K. B. (1990). Architectural innovation: The reconfiguration of existing. *Administrative science quarterly, 35*, 9–30.
14. Hinings, B., Gegenhuber, T., & Greenwood, R. (2018). Digital innovation and transformation: An institutional perspective. *Information and Organization, 28*, 52–61. https://doi.org/10.1016/j.infoandorg.2018.02.004

15. Lawrence, P. R., Lorsch, J. W. (1967). Differentiation and integration in complex organizations. *Administrative science quarterly*, 1–47

16. Meyer, J. W., & Rowan, B. (1977). Institutionalized organizations: Formal structure as myth and ceremony. *American Journal of Sociology, 83*, 340–363. https://doi.org/10.1086/226550

17. Nachira, F., Dini, P., Nicolai, A. (2007). A network of digital business ecosystems for Europe: Roots, processes and perspectives. European Commission, Bruxelles, Introductory Paper 106

18. Okhuysen, G., & Bonardi, J.-P. (2011). The challenges of building theory by combining lenses. *The Academy of Management Review, 36*, 6–11.

19. Oliver, C. (1992). The Antecedents of Deinstitutionalization. *Organization Studies, 13*, 563–588. https://doi.org/10.1177/017084069201300403

20. Oliver, C. (1991). *Strategic responses to institutional processes. AMR, 16*, 145–179. https://doi.org/10.5465/amr.1991.4279002

21. Pain, R., & Francis, P. (2003). Reflections on participatory research. *Area, 35*, 46–54.

22. Pera, R., Occhiocupo, N., & Clarke, J. (2016). Motives and resources for value co-creation in a multi-stakeholder ecosystem: A managerial perspective. *Journal of Business Research, 69*, 4033–4041. https://doi.org/10.1016/j.jbusres.2016.03.047

23. Senyo, P. K., Liu, K., & Effah, J. (2019). Digital business ecosystem: Literature review and a framework for future research. *International Journal of Information Management, 47*, 52–64. https://doi.org/10.1016/j.ijinfomgt.2019.01.002

24. Sosa, M. E., Eppinger, S. D., & Rowles, C. M. (2004). The misalignment of product architecture and organizational structure in complex product development. *Management science, 50*, 1674–1689.

25. Thompson, J. D. (1967). *Organizations in action: Social science bases of administrative theory*. McGraw-Hill.

26. Vargo, S. L., Wieland, H., & Akaka, M. A. (2015). Innovation through institutionalization: A service ecosystems perspective. *Industrial Marketing Management, 44*, 63–72. https://doi.org/10.1016/j.indmarman.2014.10.008

27. Wareham, J., Fox, P. B., Cano Giner, J. L. (2014). Technology ecosystem governance. *Organization Science 25*, 1195–1215

Building the Digital Public Administration: The Impact of Social Media in the Public Sector. The Perception of Public Employees in Italian Local Context

Todisco Lucio, Canonico Paolo, Mangia Gianluigi, and Tomo Andrea

Abstract In recent years, the diffusion of social media has revolutionized the way people live in society, communicate with each other and work in organizations. In detail, for public administrations, the diffusion and use of social media have meant a necessary rethinking of their work activities to increase the transparency of information and the services' efficiency to be provided to citizens. However, social media use is strictly linked to the way people use them and the perception of their usefulness for the work activities to be performed. This chapter aims to understand the perception that civil servants have on social media's impact on the transparency and quality of services to citizens. Furthermore, it provides interesting practical and managerial implications on the relationship between organizational change and the use of social media in public organizations and provides literature on the use of information and communication technologies in the public sector.

Keywords Social media · Public sector · Digital transformation

1 Introduction

In recent years, digital transformation has had a significant impact on public organizations and modified the interactions between the public sector and citizens [1, 2].

This digital transformation has led public administrations to increase relations between the public sector and citizenship through new forms of content sharing, widening participation, collaboration and transparency of policies [3–5].

In order to develop this digital transformation process, the public sector has tried to introduce ICT tools like social media in their organizations [6–9].

T. Lucio (✉) · C. Paolo · M. Gianluigi · T. Andrea
Department of Economics, Management, Institutions, ITA, University of Naples Federico II, Naples, Italy
e-mail: lucio.todisco@unina.it

© The Author(s), under exclusive license to Springer Nature Switzerland AG 2022
L. Solari et al. (eds.), *Do Machines Dream of Electric Workers?*, Lecture Notes in Information Systems and Organisation 49,
https://doi.org/10.1007/978-3-030-83321-3_8

The use of social media has represented a relevant change not only in the relationship between the public administration and citizens but also in the public employees' work modalities in organizations.

Therefore, in this chapter, we aim to explore the effectiveness of the implementation and use of information and communication technologies in the public sector, with specific attention paid to social media.

To this aim, we administered a structured questionnaire to 281 Italian public employees on the perception of the potential and criticalities of using social media in the public sector.

From a managerial point of view, this chapter illustrates the perception that public employees have of social media's role in creating added value in public administrations. From a theoretical point of view, this research intends to contribute to the debate on the impact of technologies in the public sector. The reminder of the chapter is structured as follows. The next section assesses previous literature on the use of social media in government and describes the research questions driving the study. The third section sets the research context and methodology. The fourth section presents the findings. The last section provides the findings discussion and final remarks concerning theoretical and practical implications emerging from the study.

2 The Social Media Impact in Public Sector

The impact of information and communication technologies in contemporary society has brought about a radical change in the organization's design and citizens' interactions.

In a time of significant technological developments, it is worth understanding how technological change has led to new social paradigms, tasks and roles in organizations. The growing use of new technologies in public organizations has resulted in more considerable research for effectiveness, efficiency and innovation of organizational processes to respond to new social and economic challenges [10–12].

The spread of social media is part of the dynamic development of the concept of e-government. With e-government, we indicate the use of information and communication technologies in the relationship between citizens, firms and public administrations to create direct ways of interaction with public institutions. The result is to make public administration services more efficient, reducing costs and delivery times [13, 14].

According to many researchers [15–18], social media are web technological tools that public organizations use to improve a two-way exchange with citizens.

In general, social media's use has a positive impact on the trust that citizens have of public administrations [19, 20].

One of the advantages of using social media relates to creating a culture of transparency [21, 22].

Furthermore, social media expand the audience of citizens reached by public information and increase the possibility of sharing information [7, 21].

According to many researchers [23–25], social media's positive impact is increasing citizens' participation in the lives of public administrations. More shared information leads to an increase in social interactions, growths collaboration between citizens, and allows express opinions to influence decision-making processes.

Also, social media encourage citizens' engagement in the public sphere, supporting them to join political debates, voting and participation in community life, thus supporting the consolidation of democracy [26–28].

Finally, a further positive aspect regards the use of social media in emergencies. In situations of health and social crisis, public administrations' social media can be fundamental in giving truthful, reliable and official information, countering fake news [29, 30].

However, implementing social media in the public sector has critical problems that can often be underestimated at an early stage.

The first critical aspect concerns privacy and brand reputation [29, 31]. The concept of privacy is connected to regulatory and management viewpoints. The potential uncertainties concern risks of loss of control over sensitive information and data of citizens or firms.

A second aspect strictly connected to privacy's topic concerns the regulation of data access. Sharing public information involves creating new rules for monitoring technical problems related to the theft of sensitive data. [32, 33].

A third aspect refers to the possibility that social media's introduction does not necessarily lead to improved communication processes and interaction with citizens [33, 34].

The ineffectiveness of the communicative message is possible due to the difficulties of citizens having a stable Internet connection or the lack of the essential skills for the recovery of information shared via social media [9].

Starting from the analysis of the positive and critical aspects of the use of social media in the public administration, it is interesting to understand what is the perception that public employees have of the effectiveness of these technological tools in the public sector.

This chapter was inspired by the following question: How do public employees evaluate the impact of social media in the public sector?

3 Research Setting and Design

3.1 Research Context

In recent decades, the implementation, management and use of information and communication technologies in the Italian public administration have been relevant. From a normative point of view, it is the CAD—Digital Administration Code—that regulates the digital rights of citizens and firms with the public administrations and the use of ICT tools in the Italian public sector.

In 2011, the FORMEZ report "public administration and social media" provided some useful indications for the correct use of social media in the public sphere. With the three-year plan for information technology in the Italian public administration (2019–2021), the dissemination of the 'digital-first" principle was established as a priority goal to design citizens' services starting from the use of digital technologies such as social media.

Currently, according to the latest ISTAT report on the Italian public administrations, in 2017, 87.9% of these used the information and communication technologies for data management and to provide services to citizens and firms.

However, the Italian public administration's digitalization process presents some criticalities. The diffusion of social media concerns 87.9% of Italian central administrations, but only 42.1% of Italian local administrations. On average, only four out of ten public institutions interact with citizens using social media. The main ICT tools used in the Italian public institutions are social networks (38.3%). Only 14.8% of public administrations use instant messaging tools and 13.8% of these use multimedia content sharing websites (e.g., Instagram, YouTube and other platform and tools). (ISTAT, 2017).

3.2 Questionnaire and Sample

For this research, the questionnaire was based on understanding the perception of the positive and critical use of social media in the Italian public sector.

Our sample, selected from a convenience sample, involved 281 public employees from different Italian public administrations (central administrations, local administrations, universities and research institutes).

These public employees participated in a high-level training course on information and communication technologies in the public sector held at the University of Naples Federico II.

This specific sample's choice is based on the assumption that public employees involved in the analysis are actively interested in developing of digital tools and social media to improve the quality of public administration.

Finally, starting from the latest official report on Italian public administrations (ISTAT, 2017), the sample analysed well replicates public employees' distribution in Italian public administrations in terms of representation of the types of public administration and the individual position held.

Public employees were asked about their perception on (i) the perception of the social media's role in public administrations, (ii) the perception of the social media's usefulness in improving the quality of services and (iii) the perception of the social media's usefulness in enhancing transparency in the management of data information. Finally, we wanted to verify whether this positive perception was more significant among young public employees than older colleagues.

A Likert scale of 1–5 was used to answer the questionnaire (1 = totally disagree, 5 = completely agree). Also, we considered the following socio-demographic variables

Table 1 Socio-demographic variables

	0	1	2	3
Age (A)	<35	35–50	>50	–
Sex (S)	Male	Female	–	–
Institution (I)	Central Administrations	Local Administrations	University and Research Institutes	-
Education (E)	High School	Bachelor's Degree	Master's Degree	Specializations
Length of Service (LS)	<5	5–10	11–15	>15

for each public employee: age, gender, administration, education and length of service (Table 1).

4 Results

The results confirm how social media tools are correlated with positive results from the viewpoint of public employees' perspectives.

As shown in Table 2, regarding the perception of social media's usefulness in public administrations (Q1), 60% of the public employees interviewed agree or completely agree on their usefulness for the improvement of public administration (agree, 27%; completely agree, 33%).

As regards the quality of services provided to citizens (Q2), the perception that public employees interviewed have on the role of social media is extremely positive.

71% agree or completely agree on the decisive role that social media have in improving the quality of public administration services provided to citizens (agree, 32%; completely agree, 41%).

Finally, 72% of public employees who responded to the questionnaire have a relevant consideration on the positive role that social media has in improving transparency in the management and use of data (Q3) (agree, 31%; completely agree, 41%).

Table 2 Perception of the social media's positive role in public administration (from 1: totally disagree to 5: completely agree)

	1	2	3	4	5
Q1	7%	13%	20%	27%*	33%*
Q2	2%	9%	16%	32%*	41%*
Q3	7%	5%	16%	31%*	41%*

Table 3 Perception of the social media's positive role in public administration (from 1: totally disagree to 5: completely agree) crossing age socio-demographic variable with the variable Q1

	1	2	3	4	5
A0	5%	5%	5%	40%*	45%*
A1	8%	6%	19%	29%	38%
A2	4%	18%	38%	22%	18%

Table 4 Perception of the social media's positive role in public administration (from 1: totally disagree to 5: completely agree) crossing age socio-demographic variable with the variable Q2

	1	2	3	4	5
AO	0%	4%	4%	35%*	57%*
A1	0%	9%	27%	33%	31%
A2	9%	14%	34%	28%	15%

Table 5 Perception of the social media's positive role in public administration (from 1: totally disagree to 5: completely agree) crossing age socio-demographic variable with the variable Q3

	1	2	3	4	5
AO	7%	3%	3%	40%*	47%*
A1	2%	9%	21%	24%	44%
A2	23%	0%	24%	33%	20%

To complete the analysis, we wanted to verify the percentage of responses related to the positive perception of social media in the public sector concerning the age socio-demographic variable.

It is interesting to verify in Tables 3, 4 and 5 how young public employees (AO) compared to older colleagues see social media as useful tools for improving public administration.

5 Discussion and Conclusions

Social media has represented an essential change in how public organizations interact with citizens and represent an opportunity for public employees to change their working modalities.

The present research results reflect how the development of a technological and open society requires a further public administration charge. The digital age provides public administrations with a significant amount of information that can be used and shared in order to improve the quality of the services offered. From the concept of e-government, public institutions are moving towards that of open government, a model according to which governments and public administrations must be transparent and their activities open and available to support and assure greater public control of public sector work through new technologies [35, 36].

This chapter aimed to understand the perception that public employees have on the effectiveness of social media applications in work contexts. From a managerial point of view, the research's results show how public employees have a positive perception of social media, seen as critical tools for implementing change processes in public organizations. Social media represents a significant challenge for the public sector to improve transparency and citizens' trust in public administrations, better use and manage data held by public administrations and define more effective interaction methods between public organizations and society [6, 37].

Young public employees mainly see this positive perception. They show a strict connection with citizens' expectations from public administrations on the use of information and communication technologies. Furthermore, this result focuses on the digital divide between young and older workers [38, 39].

From a theoretical point of view, the present study contributes to the literature on the use of social media in the public sector.

In so doing, we support an improved understanding of the role that new technologies play in the public sector, providing the reason for thinking on the role they play in defining a more open, efficient and transparent digital society.

A limitation of this research concerns the analysis of a specific context, such as the Italian one, which is still in a preliminary phase of development in the use of digital tools in the public sector and, mainly, in social media use. However, this allows, compared to the use of digital tools to be an interesting starting point for future, more in-depth research on the topic of the use of digital tools in public organizations and the digital skills of public employees.

References

1. West, D. M. (2004). E-government and the transformation of service delivery and citizen attitudes. *Public Administration Review, 64*(1), 15–27.
2. Danziger, J. N., & Andersen, K. V. (2002). The impacts of information technology on public administration: An analysis of empirical research from the "golden age" of transformation. *International Journal of Public Administration, 25*(5), 591–627.
3. Hansen, H. K., & Flyverbom, M. (2015). The politics of transparency and the calibration of knowledge in the digital age. *Organization, 22*(6), 872–889.
4. Meijer, A. (2013). Understanding the complex dynamics of transparency. *Public administration review, 73*(3), 429–439.
5. Kim, S., & Lee, J. (2012). E-participation, transparency, and trust in local government. *Public Administration Review, 72*(6), 819–828.
6. Mergel, I. (2013). A framework for interpreting social media interactions in the public sector. *Government Information Quarterly, 30*(4), 327–334.
7. Mergel, I. (2012). The social media innovation challenge in the public sector. *Information Polity, 17*(3, 4), 281–292.
8. Linders, D. (2012). From e-government to we-government: Defining a typology for citizen coproduction in the age of social media. *Government Information Quarterly, 29*(4), 446–454.

9. Picazo-Vela, S., Gutiérrez-Martínez, I., & Luna-Reyes, L. F. (2012). Understanding risks, benefits, and strategic alternatives of social media applications in the public sector. *Government Information Quarterly, 29*(4), 504–511.
10. De Vries, H., Bekkers, V., & Tummers, L. (2016). Innovation in the public sector: A systematic review and future research agenda. *Public Administration, 94*(1), 146–166.
11. Gil-Garcia, J. R., Helbig, N., & Ojo, A. (2014). Being smart: Emerging technologies and innovation in the public sector. *Government Information Quarterly, 31*, I1–I8.
12. Orlikowski, W. J., & Barley, S. R. (2001). Technology and institutions: What can research on information technology and research on organizations learn from each other? *MIS Quarterly, 25*(2), 145–165.
13. Tolbert, C. J., & Mossberger, K. (2006). The effects of e-government on trust and confidence in government. *Public Administration Review, 66*(3), 354–369.
14. Piras, P. (2005). Organizzazione, tecnologie e nuovi diritti. *Informatica e Diritto, 14*(1–2), 89–98.
15. Todisco, L., Tomo, A., Canonico, P., Mangia, G., & Sarnacchiaro, P. (2020). Exploring social media usage in the public sector: Public employees' perceptions of ICT's usefulness in delivering value added. *Socio-Economic Planning Sciences*, 100858.
16. Di Virgilio, F., Valderrama, M., & Lopez Bolas, A. (2018). Social Media Strategy within Organizational Communication Major Open Issues and Challenges. In F. Cantoni & G. Mangia (Eds.), *Human Resource Management and Digitalization* (pp. 207–227). Routledge.
17. Mergel, I. (2018). Open innovation in the public sector: drivers and barriers for the adoption of Challenge. gov. *Public Management Review, 20*(5), 726–745.
18. Mergel, I. (2010). "The use of social media to dissolve knowledge silos in government". In O' Leary, R., Kim, S., and Van Slyke, D. M. (Eds.), *The future of public administration, public management, and public service around the world*, pp. 177–187, Washington: Georgetown University Press.
19. Avery, E. J., & Graham, M. W. (2013). Political public relations and the promotion of participatory, transparent government through social media. *International Journal of Strategic Communication, 7*(4), 274–291.
20. Bonsón, E., Torres, L., Royo, S., & Flores, F. (2012). Local e-government 2.0: Social media and corporate transparency in municipalities. *Government information quarterly, 29*(2), 123–132.
21. Gandía, J. L., Marrahí, L., & Huguet, D. (2016). Digital transparency and Web 2.0 in Spanish city councils. *Government Information Quarterly, 33*(1), 28–39.
22. Gunawong, P. (2015). Open government and social media: A focus on transparency. *Social Science Computer Review, 33*(5), 587–598.
23. Wagner, S. A., Vogt, S., & Kabst, R. (2016). How IT and social change facilitates public participation: A stakeholder-oriented approach. *Government Information Quarterly, 33*(3), 435–443.
24. Wukich, C., & Mergel, I. (2016). Reusing social media information in government. *Government Information Quarterly, 33*(2), 305–312.
25. Ellison, N., & Hardey, M. (2014). Social media and local government: Citizenship, consumption and democracy. *Local Government Studies, 40*(1), 21–40.
26. Mergel, I., & Desouza, K. C. (2013). Implementing open innovation in the public sector: The case of Challenge. gov. *Public administration review, 73*(6), 882–890.
27. Mossberger, K., Wu Y., & Crawford J. (2013), Connecting citizens and local governments? Social media and interactivity in major U.S. cities, *Government Information Quarterly*, 30 (4), 351–358.
28. Bryer, T. A., & Zavattaro, S. M. (2011). Social media and public administration: Theoretical dimensions and introduction to the symposium. *Administrative Theory & Praxis, 33*(3), 325–340.
29. Fusi, F., & Feeney, M. K. (2018). Social media in the workplace: Information exchange, productivity, or waste? *The American Review of Public Administration, 48*(5), 395–412.
30. Alexander, D. E. (2014). Social media in disaster risk reduction and crisis management. *Science and Engineering Ethics, 20*(3), 717–733.

31. Clark, A. F. (2016). Toward an Entrepreneurial Public Sector: Using Social Exchange Theory to Predict Public Employee Risk Perceptions. *Public Personnel Management, 45*(4), 335–359.
32. Thornthwaite, L. (2018). Social media and dismissal: Towards a reasonable expectation of privacy? *Journal of Industrial Relations, 60*(1), 119–136.
33. Kaul, A., Chaudhri, V., Cherian, D., Freberg, K., Mishra, S., Kumar, R., & Carroll, C. E. (2015). Social Media: The New Mantra for Managing Reputation. *Vikalpa, 40*(4), 455–491.
34. Khan, G. F., Swar, B., & Lee, S. K. (2014). Social Media Risks and Benefits: A Public Sector Perspective. *Social Science Computer Review, 32*(5), 606–627.
35. Wirtz, B. W., & Birkmeyer, S. (2015). Open government: Origin, development, and conceptual perspectives. *International Journal of Public Administration, 38*(5), 381–396.
36. Lee, G., & Kwak, Y. H. (2012). An open government maturity model for social media-based public engagement. *Government Information Quarterly, 29*(4), 492–503.
37. Porumbescu, G. A. (2016). Linking public sector social media and e-government website use to trust in government. *Government Information Quarterly, 33*(2), 291–304.
38. Elias, S. M., Smith, W. L., & Barney, C. E. (2012). Age as a moderator of attitude towards technology in the workplace: Work motivation and overall job satisfaction. *Behaviour and Information Technology, 31*(5), 453–467.
39. Morris, M. G., & Venkatesh, V. (2000). Age differences in technology adoption decisions: Implications for a changing work force. *Personnel Psychology, 53*(2), 375–403.

Museums Driving Innovation by Technology, People and Organisation

Mauro Romanelli and Maria Ferrara

Abstract In embracing information technology museums are rediscovering the importance of driving innovation in services and processes in order to promote value creation within social and cultural ecosystems. Innovation is the key source for driving museums to change and develop value creation processes by using information technology in order to strengthen audience involvement and user participation, while also enhancing the role of museum professionals as user-centered mediators in order to build a bridge between information and knowledge sources so as to enhance learning and education opportunities for users by strengthening user involvement and participation. With their move from adopting technology-enabled innovation to following a knowledge- and organisation-driven innovation, museums push innovation, emerging as value-driven and innovation-led organisations that contribute to building knowledge and value creation processes strengthening technology, organisation and human resources, and engaging users and audience as sources and key driving forces that help museum to rethink and rediscover sustainable organisation-led innovation strategies which can lead to social and public value-based and innovation-driven processes within social and cultural ecosystems.

Keywords Innovation · Museums · User participation · Technology

1 Introduction

Museums as cultural organisations are using technology in order to drive innovation as a key source that helps museums to design change by incorporating systems and processes and achieving the traditional mission of education, knowledge and culture

M. Romanelli (✉) · M. Ferrara
University of Naples Parthenope, Naples, Italy
e-mail: mauro.romanelli@uniparthenope.it

M. Ferrara
e-mail: maria.ferrara@uniparthenope.it

dissemination [1] by strengthening innovation in value creation, thus promoting audience involvement and service management by enhancing the relationship between the museum and the public by involving the audience as proactive users who contribute to cultural heritage knowledge [2, 3].

Information and communication technology helps to drive innovation within museums as cultural organisations that develop a new way for promoting value creation, enhancing the museum as a community that strengthens the relationship with the audience as a source of information and knowledge creation and sharing about cultural heritage. As organisations that use the Internet, social media, and virtual and interactive technology, museums drive service and user innovation and value co-creation as issues and sources for knowledge sharing and creation, as well as learning and education within cultural ecosystems [4].

Museums are memory and educational institutions, information-driven and utilities, and knowledge- and learning-oriented organisations [5–10]. They embrace and develop technology to strengthen user engagement and support the participation of the audience in cultural activities [11, 12]. Museums develop technological innovation in order to increase organisational performance and achieve cultural and social objectives [13], while also driving value co-creation processes [14], following an audience-centered orientation [15]. As cultural institutions focused on the citizen and truth and rights, museums have a social role within the contemporary world [16], collecting, preserving, researching and displaying cultural heritage, as well as connecting the past with the present and future while also promoting social value and action [17, 18]. As audience-driven, production-centred, intensive-information and knowledge-oriented organisations [7, 8, 19, 20], museums contribute to constructing service experience within cultural ecosystems, involving the audience as active participants in the defining of cultural heritage content and strengthening the relationships between technology, the public and the museum as an innovation-driven [3, 7, 21–23] and value creation-oriented organisation [24–27]. Museums develop interactive and dialogic communication while also simultaneously legitimising information and knowledge management by using the potential of information technology [6, 8, 28]. As agents and spaces of social and cultural innovation [29], museums develop user-led innovation, strengthening cultural participation of users in order to create and share museum content and knowledge [30–32].

Investigating research regarding the relationships between innovation and the use of technology, user participation and involvement and museum staff, the idea of a museum as a driven-oriented organisation able to contribute to value creation remains an unexplored area, despite the increasing attention paid by scholars to the introduction of technology within the cultural heritage. While in the firms' sector, innovation helps improve services and processes, thus leading to the development of competitive advantages, and in the field of cultural organisations, a clear definition of innovation is lacking. With regards to cultural organisations as well as museums, some studies elucidate that innovation helps museums to improve organisational performances and achieve both social goals, such as fostering education and culture meanings and strengthening visitor motivation and satisfaction and financial goals [13]. Thereby, innovation helps to engage the audience, thus developing and improving the organisation, business model and management [33].

This study helps to identify the trajectories that museums are following in order to drive innovation by using technology for involving the audience as users in cultural heritage and developing the museum as a working community while also promoting innovation for value and knowledge creation. In transitioning from being custodial and collections-driven institutions to becoming audience and cultural heritage production-oriented institutions, museums as knowledge and information-driven organisations develop technologically and organisationally and promote users' involvement as a means to proceed toward a sustainable pathway that relies on continuous attitude and orientation to contribute to social, economic, cultural and public value within cultural ecosystems [4, 7, 8, 19, 20].

This study aims to provide an interpretive view to identify how museums are changing by using the web, digital, interactive and virtual technology and virtual environments as a source for innovation that enables value creation involving the audience in defining cultural heritage content. Studying the role of technology within museums contributes to understanding how museums are changing to enable value co-creation in the cultural heritage field. Museums contribute to developing and sharing knowledge and information regarding heritage within cultural ecosystems [4]. Museums are also embracing the Internet and interactive technology in order to drive service innovation, by opening up to the participation of the audience in order to generate new knowledge for that audience and encourage new cultural experiences as sources for promoting value co-creation. Technology helps museums to serve the educational mandate, and support learning experiences involving potential visitors who can take part in the production and value creation regarding cultural heritage [34]. Museums, through information technology, cede authority, enabling staff and users to develop interactive–collaborative processes for knowledge transfer and information sharing [2, 3].

The aim of this study is to elucidate how museums identify some certain pathways for value co-creation by using technology to enable museum professionals to interact with users who contribute to knowledge, learning and value creation. Museums develop technology to encourage user participation and build a shared authority with the active audience when it comes to the definition of cultural heritage content. The study is structured in seven sections. Following the introduction and methodological section, in the third section, museums emerge as information-based, knowledge-driven, education- and learning-oriented organisations. The fourth section elucidates how museums, as organisations driving innovation, contribute to value creation processes by using the potential offered by technology. Technology helps museums drive innovation by involving the users to participate, and strengthening them to contribute to cultural knowledge issues. In the fifth section, technology drives museums to develop innovation: technology enables museum professionals to deal with information and knowledge as advocate and user-centered mediators. Is also helps helps to develop a shared authority on cultural heritage content involving the museum and the public. Technology helps rediscover the importance of user participation in the definition of cultural heritage content and knowledge creation, by opening up to the design of virtual museums new opportunities for education and learning purposes. In the discussion, a framework of analysis is elucidated to identify some pathways for museums that evolve as driven-led organisations which contribute to value co-creation by following an innovation-oriented strategy to rethink and redesign processes of change. Finally, conclusions are outlined.

2 Methodological Section

This study aims only to provide an interpretive and qualitative framework. The research is based on archival and qualitative data, considering the literature related to the role of the Internet, virtual and interactive technology as a means of enabling museums to contribute to driving innovation so as to create social and cultural value by opening up to an increasing user involvement and participation in the definition of cultural heritage contents. The analysis tends to elucidate how museums support and drive innovation by using the potential offered by information and digital technology as applied in the cultural heritage field. The selected contributions are summarised and interpreted [35] in a narrative synthesis that accommodates differences between the questions, research design and the context of the studies considered in order to develop new perspectives on emerging issues and advance theoretical models [36]. The referred journal articles were selected from *Google Scholar*, which served the main web source and database.

3 Museums as Memory Institutions, Information-Driven, Knowledge- and Learning-Oriented Organisations

As a community of stakeholders, museums are considered information utilities and information-based institutions as well as knowledge municipalities that legitimise processes of information and knowledge acquisition, creation and dissemination [6–8]. As memory institutions serving the society, museums acquire, conserve, research, communicate and exhibit for study, education and enjoyment [37], thus enabling knowledge and critical reflection on the past [38] and offer public access to collections that «contain the memory of peoples, communities, institutions and individuals, the scientific and cultural heritage, and the products throughout time of our imagination, craft and learning» (p. 3) [3]. Museums contribute to creating social value for the public by incorporating heritage as resources inherited from the past, history, continuity, values, beliefs, knowledge and traditions [17].

Museums support social and public value creation. They contribute to an enlightened society and support economic issues and social regeneration of local communities and economies, so as to enhance cultural capacity of communities by building partnerships and involving the audience [39]. Museums of the future proceed toward sustainable innovation by strengthening branding, event-driven and local community empowering strategies [40]. Museums as institutions embedded within society and communities contribute to enhancing value by strengthening relations and exchanges within social and cultural ecosystems [41].

Museums as sustainable organisations «serve the society by helping provide the knowledge» (p. 305) [6]. As organisations that generate, perpetuate, structure and disseminate information, museums «help their audiences exploit effectively the information resources in their self-directed quest for knowledge» (p. 306) [6] because «the role of museums, in the future, that of the knowledge municipality, lies in legitimizing information and information processes and in being an advocate for knowledge as the province of the people» (p. 303) [8]. Museums, playing the role of knowledge-oriented and information-driven organisations, open up to flexible and multiple interpretations of knowledge and understanding, constantly rediscovering meanings when the truth is dependent on context [42].

As information-based and learning-oriented organisations, museums contribute to information and knowledge creation [5–8] and provide new, authentic, cultural knowledge as well as education to their audience [43] «by creating access to information, which entails both making information readily available and ensuring that its users have the ability to comprehend it» in order to increase knowledge (p. 307) [6]. Museums use the information as what can be communicated to people and the knowledge which results from the interaction [44]. Museums pay attention to information resources management and storing for new knowledge creation and sharing by using the potential offered by digital and virtual technology [3]. Museums shape knowledge, support learning and education and become learning environments that tassist with educational purposes [45] driving visitors to be active in learning action, since learners make meaning, construct concepts and have experiences that influence their understanding. Constructing learning participation as social activity facilitates the meaning-making happening in the mind of the visitor, thus mediating the way in which the objects are exhibited [9, 18].

4 Museums Driving Innovation for Creating Value by Technology

Innovation is a key source when it comes to driving museums toward strategic and organisational changes as a means of developing value creation processes. Museums develop and drive innovation so as to change and be perceived as audience-oriented, knowledge-oriented and information-based institutions providing an educational and civilising mission within society. With regards to the concept of innovation in museums, Vicente, Camarero and Garrido (2015) have defined innovation «as a tendency to incorporate new systems, technologies or processes that change both how the museum is run and how its exhibits are presented to the visitor» (p. 652) [1].

Museums contribute to democratising knowledge about cultural heritage content by developing and driving user and community innovation through following the changes within cultural ecosystems [46, 47]. In developing the potential of technology, museums promote innovation in sharing authority on cultural heritage, enabling staff and users to develop both cultural experiences and interactive–collaborative processes that rely on knowledge transfer and information sharing within the museum community, involving and engaging the audience as an active agent influencing how museums act and represent meanings and understanding [2, 3, 43]. In particular, technology-driven innovations contribute to improving museums' organisation as well as their management processes and enhancing visitor experience and involvement. Museums adopt a technology-driven, visitor-oriented and organisation-based strategy in order to drive innovation, change and value creation processes [1].

As value-driven organisations, museums fuel innovation in services and processes, strengthening human, technological, organisational and information resources [48]. In particular, technology helps organisations to drive innovation opening up to user involvement in knowledge about cultural content, and driving the audience as an active actor in knowledge content definition while also strengthening user-led innovation [43, 49].

As information and knowledge-oriented organisations, museums involve and engage the public as a creative actor driving innovation in order to improve knowledge generation and understanding. Museums promote innovation by strengthening the individual experience and creating a new public sphere of knowledge where the visitor can admire the innovation of the artist and learn to become an innovative actor [50].

As enablers of cultural change and value, as well as mediators of information and knowledge, museums use online technology as a means for innovation by driving people to strengthen communication and gathering information about knowledge sources [8]. Museums should strategically enhance and support communication [10] and interaction between museum staff, objects, artifacts and the public, engaging with a working audience in order to support active participants and involve them in an interactive, innovation-driven and value creation-oriented process [51].

Museums use technological innovation in order to increase organisational performance and achieve cultural as well as social objectives [13] and develop value co-creation processes [14]. Museums as information and knowledge-based organisations drive innovation, adopting a learning orientation in order to improve social and financial performances [22] by opening up to significant participation and contribution of the audience in the definition of cultural contents for co-production of knowledge. Driving technological innovation helps support visitor orientation, which in turn contributes to enhancing market and economic performance [21]. In particular, «visitor orientation may encourage organisations to respond to visitor expectations by focusing on the value of the collection itself, offering the cultural product (as opposed to a leisure product) that visitors expect to see. As a result, the museum will center its attention on producing content through conservation and research linked to collections and organizing exhibitions» (p. 230) [21]. Information technology helps museums to engage the audience and promote user-led innovation for knowledge sharing and creation by involving users in developing cultural interactive co-creative experiences, constructing meanings in their interaction with the museum, driving user-generated contents and encouraging the participants to contribute to digital culture creation [31, 31, 32]. «New technologies have provided opportunities for cultural institutions to re-think the ways in which they pursue their principal objectives» (p. 13) [33]. Technological innovations contribute to organisational performance of museums as market-driven and innovation-oriented cultural organisations [22]. In particular, digital technology helps stress innovation within museums, thus raising the possibility of those museums being able to expand their audience reach, to develop the art form and contribute to economic and cultural value, by designing new business models [33].

In adopting digital technology applications and innovative services, museums achieve positive impact with regard to the relationship with the audience and tend to drive innovation [52]. Technology helps museums as organisations driving innovation to contribute to value creation by strengthening culture so as to enhance the culture in terms of subjective experience and emotions, achieving social or economic purposes, using processes and techniques [53]. Museum should promote innovation–culture-driven processes by engaging the public and encouraging partnership and collaboration within the community, thus becoming a key actor playing a visible role in the service of urban development [54]. In embracing technology, museums become social agents of change spaces of cultural innovation and experimentation [29] following an audience-centered orientation by engaging and involving the public in cultural heritage contents definition and creation [15]. Museums contribute to sustaining value creation enabling the public to act as a creator of value and co-producers of knowledge [55]. As value-driven organisations, museums promote value co-creation adopting a service-centered, customer-oriented and relational view [24, 25]. Museums develop both technology and human resources for interacting with people and enhancing meanings and value co-creation [26] which relies on co-production as active participation and engagement by tailoring the visitor experience [27] and developing user-led innovation through sustaining co-creative and interactive experiences [30–32, 43].

5 How Technology Enables Museums to Drive Innovation for Creating Value

Museums, as people-oriented and communication-driven organisations, contribute to driving innovation as a source for creating value within cultural ecosystems by using the potential of technology to actively engage the audience in the knowledge and education value process. The advent of information technology helps museums to drive innovation in providing information sources which are accessible to users [6]. Technology is driving museums to drive innovation for value co-creation processes in cultural heritage helping the design of a virtual, participatory communication, learning and education-oriented museum, by developing the role of museum information professionals as users–intermediators between the public and museum's knowledge and information, meeting the changing needs of users, opening up to participation of the audience as a means of constructing cultural meanings and contributing to knowledge creation, learning and educational purposes and experiences.

5.1   Toward a 'Shared' Authority on Cultural Heritage Contents Driving Innovation by Strengthening User Participation from Virtual Museums to Learning and Education Opportunities

Museums contribute to innovation, encouraging the dialogue and conversations through technology by strengthening user involvement and audience participation, and selecting an audience-oriented strategy. As institutions dealing with technology, museums encourage user participation in cultural activities, thus enhancing information, communication and knowledge sharing. Technology helps provide an emotional space by empowering the visitors in re-understanding, re-interacting and re-reading the objects [11].

Technology helps museum to drive innovation democratising knowledge in the cultural heritage field and redefining cultural authority within a changing society [46, 47]. Museums are embracing interactive technology and changing, moving from being consumption-centered/custodial and collection-driven institutions to becoming increasingly production-centered/audience-driven institutions that support bidirectional participatory and bottom-up communication as well as dialogic interaction, fostering collective expertise and driving multidirectional collaboration and cultural contents sharing between the museum and the public, while also strengthening two-way channels, user involvement and designing visitor-friendly environments [19, 20, 28].

Museums are rediscovering a participatory approach, involving and engaging the public [12], using information technology to drive the visitor as an active participant able to contribute to knowledge creation [56]. Technology is leading museums to abandon the exclusive authority on cultural heritage, opening up to user participation and partnership with the audience and empowering the museum visitors as producers of knowledge and active contributors in value creation processes [3, 12, 55]. «Engaging the public in value identification and creation offers the potential to build the widest possible constituency for ongoing museum support» (p. 41) [55]. Museums should construct a *shared* authority on cultural heritage contents involving the audience. Museums ought to cede authority by developing the potential of interactive technology and sustaining a two-way communication with visitors, using social media for networking and collaboration between users and museum staff, and thus driving the active participation of users as producers of knowledge [2, 3, 31].

Museums contribute to building social capital and cohesion, fostering knowledge and awareness about cultural heritage and supporting community development, leading toward a shared authority between the museum and the public [3, 6]. Museums support interactive information and knowledge management, sharing collaboration and user-centred design [20], opening up to decentralisation and democratisation of knowledge and cultural production, by developing digital and interactive information technology so as to involve participants and establish multi-directional collaboration with the public [28]. In using social media and social networking services, museums develop engagement to distribute community knowledge taking into account the perspectives of the different users who interact between them [30, 31].

Computer-based and informatics-driven technology helps museums push service innovation and strengthen users' involvement and contribution to technology-driven innovation, adding a digital form to traditional and physical dimensions, reconciling and combining authority and participation for the definition of content regarding cultural heritage. The virtual museum as described and defined by Tsichritzis and Gibbs (1991), and as a place living without the barriers of space and time as hypothesised by Malraux in *Le Museè Imaginaire* helps the museums to enhance an audience-driven and visitor-centred orientation, enriching the objects with information, and leading to the virtual museum as a new form of museum [3, 57]. The virtual museum focuses on strengthening sources of information and communication: Its objects and the related information are disseminated everywhere [3]. Virtual museums drive user-oriented information and knowledge sources in order to enable interaction and communication between the visitor and museum information and knowledge sources, helping virtual visitors to connect with, and understand, museum information sources [57].

The virtual museum as an interactive and virtual space allows each artifact to be displayed, enabling people to play with artifacts which provide information and exhibit cultural objects in digital formats [3, 58]. Virtual museums contribute to enhancing the educational potential and driving the visitor to learn more about a subject *(learning)* [57]. The virtual museum design helps strengthen user-constructed and engendered experiences [59]. «In a virtual environment, the visitor is not an observer but s/he interacts with the learning objects and s/he constructs her/himself the knowledge» (p. 525) [57].

Technology is pushing the knowledge-driven museums to reinvent their educational and cultural role in society, encouraging interactive participation and strengthening the learning experience [6, 8, 9, 34]. In particular, technology helps museums to enhance knowledge and share authority on cultural heritage with the audience by encouraging active participation through sustaining the learning experience of visitors [60].

Promoting museum education using technology helps develop a shared and cultural pathway between the visitors and museum curators by enablingexhibitions which come from life experience and facilitating visitor meaning-making and driving the visitor as active learner [9]. In following a constructivist view, where the visitor chooses the meaning to make regarding the museum experience [9], museums promote educational opportunities by developing virtual-interactive environments to facilitate visitors' interaction and personalise learning activities at the museum while simultaneously enhancing visitors' interaction with the museum [61, 62]. Virtual environments contribute to increasing the learning and motivation of participants by enhancing interactive communication between the users and cultural institutions and having the audience take part in the cultural production, interacting with digital objects by personalising learning activities [63].

Styliani et al. [57] have stated that «learning is an active process and the end-users are engaged in hands-on-involvement in an engaging experience that enhances the understanding, fosters fruitful learning interactions, awakens and keeps the interest alive and enriches aesthetic sensitivities» (p. 525). Technology helps museums serve the educational mission, driving the audience to actively participate and determine their own experience. Technology supports the learning process, bringing together both entertainment and educational purposes as complementary aspects of the museum experience [64], bridging public education and recreation and enabling museum educators to proactively guide the virtual experiences for learning [61].

5.2 Museums Professionals as Users-Centered Mediators and Information Sources Enablers Within Museums as Information Environments

Technology is enabling museums to become a source of information that helps develop knowledge creation and the sharing of sources and infrastructures [19]. In particular, information technology has redefined the role of the museum as an information environment. «A museum offers a unique environment from which to study the way in which knowledge is accumulated, analyzed, and distributed by information professionals» (p. 1083) [65]. «Museum informatics has become increasingly important as advances in information science and technology offer new capabilities to help museum professionals meet changing user needs» [66]. Web advancements and digital applications facilitate interactive information sharing and user-centered design and collaboration while also contributing to changing the nature of museum work, enabling a shared authority between staff and communities and encouraging social engagement and user-led cultural content generation, making the museum a community and platform for culture and knowledge creation [2, 3].

Technology enables museums to become knowledge and intensive-information organisations that contribute to creating new knowledge about cultural heritage [8, 65]. Museums integrate technology and human resources in order to develop information policies, manage information resources, and design work changes that concern the roles of museum informational professionals in providing new knowledge generation for the audience [66]. New advanced technology and museum informatics enable museum information professionals to act as user-centered mediators who facilitate the interactions between the museum and users, making information resources available and meeting the information needs while coherently responding to expectations of museum information resource users [65, 66]. «As museum visitors and museum professionals evolve their expectations of the information resources museums and other cultural heritage organisations should provide, MIPs face serious challenges as they adapt to changing capabilities and strive to meet the changing needs and expectations of museum users» (p. 106) [66]. Museums as knowledge enablers have to support and enhance human resources and work on the skills and capabilities of museums professionals by embracing information technology. Technology drives museum information professionals to develop new methods of organising information and accessing the collections, integrating technology into the exhibits, and using virtual environments to personally tailor the experience for each individual visitor and user [8, 65].

Information technology helps empower curators to digitally preserve the artefacts of their collections, to disseminate their ideas and facilitate understandings of the complexities regarding museum exhibits. As stated by Marty (1999) «information technology has changed the way museum professionals work in-house, from collections management to exhibit design. It has changed the way museum professionals work online, from inter-institutional collaboration to educational outreach. It has changed the way museum visitors approach the museum, its holdings, and educational potential. It has changed what museum visitors expect from a museum, both in real life and online» (p. 269) [65]. Technology aids museum staff experts in interacting with motivated people and communities in order to re-construct and reinterpret knowledge and information about collections. Information technology helps improve information and knowledge management within museums, encouraging collaboration among museum professionals and museum users [2, 67]. The Internet is enabling museums as information utilities, to actively use information in terms of generation, perpetuation, organisation and dissemination to generate new knowledge for their audience [6]. Museums as repositories of knowledge and service-oriented information organisations should improve their organisational processes by strengthening the work and skills of museum professionals as curators and educators acting as user-centered mediators meeting the needs of visitors [67]. The Internet and interactive and virtual technology drive museums as information-based organisations [7, 68] and enable museum professionals to use information technology in order to meet and support changing needs and expectations of online visitors through new forms of interactivity, working to improve the museum experience for users by focusing on digitisation technology, information policy and collaboration initiatives [67]. Changing technology drives the needs of museum users to change and adapt to the new capabilities of the museum [65]. Technology is leading museum professionals to develop new capabilities working in relation to changing user needs. Moreover, technology helps museum professionals to serve as user-centred mediators and meet the changing needs of users, enabling users as active participants in the co-construction of digital knowledge and cultural heritage [7, 67, 68].

6 Discussion

Today, museums are rediscovering the importance of an organisation playing a social role within the contemporary world, emerging as a value-driven, knowledge- and information-oriented and learning institution driving innovation by employing and valuing the potential of new Internet, virtual and interactive technology applied to the interaction between objects, information, users, and the museum's communities actively cooperating for engendering new knowledge as an immediate result and issue of the value co-creation process.

Museums as a bridge between information and knowledge have to select an innovation-driven orientation in order to promote change within organisational and technological infrastructure to drive the museum as a value-driven and innovation-enabled organisation. In embracing technology, museums reinvent the method of promoting sustainable innovation in processes, services and organisation rediscovering a pathway for strengthening the relationship with the audience and fostering user's involvement and visitor engagement. In promoting innovation, museums as audience-centered and visitor-oriented institutions proceed to sustaining value creation processes by sharing knowledge and communication on cultural heritage content. Driving innovation within museums relies on bringing together technology, people and organisations to support value co-creation processes. Museums, as organisations, should develop the information technology and strengthen museum professionals in order to support participatory engagement by involving the users in contributing to knowledge and meanings in cultural heritage.

The contribution of this study is to elucidate how museums identify a pathway for driving innovation by using technology through opening up to museum professional human resources and involving the users as active participants and co-producers of knowledge as sources for driving value co-creation processes as shown in Fig. 1.

Technology enables museums to develop sources for innovation in knowledge creation and sharing, engaging the public and providing opportunities for accessible and flexible education and learning. Museums develop technology to involve the public, engage the audience and encourage user participation following a collection-oriented view for information provision and knowledge sharing. Audience-driven

	from user participation	to education and learning	
from information providers	Museums as information-oriented organisations	Museums as educational institutions	Technology for managing collections
to user-centred mediators	Museums driving communication-led innovation	Museums driving knowledge- and learning -led innovation	Technology for engaging and interaction
	from technology-enabled innovation	to organisation/knowledge-driven innovation	

Fig. 1 Toward museums driving innovation: a framework of analysis

museums contribute to strengthening the potential of user involvement and participation to drive value and knowledge creation. Museums should evolve from being audience-oriented institutions to becoming knowledge- and learning-driven organisations that contribute to the educational mission and value creation within society. As collection- and information-based institutions, museums use technology for managing collections, employing human resources to provide information to the audience or involving the users in engaging with museum professionals in order to access museum information resources by developing technology for strengthening interactive communication.

In moving from adopting a technology-enabled innovation to following a knowledge- and organisation-driven innovation, museums drive innovation emerging as value-driven and innovation-led organisations that contribute to building knowledge and value creation processes strengthening technology, organisation and human resources, as well as users and the audience as sources that help museum to rethink sustainable organisation-led innovation strategies within social and cultural ecosystems. Audience-driven museums are educational institutions that use technology for managing collections, while knowledge-driven, education- and learning-based and participatory-oriented museums communicate and interact with the audience to promote knowledge creation and support learning following a constructivist view. Museums are rediscovering the learning mission, encouraging user participation and providing the museum as a learning environment to drive users to live an educational experience by employing technology and interacting with museum professionals to access information for new knowledge and value creation.

7   Conclusions

Technology helps museums to promote innovation as a source for driving value co-creation strengthening the human capital of museum professionals, and engaging the users in participating so as to define cultural heritage contents, thus reinventing the educational mission by leading to new learning opportunities for users acting as co-producers of knowledge and co-creators of value. Technology helps support processes of value co-creation in cultural heritage driving museums to evolve and innovate as communities where the interaction between the audience and visitors and museum staff is emerging as a key value and driving force for sustainable cultural heritage production and sharing within social and cultural ecosystems.

Technology enables museum professionals to support the changing needs of visitors and develop capabilities because of engaging and interacting with users. Museums embracing new technology sustain service innovation by promoting value co-creation as an organisational capability to support service experience and innovation through encouraging interactive participation. Technology helps museums enhance the learning experience by promoting user-generated content, and driving participants to contribute in creating digital culture. As audience- or collection-driven organisations, museums select a different pathway, sharing and combining authority and participation on cultural heritage content, developing the capabilities of museum professionals as human resources, and strengthening the opportunities provided by new virtual and interactive technology designed to give rise to a participatory museum as a learning and educational institution.

There are some limitations. The aim of this research is only to provide a theoretical framework to help understand the trajectories of development for museums aiming to drive change using technology to develop user participation as innovation and a source to lead museums as community-based organisations within cultural ecosystems. The study is descriptive, and solely exploratory. Further research perspectives should investigate how the advent of technology helps drive innovation within the organisational design and human resource management within museums by interacting with users as active co-producers of knowledge and value.

References

1. Vicente, E., Camarero, C., & Garrido, M. J. (2012). Insights into innovation in european museums. *Public Management Review, 14*(5), 649–679.
2. Kelly, L. (2010). How Web 2.0 is changing the nature of museum work. *Curator: The Museum Journal, 53*(4), 405–410
3. Schweibenz, W. (2011) Museum and Web 2.0: Some thoughts about authority, Communication, Participation and Trust. In G. Styliaras, D. Koukopoulos, & F. Lazarinis (Eds.), *Handbook of Research on Technologies and Cultural Heritage: Application and Environments* (pp. 1–15). IGI Global.
4. Borin, E., & Donato, F. (2015). Unlocking the potential of IC in Italian cultural ecosystems. *Journal of Intellectual Capital, 16*(2), 285–304.
5. Bagdadly, S. (1997). Il museo come azienda. Management e organizzazione al servizio della cultura, Etas, Milano.
6. MacDonald, G. F., & Alsford, S. (1991). The Museum as information utility. *Museum Management and Curatorship, 10*(3), 305–311.
7. Marty, P. F. (2007). Finding the skills for tomorrow: information literacy and museum information professionals. *Museum, Management and Curatorship, 21*(4), 317–335.
8. Freedman, G. (2000). The changing nature of museums. *Curator: The Museum Journal, 43*(4), 295–306.
9. Hein, G.E.: Museum education. In S. Macdonald, (Ed.), A companion to museum studies(pp. 340–352), Oxfod, Blackwell (2006)
10. Hooper-Greenhill, E. (2007). Museums: learning and culture. In E. Hooper-Greenhill (ed.), *Museum and Education. Purpose, Pedagogy, Performance* (pp. 1–14), London, Routledge.
11. Bearman, D., & Gebra, K. (2008). Transforming Cultural Heritage Institutions through New Media. *Museum Management and Curatorship, 23*(4), 385–399.
12. Simon, N. (2010). The participatory museum, Museum 2.0, Santa Cruz.
13. Camarero, C., & Garrido, M. J. (2008). The role of technological and organizational innovation in the relation between market orientation and performance in cultural organizations. *European Journal of Innovation Management, 11*(3), 413–434.
14. Antòn, C., Camarero, C., & Garrido, M. J. (2018). Exploring the experience value of museum visitors as a co-creation process. *Current Issues in Tourism, 21*(12), 1406–1425.
15. Consiglio, S., Cicellin, M., Scuotto, A., & Ricchezza, D. (2017). L'approccio audience-centric dei musei: Un processo di innovazione sociale. *Prospettiveinorganizzazione, 8*
16. Knell, S. (2019). *The Contemporary Museum*. Routledge.

17. Burton, C., & Scott, C. (2007). Museums. Challenges for the 21st century. In R. Sandell, &R. R. Janes (Eds.), *Museum Management and Marketing* (pp. 56–68), London: Routledge.
18. Hein, G. E. (2005) The role of museums in society: Education and social action. *Curator: The Museum Journal, 48*(4), 357–363.
19. Gilmore, A., & Rentschler, R. (2002). Changes in museum management: A custodial or marketing emphasis. *Journal of Management Development, 21*(10), 745–760.
20. Bonacini, E. (2012). Il museo partecipativo sul web: forme di partecipazione dell'utente alla produzione cultural e alla creazione di valore culturale. The participatory museum on the Web: forms of user participation in cultural production and the creation of cultural value. *Il Capitale Culturale, 5*, 93–125.
21. Camarero, C., Garrido, M. J., & Vicente, E. (2011). How cultural organizations' size and funding influence innovation and performance: The case of museums. *Journal of Cultural Economics, 35*(4), 247–266.
22. Garrido, M. J., & Camarero, C. (2010). Assessing the impact of organizational learning and innovation on performance in cultural organizations. *International Journal of Nonprofit and Voluntary Sector Marketing, 15*(3), 215–232.
23. Camarero, C., Garrido, M.J., & Vicente, E. (2015). Achievng effective visitor orientation in European museums. Innovation versus custodial. *Journal of Cultural Heritage, 16*(2), 228–235.
24. Prahalad, C. K., & Ramaswamy, V. (2013). *The future of competition: Co-creating unique value with customers.* Harvard Business Press.
25. Vargo, S. L., Maglio, P. P., & Akaka, M. A. (2008). On value and value co-creation: A service systems and service logic perspective. *European Management Journal, 26*(3), 145–152.
26. Ind, N., & Coates, N. (2013). The meanings of co-creation. *European Business Review, 25*(1), 86–95.
27. Minkiewicz, J., Evans, J., & Bridson, K. (2014). How do consumers co-create their experiences? An exploration in the heritage sector. *Journal of Marketing Management, 30*(1–2), 30–59.
28. Capriotti, P., & Kuklinski, H. P. (2012). Assessing dialogic communication through the Internet in Spanish museums. *Public Relations Review, 38*(4), 619–626.
29. Castells, M. (2001). *Museums in the information era* (pp. 1–4). Cultural connectors of time and space. ICOM News.
30. Russo, A. (2011). Transformation in cultural communication: social media, cultural exchange, and creative connections. *Curator: The Museum Journal, 54*(3), 327–346.
31. Russo, A., Watkins, J., Kelly, L., & Chan, S. (2008). Participatory communication with social media. *Curator: The Museum Journal, 51*(1), 21–31.
32. Russo, A., Watkins, J., Kelly, L., & Chan, S. (2007). Social media and cultural interactive experiences in museums. *Nordisk Museologi, 1*, 19–29.
33. Bakhshi, H., & Throsby, D. (2010). Culture of innovation. An economic analysis of innovation in arts and cultural organisations. Londres, NESTA.
34. Anderson, M. L. (1999). Museums of the future: The impact of technology on museum practices. *Daedalus, 128*(3), 129–162.
35. Denyer, D., & Tranfield, D. (2006). Using qualitative research synthesis to build an actionable knowledge base. *Management Decision, 44*(2), 213–227.
36. Dixon-Woods, M., Agarwal, S., Young, B., Jones, D., & Sutton, A. (2004). *Integrative Approaches to Qualitative and Quantitative Evidence.* Health Development Agency.
37. ICOM News, no. 3, 2004, http://icom.museum/pdf/E_news2004/p3_2004-3.pdf.
38. Hooper-Greenhill, E. (1995). Museums and communication: an introductory essay. In E. Hooper-Greenhill, (ed.), *Museum, Media, Message* (pp. 1–12), Routledge, London
39. Scott, C. (2006). Museums: Impact and value. *Cultural Trends, 15*(1), 45–75.
40. Greffe, X., Krebs, A., & Pflieger, S. (2017). The future of the museum in the twenty-first century: Recent clues from France. *Museum Management and Curatorship, 32*(4), 319–334.
41. Sabiescu, A., Charatzopoulou, K. (2018). The Museum as ecosystem and museums in learning ecosystems. In A. Vermeeren, L. Calvi, A. Sabiescu, (Eds.), *Experience Design. Crowds, Ecosystems and Novel Technologies* (pp. 325–345), Springer, Cham

42. Davies, S. M., Paton, R., & O'Sullivan, T. J. (2013). The museum values framework: A framework for understanding organisational culture in museums. *Museum Management and Curatorship, 28*(4), 345–361.
43. Russo, A., & Watkins, J. (2007). Digital cultural communication: Audience and remediation, in theorizing digital cultural heritage. In F. Cameron, & S. Kenderline (Eds.), *A Critical Discourse* (pp. 149–164), Cambridge: The MIT Press
44. Orna, E., & Pettitt, C. (2010). What is information in the museum context? In R. Parry, (Ed.), *Museums in a digital age* (pp. 28–38), Routledge, London
45. Hooper-Greenhill, E. (1992). *Museums and the shaping of knowledge.* Routledge.
46. Von Hippel, E. (2005). Democratizing innovation: The evolving phenomenon of user innovation. *Journal für Betriebswirtschaft, 55*(1), 63–78.
47. Bautista, S. S. (2014) *Museums in the Digital Age. Changing Meanings of Place, Community, and Culture.* AltaMira Press
48. Magnusson, P. R., Matthing, J., & Kristensson, P. (2003). Managing user involvement in service innovation: Experiments with innovating end users. *Journal of Service Research, 6*(2), 111–124.
49. Maglio, P. P., & Spohrer, J. (2008). Fundamentals of service science. *Journal of the Academy of Marketing Science, 36*(1), 18–20.
50. Weibel, P. (2018). Manifesto for a New Museum. In G. Bast, E. G. Carayannis, D. F. J. Cambpbell (Eds.), *The Future of Museums* (pp. 49–52), Springer, Cham
51. Balogun, J., Best, K., & Lê, J. (2015). Selling the object of strategy: How frontline workers realize strategy through their daily work. *Organization Studies, 36*(10), 1285–1313.
52. Tsaih, R. H., Lin, J. Q. P., & Chang, Y. C. (2014) National Palace Museum and service innovations. Emerald Emerging Markets Case Studies (2014)
53. Holden, J. (2006). *Cultural Value and the Crisis of Legitimacy.* Why culture need a democratic mandate, Demos, London
54. Søndergaard, M. K., & Veirum, N. E. (2012). Museums and culture-driven innovation in public–private consortia. *Museum management and curatorship, 27*(4), 341–356.
55. Scott, C. (2010). Museums, the public, and public value. *Journal of Museum Education, 35*(1), 33–42.
56. Mancini, F., & Carreras, C. (2010). Techno-society at the service of memory institutions: Web 2.0 in museums. *Catalan Journal of Communication & Cultural Studies, 2*(1), 59–76
57. Styliani, S., Fotis, L., Kostas, K., & Petros, P. (2009). Virtual museums, a survey and some issues for consideration. *Journal of Cultural Heritage, 10*(4), 520–528.
58. Schweibenz, W. (1998). "The Virtual Museum": New perspectives for museums to present objects and information using the internet as a knowledge base and communication system. In *Proceedings des 6. Internationalen Symposiums für Informationswissenschaft, Prag,* 3–7, November, pp. 185–200
59. Deshpande, S., Geber, K., & Timpson, C. (2007). Engaged dialogism in virtual space: An exploration of research strategies for virtual museums. In F. Cameron, & S. Kenderline (Eds.), *Theorizing Digital Cultural Heritage. A Critical Discourse* (pp. 261–279), The MIT Press, Cambridge
60. Hazan, S. (2007). A crisis of authority: New Lamps for old. In F. Cameron & S. Kenderline (Eds.), *Theorizing Digital Cultural Heritage. A Critical Discourse* (pp. 133–147), The MIT Press, Cambridge
61. Roussou, M. (2010). Learning by doing and learning through play: An exploration of interactivity in virtual environments for children. *ACM Computers in Entertainment, 2*(1), 1–23.
62. Ott, M., & Pozzi, F. (2010). Towards a new era for cultural heritage education: Discussing the role of ICT. *Computers in Human Behavior, 27*(4), 1365–1371.
63. Carrozzino, M., & Bergamasco, M. (2010). Beyond virtual museum: Experiencing immersive virtual reality in real museums. *Journal of Cultural Heritage, 11*(4), 452–458.
64. Addis, M. (2005). New technologies and cultural consumption—Edutainment is born! *European Journal of Marketing, 39*(7–8), 729–736.

65. Marty, P. F. (2007). The changing nature of information work in museums. *Journal of the American Society for Information Science and Technology, 58*(1), 97–107.
66. Marty, P. F. (1999). Museum informatics and collaborative technologies: The emerging socio-technological dimension of information science in museum environments. *Journal of the American Society for Information Science, 50*(2), 1083–1091.
67. Marty, P. F. (2011). My lost museum: User expectations and motivations for creating personal digital collections on museum websites. *Library and Information Science Research, 33*(3), 211–219.
68. Marty, P. F. (2006). Meeting user needs in the modern museum: Profiles of the new museum information professional. *Library and Information Science Research, 28*(1), 128–144.

Measuring Healthcare Performance in Digitalization Era an Empirical Analysis

Concetta Lucia Cristofaro, Marzia Ventura, Rocco Reina, and Teresa Gentile

Abstract The field of performance has grown so much over the years that in the various organizational contexts the awareness, and use of performance measurement (PM) systems has increased. This change occurs also in health care. Performance measurement emerged in healthcare organizations to better quantify the achievement of objectives, to evaluate overall performance and promote excellence. Meanwhile, organizations have increasingly refined ICT technologies and data collection and flows, in order to better configure performance measurement systems for the organizational units and processes. The focus of this research is to understand how technology can facilitate the monitoring of the indicators used in the measurement of health services, through an exploratory study on one specific hospital ward. In this case, the focus was on Academic Hospital of Catanzaro, where the performance measurement system was implemented in order to improve the quality of the offered services.

Keywords Health digitalization · Performance measurement · Hospital pharmacy

1 Purpose of Research

In recent decades, Italy and other European countries have been fertile ground for numerous New Public Management (NPM) initiatives, with the aim to improve performance in various areas of public administration. NPM tools based on management's principles and techniques are related to the reorganization of processes and objectives of public companies, performance measurement and performance control [1–3]. Growth in the field of performance measurement has raised awareness and use of performance measurement systems in different organizational settings [4]. This change occurs also in health care [5] by introducing at the legislative level principles and criteria of effectiveness and efficiency typical of the business context [6].

C. L. Cristofaro (✉) · M. Ventura · R. Reina · T. Gentile
Magna Graecia University, 88110 Catanzaro, Italy
e-mail: concetta.cristofaro@unicz.it

© The Author(s), under exclusive license to Springer Nature Switzerland AG 2022
L. Solari et al. (eds.), *Do Machines Dream of Electric Workers?*, Lecture Notes in Information Systems and Organisation 49,
https://doi.org/10.1007/978-3-030-83321-3_10

To quantify how well the objectives are achieved, performance measurement has emerged in healthcare organizations to evaluate overall performance and drive excellence [7]. Systems able to measure performance in complex organizations have been exposed to unprecedented interest, also in healthcare system with the management of information flows. So, such levels supported coherent healthcare management processes through the design of new application and technology platforms. The development of information and communication technology (ICT) increased these opportunities; in fact, the European Commission defined e-Health such as "the use of ICT in products, services and healthcare processes, accompanied by organizational changes and new skills developments, all aimed at improving health, efficiency and productivity in the health sector, as well as greater economic and social value of health." In healthcare organizations, the measurement of performance can identify sub-optimized treatments and improve the quality of services. Due to major reforms put in place in the area, performance measurement in healthcare has received growing attention from practitioners and academics in the recent years.

So, the purpose of this research is to try to understand how important ICT can be for measuring performance in health care. To try to measure this impact, attention was focused on the Academic Hospital of Catanzaro, where an implementation process of the performance measurement system is being carried out in terms of improving the quality of the services offered.

2   Theoretical Framework and Applied Theories

2.1   Digitalization in Healthcare

The healthcare sector is undergoing major digital transformation, as an innovation engine of the twenty-first century which affects every organizations. One core area where this is taking place is the use of digital technologies to increase patient experiences and access to medical care [8–11]. The digitalization of health care is included among the priority actions in the recent 2014–2020 Digital Growth Strategy, as a "fundamental step to improving the cost–quality ratio of health services, limiting waste and inefficiencies, reducing differences between territories, as well as innovating front-end relationships to improve the perceived quality of the citizen" (Italian Parliament communication, 2019). The motivations behind the priority assigned to the digitalization process in health care are to make citizen able to play a more active role in managing their health. Therefore, the increasing use of a digitized healthcare system involves the adoption of a new and modern information and communication technology (ICT) that opens new possibilities to improve the different aspects of health care such as the ability to provide better access to patient information, greater transparency, ability to support and reconstruct business systems and processes [12]. ICT in health care plays a central and pivotal role in influencing infrastructures, organizational models, work processes and professionalism [13]; so, their dissemination in clinical practice generally occurs in an unorganized and unpublished way, avoiding in most cases pathways that allow timely empirical assessment of their effectiveness and their clinical and organizational impact [14].

In order to find the right balance between technology pushes—which inevitably increase healthcare costs—and new health policies that focus on the patient's centrality, it is necessary to have an interpretative framework that supports the strategic use of ICT in the business processes of healthcare companies, in external relationships such as business relationships with patients, suppliers, other companies and finally in the overall information flows of the healthcare system as a whole. The benefits include not only cost reduction through dematerialization procedures but also fair access to the population at essential levels of health information and personal data. All this allows to influence and expand the horizon to measure quality and performance [15, 16].

2.2 Measuring Performance in Health Care

Performance can be defined as the maintenance of a functional state that corresponds to social, patient and professional standards [17]. Performance management is defined as a technology capable of handling behaviors and results, two critical elements of what is known as performance [18].

The Italian healthcare system underwent significant reforms that promise to produce greater access to and better outcomes from health care than their previous policies do. The system aims to create new efficient healthcare system that are equitable, patient-focused, results-driven, accessible and sustainable. The Ministry of Health has created conceptually sound performance indicator frameworks to actively measure, manage and operationalize the performance of their health systems, thereby linking them to the performance measurement. In an effort to promote common learning and best practice [19], performance management (PM) processes have become a potent part of strategic and service quality decisions in healthcare organizations.

In the healthcare sector, in fact, performance management is a set of management tools designed to ensure optimal healthcare performance in line with policy goals [20]. Health system performance management includes both tools and processes able to improve healthcare performance [21]. Performance monitoring and management must be carried out based on quantitative indicators able to understand the effects of the organizational actions. This may also assist in the benchmarking process, by which the facility's performance can be compared to other facilities, and thus enable to identify the points of strengths and weakness of each facility. This procedure requires the identification, characterization and definition of several key performance indicators (KPIs), which are suitable for either public or private facilities as benchmarks for performance cost effectiveness [22, 23]. The current state of the art indicates a need to develop integrated KPIs for healthcare facilities, seeking links between performance, maintenance, operations and energy expenditure and cost effectiveness [24].

There is significant consensus in literature that a number of indicators are necessary to capture all relevant aspects of a particular system. A multiple stakeholder perspective has been indicated as one of the most important characteristics that contribute to the success of performance evaluation models, considering the complexity of healthcare operations [25]. Performance indicators should represent an integrated information network that is the source for benchmarking and strategic planning. Performance indicators raise issue awareness and understanding, inform the decision-making and measure the achievement of goals. Specific indicators characteristics are required to evaluate performance efficiently: measurability, relevance, clarity, reliability, data accessibility, opportunity and long-term view [26]. The existence of a framework dealing with measure deployment in the strategic, tactical and operational levels to include tangible, intangible, financial and non-financial aspects is also questioned by literature [27].

This emphasizes the increased need and interest in the development of ICT applications for the domain of healthcare facilities management. Moreover, the complexities involved in the different facilities management themes and their interrelations can be solved and better understood if ICT is implemented [28, 29]. In order to implement the principles that must be based on the health performance assessment system, it is necessary to define the management cycle, which is divided into six phases over time (Fig. 1).

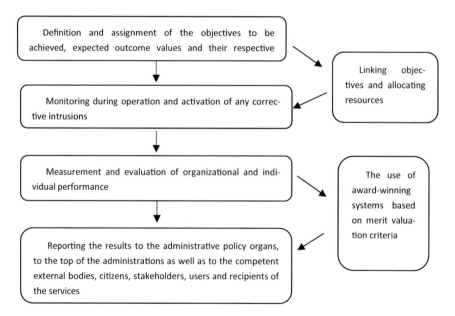

Fig. 1 Performance management cycle [30] *Source* our adaptation on "Misurazione e valutazione della performance: principi, struttura e metodi"

It is interesting to note how well the phase of the objectives are to be expressed in technical terms (quality, volumetric, efficacy, user satisfaction, efficiency, etc.) and subsequently refer to the negotiation of the financial resources necessary for their achievement [16, 31]. In order to support the planning and evaluation processes of the regional health systems and those who compile it, it is necessary to introduce both at regional and business management level, tools able to measure the most important dimensions of the healthcare system and provision of social services. Overcoming auto reference by systematically comparing results among operators permits to enhance best practices and engage in learning processes able to improve the quality of services, ensure citizen's transparency on the results achieved and work because the levels essential assistance is fairly guaranteed, such as strategic goals of the national health system.

In order to evaluate performance, it is necessary for the public health context to have multiple results measurement mechanisms for an integrated evaluation of the achieved performance. Any measure selected to monitor a goal is never exhaustive in the representation of the phenomenon.

So, management usually selects the indicators that fit better with respect to a number of requirements, such as

- The relative significance of the target to be monitored
- The ease of measurement with simple and comprehensible algorithms
- The availability of data.

Regarding measurability of the results, the MES—Laboratory of Management and Health of Scuola Superiore Sant'Anna of Pisa[1]—proposed the adoption of a set of indicators that should meet the following requirements:

- Validity: The indicator must be able to measure what it wants to measure and be consistent with other related indicators.
- Sensitivity: The indicator must be able to record the changes in time correctly and in the space.
- Comparability: The indicator must keep the same meaning over time and in different local realities.
- Consistency: Changing the value of the indicator does not have to be due to random errors.

These requirements, though important, do not guarantee the capability of the indicator to measure the universe, in fact, the number is always a more or less significant simplification of the complexity of reality.

---

[1] Laboratory of Management and Health of Scuola Superiore Sant'Anna of Pisa works by elaborating, experimentally, the analysis of a first set of indicators able to measure the appropriateness, efficiency and the quality of healthcare services provided at regional level and single delivery providers level (www.s lute.gov.it).

3   Research Methods

The article uses a case study methodology developed in two phases: The first phase—on the desk—analyzed research literature and academic publications that have focused on implementation performance measurement systems within the healthcare organizations through the support information system.

The systematic search used the advanced search option in all of the databases, using the terms "digitalization in healthcare," "measuring performance" and "health care organization." The search was limited to publications in the English language without any restrictions on year of publication. The literature search was performed electronically, using the portal of the university library. The search was conducted in different databases that were classified as discipline-specific databases include Scopus, ProQuest social science; Elsevier, "Emerald" and "All Springer Link2018." In this way, we collected about n° 200 academic documents. Subsequently, we selected the most relevant documents by keywords and identified 90 documents. At the end of the selection process, we based review on 33 academic documents. In the second phase—on the job—analysis starts from the measurable study of a set of impact indicators of the Academic Hospital of Catanzaro. Specifically, the present working progress paper focused on pharmaceutical unit. The choice was made with respect to: (a) the relative independence of organizational unit, (b) the small dimension of observed ward, (c) a similarity in the process management with respect to other clinical wards and (d) the impact of pharmaceutical expenditure on hospital balance. So that, it could be easier understand the possibility—through small operational changes—to impact deeply on general performance of academic hospital. In this way, it is possible to front the topic easily and verify if and how the performance management takes place and its measurement. In fact, for example, the relation between the pharmaceutical unit and the others clinical units could permit to verify how cost reduction activities impact on general performance of hospital. So, all this can contribute to understand the different possibilities to act regarding performance management in health sector by stimulating new fields of research.

4   Case Study

The organizational unit "hospital pharmacy" is part of the "Mater Domini" hospital and operates on two structures located on the territory of the province of Catanzaro. The main activities it carries out can be summarized as follows:

1.   Information on drugs and medical devices and consultancy activities for other organizational units
2.   Procurement and supply of medicines and medical devices to other organizational units and patients
3.   Assistance: Development, drafting, validation and disclosure of corporate and regional guidelines

4. Pharmaceutical and regulatory consultancy: Elaboration, drafting, drafting and diffusion of therapeutic handbooks, repertoire of medical devices, repertoire of disinfectants
5. Management of AIFA monitoring records—payback and refunds from negotiated procedures
6. Supervision: Supervision, inspection and control within the company on the correct conservation of drugs, medical devices, drugs and control of the adequacy of the quantities of the pharmaceutical material required
7. Statistics: Processing of drug and medical device consumption data by therapeutic group, by product class, by cost center, etc.
8. Monitoring of hospital pharmaceutical expenditure: Analysis of expenditure by drug, by active ingredient, by therapeutic group, by cost center
9. Technical/pharmaceutical assistance for purchases: Preparation and drafting of technical specifications for the purchase of the relevant materials; drugs and medical devices
10. Logistics: Proposal to resolve problems relating to the supply of medicines and medical devices in pharmacies and departments
11. Tutor: Pharmacists perform tutor activities for students of the school of specialization in the hospital pharmacy of the University Magna Graecia—Catanzaro—and students in the pharmacy who must carry out the pre-graduate internship
12. Study and research: Scientific publications, active participation in scientific conferences and company training courses with original contributions.

These activities are carried out by 13 people who cover different roles as can be seen in the following Table 1:

In order to guarantee continuity of care and avoid emergencies that can generate risk factors, it was necessary to prepare a regulation aimed at standardizing the pathways and procedures of drugs and medical devices operating within the company and to comply with all the obligations due in an appropriate manner. So 18 procedures were developed as listed below:

Planning and Programming Process—Definition of Requirements.

1. Procedure for the supply and storage of medicines and medical devices
2. Procedure for the supply and delivery of off-label medicines
3. Procedure for the procurement and delivery of cancer drugs
4. Procedure for the supply and delivery of off-label medicines
5. Procedure for the supply and delivery of foreign medicines

Table 1 People who cover different roles in pharmaceutical unit of academic hospital of Catanzaro. Our elaboration

Role	Number of people
Pharmacy director	1
Pharmacy manager	3
Administrative	5
Warehouse technician	4

6. Procedure for the supply and delivery of medicines and medical devices in transit
7. Procedure for the purchase of products not present in the hospital pharmacy
8. Storage, handling and transport of medicines procedure
9. Procedure for the acceptance and fulfillment of supply requests of the organizational units of drugs and devices
10. Sending and processing requests for drugs under monitoring
11. Procedure for the statistical evaluation of consumption, reports by cost center, sending information flows
12. Pharmacovigilance activity
13. Management of experimental drugs
14. Expired management
15. Process of purchasing exclusive products and fungible goods
16. Deposit purchase/delivery process
17. Secretarial activities
18. Medical gas management

Procedures had to be prepared as the activity of the hospital pharmacy is based, in particular, on established paths and on choices that imply checks, controls and responsibilities. The checks and controls are fundamental for monitoring the activity and pharmaceutical expenditure of the organizational units with subsequent economic impact also on the territory, while responsibility means the ability to respond appropriately to any event in order to always guarantee the best the assistance activity.

Subsequently, 15 indicators were identified, listed below, for the measurement of each one of them contributes one or more procedures.

(1) Number of needs forwarded to the health department of supervision/total needs
(2) Number of purchase requests sent to UABS/total of requests
(3) Number of reminders sent to the competent unit for non-receipt of direct management devices/drugs/total of requests sent
(4) Percentage value of the number of bubbles without order references/total of the bubbles
(5) Number of bubbles on which discrepancies were noted between ordered and received/total of the bubbles
(6) Number of operations performed on the computerized system per qualified operator
(7) Number of delivery notes delivered by the operating units relating to deliveries not made to the pharmacy/per operating unit
(8) Number of drug/device return procedures initiated by the pharmacy/total deliveries
(9) Number of off-label and foreign drug requests forwarded to the health department
(10) Number of record paths relating to the information flows sent to the competent company contacts
(11) Number of requests assessed for purchase with financial funds

(12) Number of dispensations of drugs/devices carried out
(13) Number of requests processed for monitored drugs (nominative requests)/total of requests
(14) Number of shipments received relating to clinical trials/compassionate use
(15) Number of inquiries drawn up by the pharmacy for exclusive products/fungible goods.

The percentage of realization is calculated through an information system in which the data of the procedures linked to the indicator flow together.

The hospital business unit started this project in 2016, and from a first analysis of the results obtained from 2016 to 2018, there is a positive increase for each year of implementation of the indicators.

5 First Consideration

At this step work in progress, our research—beyond the survey of literature on specific topic and sector—focused on possibility to measure the performance through some specific clinical indicators. In order to do this, the starting point was the comparative analysis developed in similar situation in another clinical context; the pharmaceutical case study provides in-depth analysis of some indicators, highlighting how these tend to detect the ability to implement policies to curb pharmaceutical spending. The indicators considered were have been studied because they are the most reliable in both data and calculation criteria the most representative of the performance of pharmaceuticals and those normally used at national level for the evaluation of comparative health systems.

The chosen indicators have the ability to explain specific aspects related to performance measurement in health context. So, at this stage our aim is to measure these indicators and verify its trend on time. Once knowledge becomes more specific and larger than before, in the future, the research could focus on specific aspects and could be introduced indicators of the appropriateness of delivered pharmaceutical, certainly more significant than the central goal of ensuring the best care for the patient's need.

6 Conclusion

The paper aims to contribute both theoretically and practically on the topic practices of digitization in healthcare heritage. The outcome of this study provides implications for future research on the role and the impact of innovation in the healthcare sector; in addition, it is possible to suggest and test other empirical tools that can be used in organizations. In fact, once knowledge becomes more specific and larger than before, in the future, the research could focus on specific aspects, and next step could introduce indicators of the appropriateness of delivered pharmaceutical, certainly more significant than the central goal of ensuring the best care for the patient's need. The results of this research can be utilized for further research which can later result in a refined framework with high practical relevance.

References

1. Di Paolo, A. (2007). L'introduzione del New Public Management e della Balanced Scorecard nel processo di riforma dell'Amministrazione pubblica italiana. Economia pubblica.
2. Dunleavy, P., & Hood, C. (1994). From old public administration to new public management. *Public Money & Management, 14*(3), 9–16.
3. Voorberg, W. H., Bekkers, V. J., & Tummers, L. G. (2015). A systematic review of co-creation and co-production: Embarking on the social innovation journey. *Public Management Review, 17*(9), 1333–1357
4. Anjomshoae, A., Hassan, A., & Wong, K. Y. (2019). An: integrated AHP-based scheme for performance measurement in humanitarian supply chains. International Journal of Productivity and Performance Management.
5. Pollitt, C. (2007). Convergence or divergence: what has been happening in Europe? In *New public management in Europe*, pp. 10–25. London: Palgrave Macmillan.
6. Borgonovi, E. (2005). Principi e sistemi aziendali per le amministrazioni pubbliche, Egea.
7. Gu, X., & Itoh, K. (2016). Performance indicators: healthcare professionals' views. *International Journal of Health Care Quality Assurance.*
8. Fiore-Gartland, B., & Neff, G. (2015). Communication, mediation, and the expectations of data: Data valences across health and wellness communities. *International Journal of Communication, 9*, 19.
9. Gottlieb, M., Utesch, M. C., & Böhm, M. (2019). Beyond 2030 Challenges of engineering education in an information systems driven world-an extraction based on research topics. In *2019 IEEE Global Engineering Education Conference*, pp. 458–466.
10. Hess, C. E. E., & Ribeiro, W. C. (2016). Energy and environmental justice: Closing the gap. *Environmental Justice, 9*(5), 153–158.
11. Mentis, D., Howells, M., Rogner, H., Korkovelos, A., Arderne, C., Zepeda, E., Siyal, S., Taliotis, C., Bazilian, M., De Roo, A., & Tanvez, Y. (2017). Lighting the World: the first application of an open source, spatial electrification tool (OnSSET) on Sub-Saharan Africa. *Environmental Research Letters, 12*(8), 085003.
12. Cucciniello, M., Guerrazzi, C., Nasi, G., & Claudio, C. (2014) Fabbisogni informativi nelle aziende sanitarie: quale coerenza tra stato di maturità, propensione all' investimento e soluzioni offerte, Rapporto Oasi.
13. Cicchetti, A. (2004). La progettazione organizzativa: principi, strumenti e applicazioni nelle organizzazioni sanitarie, FrancoAngeli.
14. Grilli, F., & Willenegger, S. (2004). U.S. Patent No. 6,697,629. Washington, DC: U.S. Patent and Trademark Office.
15. European Commission eHealth Action Plan 2012–2020. (2004). Innovation e healthcare for the 21st century.
16. Nuti, S. (2008). Le misure della valutazione. Nuti S. (a cura di), La valutazione della performance in sanità, Il Mulino, Bologna.
17. Veillard, J., Champagne, F., Klazinga, N., Kazandjian, V., Arah, O. A., & Guisset, A. L. (2005). A performance assessment framework for hospitals: The WHO regional office for Europe PATH project. *International Journal for Quality in Health Care, 17*(6), 487–496.
18. Daniels, A. C., & Daniels, J. E. (2004). Performance management: Changing behavior that drives organizational effectiveness.

19. Mulgan, G., Tucker, S., Ali, R., & Sanders, B. (2007). Social innovation: What it is, why it matters and how it can be accelerated.
20. Smith, P. C. (2006). Performance management in British health care: Will it deliver? *Health affairs, 21*(3), 103–115.
21. Veillard, J., Huynh, T., Ardal, S., Kadandale, S., Klazinga, N. S., & Brown, A. D. (2010). Making health system performance measurement useful to policy makers: Aligning strategies, measurement and local health system accountability in Ontario. *Healthcare Policy, 5*(3), 49.
22. Alexander, K. (2013). *Facilities management: theory and practice.* Routledge.
23. Williams, R., & Menduni, E. (2000). Televisione, tecnologia e forma culturale: e altri scritti sulla TV. Ed. Riuniti.
24. Pullen, S., Atkinson, D., & Tucker, S. (2000). Improvements in benchmarking the asset management of medical facilities. In *Proceedings of the International Symposium on Facilities Management and Maintenance, Brisbane,* pp. 265–271.
25. Tawfik-Shukor, A. R., Klazinga, N. S., & Arah, O. A. (2014). Comparing health system performance assessment and management approaches in the Netherlands and Ontario. *Canada. BMC Health Services Research, 7*(1), 25.
26. Feng, S. C., & Joung, C. B. (2011). A measurement infrastructure for sustainable manufacturing. *International Journal of Sustainable Manufacturing, 2*(2–3), 204–221.
27. Lavastre, O., Gunasekaran, A., & Spalanzani, A. (2014). Effect of firm characteristics, supplier relationships and techniques used on Supply Chain Risk Management (SCRM): An empirical investigation on French industrial firms. *International Journal of Production Research, 52*(11), 3381–3403.
28. Waring, T., & Wainwright, D. (2002). Enhancing clinical and management discourse in ICT implementation. *Journal of management in Medicine.*
29. Yu, K., Froese, T. M., & Vinet, B. (1997). Facilities management core models. In *Conference of the Canadian Society for Civil Engineers.*
30. Nuti, S. (2010). Misurazione e valutazione della performance: principi, struttura e metodi. Piano industriale della pubblica amministrazione Il nuovo testo unico sul pubblico impiego, pp. 321–354.
31. Nuti, S. (2008). *La valutazione della performance in sanità.* Il Mulino.

Practice Enterprise and MOOCs in Higher Education Real and Perceived Performances

Massimo Bianchi

Abstract The paper aims to present and discuss the results of a performance research related to the fusion between two advanced teaching methodologies and their latest evolutions: the practice enterprise (PE) and the massive open online courses (MOOC). Ongoing practices encourage the extension of experience to the synergy between PE and MOOC with particular attention to the preparation of different roles of the teaching staff represented by teachers, tutors and mentors. The hypothesis concerns how to evaluate PE and MOOC with the same methodology, distinguishing the real performances from the perceived ones. This result would pave the way for a common platform to use these advanced teachings together, perfecting their implementation. The document wants to argue that this fusion is not only possible but also necessary to implement the preparation of teachers for further diffusion of these innovative didactics in higher education programmes.

Keywords Practice enterprise · MOOCs · Blended learning · Connectivism · Learning analytics · Performance analysis

1 From Simulimpresa to PE

The diffusion of practice management as. didactical approach started at the beginning of 80' years in schools of different order and degree. In Mediterranean countries, it was generally named Simulimpresa, and in last year the variety of realizations was reunified under the term practice enterprise (PE). It was also the subject of many experiences realized on this subjects in Erasmus projects and particularly in the HEIPNET project[1]. The research was based on the perceptions of students in the

M. Bianchi (✉)
Department of Management, University of Bologna, Bologna, Italy
e-mail: massimo.bianchi@unibo.it

[1] HEIPNET: Inclusion of Innovative Work-Based-Learning and Business Partnerships in HEI Curricula Development, Erasmus + Project 2019–2021. n° 2019-1-LT01-KA203-060,514—999,893,752 Partners: University of Graz, Utena University Lithuania,LIBA Association Lithuania, EUROPEN-PEN International, University of Pavia.

© The Author(s), under exclusive license to Springer Nature Switzerland AG 2022
L. Solari et al. (eds.), *Do Machines Dream of Electric Workers?*, Lecture Notes in Information Systems and Organisation 49,
https://doi.org/10.1007/978-3-030-83321-3_11

acquisition of entrepreneurial competences for the creation of start-ups and on the comparison among results obtained in main functional units.

The above-mentioned research was developed within projects involving firstly the practice management by Simulimpresa and, in the recent phases, the use of MOOCs (Table 1).

The purpose of the research was to better the preparation and competence of the teaching staff in the use of new didactics with a more attentive consideration of learners feedback, not only as it concerns the knowledge acquired particularly as it concerns the "soft skills" [1] but on the change of their attitudes and on the persistence of motivations acquired during the learning process.

Table 1 Projects with practice management and MOOCs experiences

CHTMBAL—Tempus			
Network for Post Graduate Masters in Cultural Heritage and Tourism Management in Balkan Countries	University D'Annunzio of Chieti-Pescara (IT)	Albania, Italy, Kosovo, Poland, Spain	2012–2014
CEN-EAST—Tempus			
CEN-EAST "Reformation of the Curriculum on Built Environment in the Eastern Neighbouring"	Vilnius Gedeminias Technical University Vilnius (LT)	Bielorussia, Italy, Lithuania, Russia, UK, Ukraine	2012–2015
CASCADE—Seventh Framework Programme			
Collaborative Action towards Societal Challenges through Awareness,	Salford/Huddersfield University (UK)	Afghanistan, Bangladesh, Bhutan, Estonia, Italy, France, Lithuania, Maldives, Nepal, Sri Lanka, Thailand, UK	2013–2015
Development and Education			
RESINT—Lifelong Learning Programme Erasmus Multilateral Projects			
Collaborative Reformation of Curricula on Resilience Management with Intelligent Systems in Open Source and Augmented Reality	Unibo Campus Forlì (IT)	Italy, Lithuania, Spain, UK	2013–2015
BECK—Erasmus + Capacity Building in the Field of Higher Education			
BECK Integrating Education with Consumer Behaviour Relevant to Energy Efficiency and Climate Change at the Universities of Russia, Sri Lanka and Bangladesh	Vilnius Gedeminias Technical University Vilnius (LT)	Bangladesh, Italy, Lithuania, Russia, Sri Lanka, UK	2019–2022

Among the undertaken experiences, the BECK project, currently underway, is included specifically within this scenario. Co-financed by the Erasmus + programme of the European Union, this transdisciplinary project promotes a capacity-building action in the university education and third level.

The purpose was the improvement of the teaching approach in digital learning according to the functional destination of competencies and to the implication for the teacher leadership according to last contributions in the field [2]. The management of these business relationships represents the more characteristic feature of PE as it ensures a realistic commitment to learners that, within the period of learning, has to join for their PE a positive balance between costs and revenues and prepare a balance sheet with the economic results.

In particular, the subjects are the methodologies to integrate education on consumer behaviour, in terms of energy efficiency and climate change in the universities of Russia, Sri Lanka and Bangladesh. On this, target is focused on the BECK project with the didactical experience of the European states involved as it concerns the specific skills of human resources, transferred in beneficiary partners.

The objective of BECK is to implement entrepreneurial competencies able to use the skills acquired in local contexts. In this project, the University of Bologna focused the application of the PE and of the MOOCs, on the compatibility between the protection of the cultural heritage and of the improvement of the energy performance.

To this purpose, the attention was focused on the education to organizational functions that, in PE, ensure the managerial process. In the didactics of PE, these functions are distinguished in two main areas: the technical, prevalently using dedicated software (Managerial Control Finance, Accounting, Sales) and the creative one mostly applying Internet connections (Marketing, Human Resources).

The PE is a learning by doing didactics with a classroom that creates and manages a simulated enterprise or an organization with all organizational functions as a real one. The business is ensured by the exchanges with other participants of the PE network that groups more than 4.000 PEs in the world and organized in the network EUROPEN-PEN[2].

In PE, the teaching, as analysed in the next paragraph, is managed by three kind of roles: the teacher, the tutor and the mentor. As blended learning, the traditional approach to the teaching changed completely as the didactical process of PE is centred on the learner, and this requires a specific preparation.

2 New Didactical Technologies and the Evolution of Learning Approach

MOOC is a methodology of online lessons that allows, anyone and anywhere, to participate freely through video lectures, discussion forums and tests which, in case of a positive result and a minimum of attendance, concludes with the issue of a

---

[2] EUROPEN-PEN International Worldwide Practice Enterprise Network, Essen Germany.

certificate. While PE could be managed, as it happened at the beginning, by traditional tools of connections like phone, fax and post mail, the MOOCs are intrinsically related to the employment of advanced platforms which allow a strict connections among the teachers and the learners with the relevant opportunity of managing forums and discussions among participants.

A relevant aspect of MOOCs is their potential diffusion in countries whose educational structures are weak and/or subject to endemic and creeping conflicts. Furthermore, these situations are a source of risks for the cultural heritage, historical or contemporary, seen as an expression of a culture that one part wants to destroy. Also in the richest countries, with recent restraints in resources dedicated to HEIs, MOOCs gain some audience owing their reduced cost compared to its diffusion and results [3]. Before examining the experiences of PE and MOOCs in progress and evaluating their extension to education in the field of cultural heritage and energy efficiency, it is appropriate to examine and discuss its theoretical roots.

The methodological basis of learning by doing is traditionally represented by the pragmatism of John Dewey [4] and next approaches derived from Behaviourism and Connectivism. All these theories underline the relevance in the learning approach, of the experimentation, of the valorisation of learners' previous experiences and of the link between theory and practice.

The introduction in education of information and Internet technologies inspired to George Siemens [5] a learning theory for the digital age defined Connectivism. The basis was a learning that combines digital technology with open educational resources. The other innovation was the teaching approach centred on students and on a great interconnection between the participants' knowledge and transversal competences with the opportunity to interact with the result of the learning. The attempt made by Connectivism aims, on the one hand, to a more conscious and adequate use of the possibilities offered by interconnection and, on the other, to overcome what are considered the limits of previous theories such as Behaviourism, Cognitivism and Constructivism [6]. Behaviourism, from its founder Watson to his eponymous Skinner, focused learning on the relationship between stimuli and conditions in which the educational process takes place and the results expressed by the manifest individuals' behaviour.

Chomsky [7] severely criticizes this approach from an epistemological point on view, not based on experimental data, but on the discussion of the principles of Behaviourism. The argument was the separation of the stimuli received from the complex environment in which the stimuli were produced and that was not necessarily neutral. Really the limits of Chomsky position against Behaviourism and, in general, about Connectivism represent the starting point of opportunities to consider integrable PEs and MOOCs in a single learning process while considering the limits of technology from the beginning present in its use in education [8].

Similar consequences derive from the limits of Behaviourism, in particular in relation to the evolution of learning in the meantime in progress. From this development emerges the Cognitivism that metaphorically assimilates the functioning of the mind to that of a software and consequently analyses the learning process in a neurophysiological key.

In last ten years, the discussion about MOOCs increases constantly [9] but is away from an unique orientation.

From a more oriented practice, we have to mention the Hiim and Hippe's model of interconnections [10] that introduces some qualitative models to highlight the complexity of the didactics once the learner is located at the centre of the didactical process [11].

The didactic relation model was used for the planning education in Norway with the purpose to support educators in planning, teaching and evaluating activities. It is based on nine key factors which describe the teaching situation as ICT, learners, teachers, time, goals, evaluation, contents, activities and contexts and make visible their interrelations. This framework (Fig. 1) would increase the awareness and understanding teaching practices and the individuation of key interrelationships and their combinations (9! = 986,400).

The framework really is not a scientific tool but a useful descriptive instrument having the aim to express the complexity of interrelationships in a suitable way.

The common orientation of all these analyses and proposals is the dissatisfaction on teaching approaches particularly as it concerns the managerial education. Even most famous MBA schools were accused of a persistent gap between didactical objectives and results. Main reason of this situation was indicated as the prevailing of traditional didactics, frontal lectures and mannerist use of case discussion.

A diffused criticism on MBA didactics and unsatisfactory results complained of by companies [12] confirmed efforts in improving new methods of learning particularly as it concerns the entrepreneurial and managerial skills and the improving of relational side of learning [13].

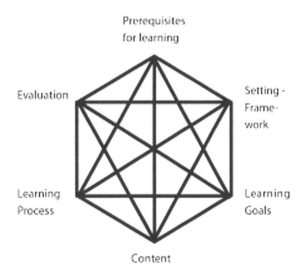

Fig. 1 Didactical model of Hiim and Hippe[3]

Prerequisites for learning

Evaluation

Setting - Frame-work

Learning Process

Learning Goals

Content

---

[3] Hiim, H., and Hippe, E. 2006. "*Praksisveiledning i lærerutdanningen: En didaktisk veiledningsstrategi.*" Oslo: Gyldendal akademisk.

A relevant advancement in the field was represented by the distinction between the enterprise education and enterprise training [14]. The enterprise education broadly includes practices to increase the self-achievement and confidence according to individual talents. The entrepreneurial training is focused on the building of relevant skills and values supporting learners in the exploitation of opportunities existing in the environment. This leads to the first experimental applications of PEs and MOOCs.

For our purposes, the model underlines the compatibility of PE and MOOC as it considers relevant the same topics.

3 MOOCs and Connective Didactics

In last ten years, the discussion about MOOCs increases constantly [15, 16]. As innovative approach that changes the relationships of the teacher with the classroom and involves evaluation methods and didactical assessment systems, PE encountered and still encounters difficulties in its insertion in curricula particularly in High Education Institutions [17].

In Italy, PE was promoted in 2001 by the first Simulimpresa course in the University of Bologna [18][4] and till now is going on with a similar experience in the University of Parma [19][5] just to evidence the difficulties in the spreading of this methodology in HEIs.

One of the obstacles derives from the scarce preparation of teaching staff. Furthermore, observations conducted in different countries highlight that the best promoter of PE in HEIs is the teacher who casually knew the approach and become enthusiastic of it, although a specific knowledge of the methodology.

This was the main reason of a MOOC having this didactical programme, in the research programme of BECK project,[6] based on the introduction of MOOCs, for the education in teaching on PE. Especially, the MOOC "Practice Management in sustainable fruition of Cultural Heritage" was scheduled at BSc level to be managed by the preparation of the PE courses for teaching staffs. The syllabus includes the energy efficiency as the first step to increase the sustainability of cultural heritage at BSc level to be managed for the preparation of the PE courses for teaching staffs. The syllabus includes the energy efficiency as the first step to increase the sustainability of cultural heritage.

Each subject involves the appliance of connective didactics starting from the planning of didactical practices. One of the most diffused mistakes of the teaching

---

[4] Perting Ltd., operates in the field of organizational consulting, network and merchandising of ICT products, is the first unit of certified Simulated Enterprise, established by an Italian University. It started up on October 2001 in Forlì Faculty of Economics—Bologna University. http://perting.pol oforli.unibo.it/.

[5] No Risk Agency, operating from 2008 in Risk Insurance.

[6] BECK project integrating education with consumer behaviour relevant to energy efficiency and climate change at the Universities of Russia, Sri Lanka and Bangladesh KA 2 Capacity Building in higher education 01/10/2019—31/11/2021.

in learning by doing and particularly in PE is to start the teaching in the classroom with no or scarce preparation and trusting in the improvisation and/or in the cultural base possessed.

On the contrary, just the evaluation sheet proposed to PE teachers (Table 2) and students (Table 3) demonstrates which and how many are the elements to consider for a good teaching positioning in PE.

The proposed syllabus of MOOC on PE contains the following:

- The aims and contents of the business simulation.
- The market and the simulated business competition.
- The formalization of the business plan and the operating budget.
- The personnel selection and assignment of individual tasks.
- Drafting of the company communication project.
- The determination of company financial needs.
- The support services for business creation and start-up.

Although the increasing relevance is in the education of the instructional designers and of the educational practitioners, together with the strategy of learning, we concentrate our attention to the different roles existing in the teaching staff operating in the classroom, owing to its direct impact on didactics and results.

PE classrooms, normally composed by no more than 25 students, are committed to create a start-up or an enterprise within the period of lectures that can be extended from 40 to 80 h. Teachers, tutors and mentors compose the teaching staff, who coordinate the didactics, with different roles synthetized at Fig. 2 in which skills are analytically listed.

Students and teaching staff are both considered two main components of the didactical triangle, but the relevance in the PEs and MOOCs management of ICT technicians and administrative staff is increasingly referred as determinant factor to produce the quality of the learning process [20].

4 Roles in PE Quality Assurance

The quality assurance in PE needs a specific approach connected to the evaluation of the performance that which in turn are a source of debate on the validity of the didactical method.

The teaching staff of PE is inserted in a more extended structure of roles involved in the didactical process with students and the environment which participate to different purposes to the learning process (Fig. 3).

Table 2 Teachers questionnaire on the didactical approach in PE

How much you agree or disagree with the following statements?	Strongly agree	Agree	Neutral	Disagree	Strongly disagree
Timetable of the PE selection of participants and lectures was announced well in advance					
The teacher was informed well in advance for the timetable of PE selection and lectures					
The room to hold the class was adequate for PE activities					
The assigned room was well equipped to successfully hold PE activities					
Administrative and technical staff was cooperative, punctual and effective in delivering information to successfully hold PE activities					
Students demonstrate an active interest for the PE activities					
Students interact with the teaching staff and colleagues					
Students grip the English language					

Table 3 Students questionnaire on the didactical approach in PE

How much you agree or disagree with the following statements?	Strongly agree	Agree	Neutral	Disagree	Strongly disagree
Effective/good teacher demonstrates the correct way to solve the problem					
It is better when the teacher (not the student) decides what activities have to be undertaken					
Teachers know a lot more than students. They should not answer that may be incorrect when they can just explain the answer directly					
Students learn best by finding solutions to their problems on their own					
How much students learn depend on how much background knowledge they have. That is the way teaching facts are so necessary					
Students should be allowed to think of solutions of practical problems themselves before the teacher shows them how they are solved					
A quite classroom is generally needed for effective learning					

These different roles are involved not only directly in the learning but also in the evaluation of the didactical performance with an integrated system based on the categories of efficiency, effectiveness and adequacy (Fig. 4).

This further triangle of elements, here represented by main categories of indexes for the control and evaluation of performances, can be used to simplify the number of indexes used to this purpose substituting the numerosity by the interdependency of

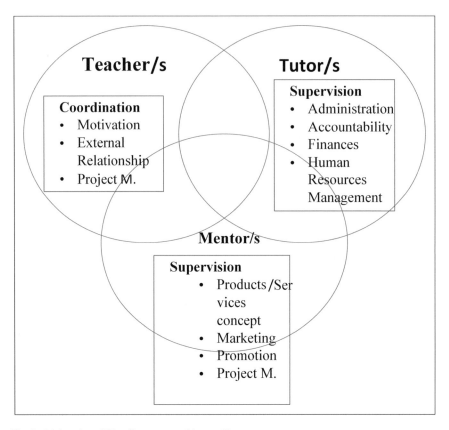

Fig. 2 Main roles of Simulimpresa teaching staff

items which adds more opportunities to keep organizational processes under control. In the particular case of PE and MOOCs learning performances, this can offer more chances for the research.

Particularly, the integrated system of performance indexes allows distinguishing the real from the perceived performance using the formula:

$$Ad = Ec/Ez$$

derived from the transform (1):

$$\text{Adequacy} = \frac{\text{Efficacy}}{\text{Efficiency}} = \frac{\frac{\text{Results}}{\text{Objectives}}}{\frac{\text{Results}}{\text{Objectives}}} \tag{1}$$

---

[7] Strategic Integration of Learning Models-Needs Assessment Analysis.8.06.2015 ISPEHE Innovate Strategic Partnership for European Higher Education Erasmus + Project KA2—Cooperation and Innovation for Good Practices 1/1/2015–31/12/2016.

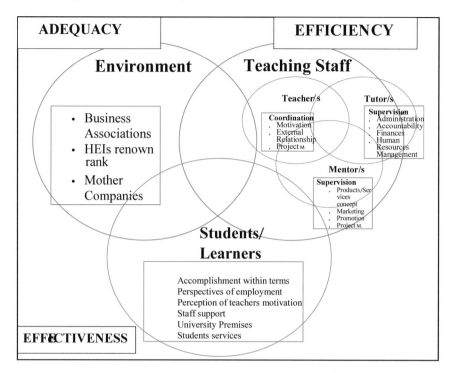

Fig. 3 Positioning of the variety of PE roles in the process of evaluation[7]

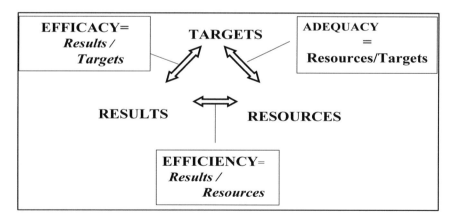

Fig. 4 Integrated system of basic performance indexes

This process allows comparing the perceived Ad, detected by questionnaires, with the real Ad obtained by the Bianchi et al. [21, 22].

The connections among these indexes and the performance in PE were built by the assignment of leading interests to parts involved in the process (Fig. 5).

Fig. 5 PE actors in the process of performance evaluation

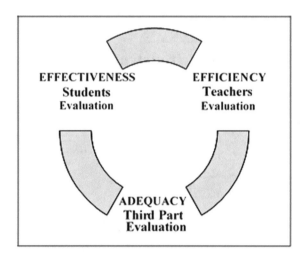

Really the actors of the learning process, students, teachers and institutions or third part evaluators like the one in charge of the expression of the rank of the HGEIs, can be considered as bearers of specific interests and prevalent expression of one of the three categories of indices proposed in the integrated evaluation system.

This identification process was observed during the mentioned projects and formed the basis for the evaluation of the results [19].

Independently from this, the attribution of indexes categories to groups of actors of learning process was used as a methodological bridge for the transition from the opinions expressed by roles involved in the learning process to the treatment of performance indexes having the purpose to distinguish the real performances from perceived ones and enabling to calculate the eventual gap between them.

5 The Evaluation of Performances of PE and MOOCs Projects

It would also be appropriate, in order to make the performance indexes used more comparable, to apply the protocol accepted by the scientific community and the international organizations working on the quality assurance. Those quality assurance procedures, very strictly and detailed defined, enable a comparable measurement of Ec, Ez and Ad indexes, taking up a debate too much soon abandoned after Cameron's studies on the subject [23].

A relevant topic introduced in Italian PE and MOOCs was the legal chartering according to ISA510[8] together with the integrated system of indexes experimented in other projects. In this way, it is possible to classify main quality indicators according to three categories Ec, Ez and Ad as given in Table 4 and to make additional comparison between real and perceived performance.

Table 4 Qualifications of performance indexes in terms of efficacy (Ec), efficiency (Ez) and adequacy (Ad)

EC	Number of trainers in the training of trainers programme
EC	Student entrepreneurial skills tested
EC	Test questions positively fulfilled
EC	Publications about project online and in printed media
EZ	Students, involved in the PE/MOOCs activities
EZ	Internal evaluation surveys conducted
EZ	Project meetings (online and international)
EZ	General education schools, teachers, students, parents staff and other stakeholders involved
AD	People participating in the round tables
AD	Tips and lessons learnt collected
AD	Improvement actions undertaken within the internal pilot implementation in schools of PE/MOOCs
AD	People attending project final conference

With this approach, in projects examined, the constant finding was the prevalence of adequacy of learning process to the perceived one, a finding that could induce to reflect about the diffused pessimism of teacher about the effective results of their job, not so evident in immediate results but not so poor if considered in a more extended length of time.

6 Conclusions

The performance evaluation applied to the new didactics represented by PE and MOOCs can be carried out following similar criteria. This process can represent an opportunity to face the difficulties encountered so far in didactic innovation aimed at mitigating some critical aspects of managerial education especially regarding the gap between theory and practice. However, with the technical opportunity to compare real with perceived performance, so often the basis for discussions on the transition from traditional teaching to new teaching, a contribution could be made to the advancement of management and entrepreneurship teaching.

Generally speaking, based on the considerations discussed in this paper, it would be advisable to extend the application of integrated systems of evaluation, supported by tools of learning analytics, for a more consistent evaluation of the didactics with an especial attention for innovative approaches [24, 25, 26, 4, 27].

References

1. Strazzeri, L. (2020). Soft skills in university education: A real experience. Behave yourself! Soft Skills Development Student Program at the Department of Economics and Business Studies, University of Genoa, *Impresa Progetto* n 1.Publ. on Line (2020). https://doi.org/10.15167/1824-3576/IPEJM2020.1.1259.
2. Bratton, J. (Ed.) (2020). Organizational Leadership. SAGE Publications Ltd, ISBN: 9781526460127
3. Yuan, L., Powell, S., & Olivier, B. (2014). Beyond MOOCs: Sustainable online learning in institutions. *CETIS.* https://doi.org/10.13140/2.1.1075.1364
4. Smart, K. L., & Csapo, N. (2007) Learning by doing: Engaging students through learner-centered activities. Business and Professionals Communication Quarterly December 1.
5. Siemens, G. (2005). Connectivism: A learning theory for the digital age. *International Journal of Instructional Technology and Distance Learning, 2*(1), 3–10.
6. Ertmer Timothy, P.A., &. Newby, J. (2013). Behaviorism, cognitivism, constructivism: comparing critical features from an instructional design perspective, performance improvement quality, performance improvement quarterly. *J. Wiley, 26*(2), 43–71.
7. Chomsky, N. (1967). Preface to the reprint of A Review of Skinner's Verbal Behavio. In L. A. Jakobovits & M. S. Miron (Eds.), *Readings in the psychology of language* (pp. 142–143). Prentice Hall.
8. Jonassen, D. H. (1990). Thinking technology: Toward a Constructivist View of Instructional Design. *Educational Technology, 30*(9). ISSN 0013-1962.
9. Jona, K., & Naidu S. (eds.). (2014). MOOCs: emerging research. Distance Education, *35*(2), 141–144. Publ. on line.https://doi.org/10.1177/10805699070700040302.
10. Kolmos, A. (2002). Facilitating change to a problem-based model. *International Journal for Academic Development, 7*(1). Publ. On Line 10 Dec 2010.
11. Hiim, H., & Hippe, E. (2006). *Praksisveiledning i lærerutdanningen: En didaktisk veiledningsstrategi.* Gyldendal akademisk.
12. Martin, M. (2018). Why we should buldoze business school. The Guardian, Fri 27 Apr (2018) https://www.theguardian.com/news/2018/apr/27
13. Boyatzis R. E., Stubbs E. C., & Taylor S. N. (2017). Learning cognitive and emotional intelligence competencies through graduate management education. *Academy of Management Learning & Education, Academy of Management Learning & Education, 1*(2), https://doi.org/10.5465/amle.2002.8509345.
14. Morselli, D. (2016). La pedagogia dell'imprenditività nell'educazione secondaria. *Formazione & Insegnamento, 14*(2), 173–186.
15. Bonk, C. J., Lee, M. M., Reeves T.C. Reynolds, T. H.(eds.) (2015a). Global reach and local practice. In *The Promise of MOOCs. Language Learning & Technology.* http://llt.msu.edu/issues.
16. Brown, M. (2016). MOOCs as social practice: a kaleidoscope of perspectives. Portland Press Ltd.
17. Bonk, C. J., Lee, M. M., Reeves, T. C., & Reynolds, T. H. (eds.) (2015b). *MOOCs and open education around the world.* Routledge NY
18. Bianchi, M., Gualdi, D., & Tampieri, L. (2017). The role of organizational ties managed by Practice. The case of Perting Ltd. *International Journal of Organizations, 18,* 11–28.
19. Bianchi, M., Hernandez-Lara, A. B., & Gualdi, D. (2015). The contribution of virtual enterprises to competence-based learning: An assessment from the students' perspective. *Technology, Innovation and Educational Journal, 1*(4), 1–16.
20. Ciappei, C., Laudano, M. C., Zollo, L., & Rialti, R. (2016) Evaluating the quality of entrepreneurial education analysing its ability to increase entrepreneurial attitude and intent of students, Excellence in Services. In 1*9th Toulon-Verona International Conference, Conference Proceedings* (pp. 117–132). Huelva.

21. Bianchi, M., Tampieri, L., Valli Casadei, D., & Paganelli, G. (2016). Real and perceived performances. *Journal of Modern Accounting and Auditing, 10*(10), 1038–1047. ISSN 1548-4583.
22. Bianchi, M., Baseska, M., Tampieri, L Ngo Mai, S., &.Verges J., (eds.) (2014). Beyond the horizon of Tempus Projects. In *Theory and practice of project management*. Il Ponte Vecchio. ISBN 978-88-654&1-407-1.
23. Cameron, K. (1986). Effectiveness as paradox: Consensus and conflict in conceptions of organizational effectiveness. *Management Science, 32*(5), 539–553.
24. Cameron, K., & Whetten, D. (1977). Some conclusions about organizational effectiveness 1983. In K. Cameron & D. Whetten (Eds.), *Organizational effectiveness: A comparison of multiple* (pp. 61–278). Academic Press.
25. Djalali, A. (2017). A didactic perspective on leadership education—focussing on the development of competencies within MBA programs, SteinBeis Edition
26. Powell, S. (2016). MOOCs and open education: Implications for higher education. Manchester Metropolitan University's Research, e-space.mmu.ac.uk.
27. Tampieri, L. (2020). *La valutazione delle performance nel project management*. Wolters Kluwer Italia.

Organizational Followership: How Social Media Communication Affects Employees' Behavior

Paola Adinolfi, Gabriella Piscopo, Davide de Gennaro, Nicola Capolupo, and Valerio Giampaola

Abstract The communication process between organizations and employees is going through a deep systemic revolution. Over time, the environments in which communication occurs have totally changed, also with new interdependencies between the actors involved in this dynamic information's exchange. Drawing from the literature on social network and organizational behaviors, this study aims at rethinking the concept of organizational followership, starting from Kelley's studies (1988), considering a perspective focused on the use of digital tools. The study is structured in two moments: an experiment on a social media account (Instagram), showing online users a series of pictures with cognitive bias to verify the ability to analyze targeted digital followership, and a qualitative approach with semi-structured interviews to a sample of native-digital people, to investigate possible behaviors and hidden motivations in digital ecosystems. The results suggest the possibility of cognitive biases in communication via social networks between leaders and followers, so the aim is to start the debate about the possibility that the phenomenon of communication via digital channels can overturn within organizations.

Keywords Organizational followership · Social media communication · Communication bias

1 Introduction

The communication process between organizations and within them is undergoing a constant revolution [1–3]. Communication is a phenomenon in constant change and evolution that follows a linear, but also tortuous, trend; a peculiar example, probably unique of this kind, is the emergency caused in 2020 by the Coronavirus pandemic, which has overturned all the existing traditional methods of work organization and communication.

P. Adinolfi · G. Piscopo · D. de Gennaro (✉) · N. Capolupo · V. Giampaola
University of Salerno, 84084 Fisciano, Italy
e-mail: ddegennaro@unisa.it

© The Author(s), under exclusive license to Springer Nature Switzerland AG 2022
L. Solari et al. (eds.), *Do Machines Dream of Electric Workers?*, Lecture Notes in Information Systems and Organisation 49,
https://doi.org/10.1007/978-3-030-83321-3_12

It should be taken into account that the organization, in the part, performed its own communications activities "*in-house*" [4], to meet marketing managers' needs to keep outputs under control and standardized (press releases, interviews, market surveys). This process is deeply in contrast to what happens nowadays: organizations delegate those social interaction with customers and followers to external agents, specialized and accomplished to involve employees in the communication processes [5]. Inward and outward communication has played an increasingly important role and consequently leadership is also called to adopt a new communication style based on a bottom-up approach that recognizes the key role played by the company's employees [6, 7].

According to the literature [8], the "*act of communicate*" is grounded in purposeful social interaction; it is the act of conveying information for the purpose of creating a shared understanding [9]. Nowadays, communication is increasingly mediated by social networks, providing people a comprehensive communication platform of interaction, knowledge sharing, information dissemination, and so on [10]. The use of social media helps the creation of social exchanges and improves communication; social media are increasingly implemented in work organizations as a tool for communication among employees [11, 12]. Furthermore, this emergence of digital ecosystems generates sub-systems which, by "*exploiting the democratic structure of social media*" [13], configure themselves as self-systems: a self-organized system [14] concerns groups of individual aggregating between each other into informal groups without any sort of influences [15], eventually sharing common languages, goals, and interests [16]. Oddly enough, but this is due to the relatively new discipline on the subject, conversation, sharing, and presence which occur on ecosystems like Instagram, Twitter, or Facebook represent a factor that has not yet been fully investigated, although they are potentially revolutionary in scope and methods [17, 18].

Accordingly, social media structure leads to generate strong bonds between actors [19]. Social networks derive from the study of interpersonal relationships and are aimed at building continuous and harmonious interpersonal relationships. However, it is fundamental to distinguish between active and passive users: the literature suggests [20] that active social users postulate social trends and agendas in different topics and decide to interact with leaders and/or organizations closely related to their personal aims and interests. Furthermore, they perform an effective communication especially if they share common semantic rules [21]. On the contrary users, by receiving information from other and deciding to not responding are listed as passive, or at least this behavior may be considered "*as evidence for passivity*" [22].

Based on previous assumptions, the leader/follower relation (e.g., manager/employee, manager/consumer) cannot be analyzed by merely focusing on the leader perspective any longer because communicative environments are dynamically changing for two main reasons: first, because the sub-system of social media led to the emergence of behaviors which would not show up in other circumstances for different motivations (e.g., psychological factors, subordination to the manager/organizational management); secondly, it should be considered that communication tools tend to reduce critical thinking because of the immediacy in consuming information.

The aim of this study is to analyze and contextualize the theme of organizational followership, starting from Kelley's studies [23–26], in light of the modern meaning of follower in the presence of the current digital communication tools used or potentially used by organizations. The original matrix [23, 24] was made of five categories of organizational followers based on the levels of behavioral activity/passivity and dependence/independence of thought: (i) sheep (passive and uncritical, lacking in initiative and sense of responsibility), (ii) yes man (dependent on a leader for inspiration, they can be aggressively deferential, even servile), (iii) alienated follower (critical and independent in thinking but passive in carrying out the role), (iv) survivor (living by the slogan "better safe than sorry"), and (v) effective followers (thinking for themselves and carrying out the own duties and assignments with energy and assertiveness). These categories, in addition to defining the specific characteristics of the organizational follower, identified for the first time the co-responsibility of these figures in relation to the organizational processes, without leaving the success of the intra-organizational relationships to the effectiveness or otherwise of the leader's action. Some different types of followership are generated (alienated, effective, passive, and conformist), which can be represented graphically as follows (Fig. 1).

The study of followership, little re-proposed by the scientific literature in the organizational field [27], has recently experienced a new life thanks to the spread of social networks and the identification of the user/consumer as a follower. In fact, there are studies that deepen and put together the organizational and sociological literature in order to identify a new role for the followers [28–30], but other studies are needed that address the theme, especially in the digital age. Furthermore, extant literature has mainly explored the positive followership paradigm, and there are few studies that have systematically examined the antecedents that elicit employees to choose different followership behaviors and different consequences on job performance [10] and it could be interesting also to fill this gap.

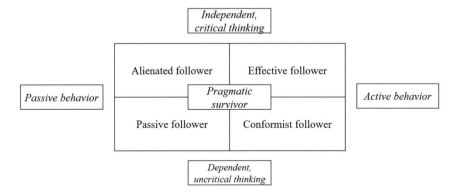

Fig. 1 A graphical representation of Kelley's followership styles [23, 24]. *Source* Our elaboration

The goal of this exploratory study is to analyze the principle of followership in the era of social communication by experimenting the effects of low-frequency organizational communication on the persecution of self-systems purposes. Thus, authors will try to imagine what effects such behaviors—if borrowed in organizations—would produce by imagining the emergence of a new figure of follower who is also the uncritical protagonist of the scenarios and contexts of the digital organization. Through a qualitative investigation, the focus will be on organizational followership through the analysis of some cognitive errors on which the groups of stakeholders fall, and how these biases can translate into work organizational dynamics when digital tools to conduct communication are used. Therefore, the final aim is to start the debate regarding digital communication, and any distortions in the communication process, in businesses.

Implications for theory and practice will be discussed.

2 Method

Following these objectives, research design has been structured by following a twofold explorative methodology which refers to the inductive content analysis proposed by Elo and Kyngäs [31]. Content analysis is a method that may be used with either qualitative or quantitative data, and it follows an inductive approach when there is not enough former knowledge about the phenomenon to be investigated [32].

The methodology of this study followed three main steps [31].

The first step was of preparation: Starting from the selection of the analysis unit [33], it was possible to decide the topic to be investigated and the most suitable channel to do it. The choice of social media fell on Instagram. Instagram is a social network born in 2010, acquired a few years later by Facebook Inc., the company founded by Mark Zuckerberg. Instagram is a communication channel that allows you to interact with other people who are part of a social network. The Instagram platform differs slightly from the social networks that preceded it, referring to a setting much closer to the new social media focused on photographs and videos of all kinds. Indeed, Instagram users have a personal profile on which to upload photos and videos, thus sharing with the people of their network (followers) the moments of their day. Being a very popular platform, in recent years, in addition to representing a communication channel, Instagram has become a real marketing tool [34, 35] and in general a tool for business management [36–39]. At this stage, the social profile from which to post the photos was also selected, thus trying to select a representative sample of the universe [40, 41]; the final sample is composed of 248 digital native students—enrolled in three-year and master's degree courses at the University of Salerno—and young employees.

The second step was of collection and organization of data:

- first, by setting a social media experiment on an Instagram individual account, showing to online users (both general users and users being "followers" of that account) a specific set of pictures of places containing cognitive bias about the single place' location—showing misleading tags and geolocation from the image subject—the aim was at verifying the digital followership ability to critically analyze and process leader's communication. The quantitative amount of interactions reached by each single post seemed to be an adequate indicator useful to explain the existence of two different conceptualizations of digital followers, namely the active and the passive one;

- secondly, by setting-up a semi-structured interview, authors' aim was at investigating and better defining the reasons for certain choices made by the followership in the new social—and especially social media—contexts (in a behavioral and/or organizational scenario). A set of three semi-structured questions was asked: (i) Look at image number … as a whole (image, location, tag, quotes, etc.). How would you react? (ii) If you opted for an interaction, which aspect drew your attention the most? (iii) Based on this picture and your interaction, would you choose to follow this Instagram account? Explain the reason for your choice.

Therefore, the expected methodological outputs will allow the authors to trace a communicative followership profile which, if applied to organizations, would configure a new follower profile in Kelley's matrix, opening new research horizons to organizational followership studies.

The final step was of analysis, in which we strived to make sense of the data. According to Dey [42], we asked ourselves: "Who is telling? Where is this happening? When did it happen? What is happening? Why?" with the aim of "being immersed" in the data [43]. This process included open coding, creating categories, and abstraction: in this way the categories were freely generated [44] and then grouped together [45] so as not only to put together observations that are similar or related, but also those that "belong" to a certain group [42] in order to describe widely the phenomenon to be investigated [46].

The results of this study will be presented and discussed in the next sections.

3   Results

3.1   The Social Media Experiment

In order to correctly present the first part of the evidence collected, it was deemed useful for synthesis needs to report the most representative post of the social media experiment through the Instagram profile. Three images will be shown below, about three different phases particularly explanatory of the empirical path carried out.

The image shown in Fig. 2 reports the first "test" posted on Instagram for the purpose of the experiment.

Figure 2 shows the Gulf of Reykjavik (Iceland), but it is accompanied by the geolocation "Lungomare Caracciolo" of Naples (Italy) and described with the caption "Everything is blue in Naples," thus creating a conflict between the image and the

secondo_giampaola
Lungomare Caracciolo

#napoli #lungomare
#lungomarecaracciolo
#campania #campaniadavivere
#campaniadascoprire #igersnapoli
#yallerscampania #campania_super_pics
#pics #picsart #photooftheday
#picoftheday #likeforlikes #likeforfollow
#naples #vedinapolipoimuori #travel
#travelblogger #destinations #tourism
#tourist #iceland #tripadvisor #viaggiare
#mare #seascape #cityscape #cityview
#reykjavik

secondo_giampaola Tutto è azzurro a Napoli,
anche la malinconia è azzurra
(Libero Bovio)

Fig. 2 First example of the experiment via social media: Naples/Reykjavik

description. The tags used also refer to the brand and the perceived image of the Neapolitan territory, with only two references to the true image (i.e., #iceland and #reykjavik). This post was viewed by about 500 followers, and it received 83 likes, 2 comments, and 1 share, generating a total of 1076 impressions on Instagram. Nevertheless, none of the photo viewers noticed, or at least questioned, the misleading nature of the "information" transmitted.

This first step allowed us to test the actual functioning of the tags and captions systems for images of this type, generating a stream of likes which will remain constant throughout the experiment, and will be around 100 per photo.

The image shown in Fig. 3 reproduces the same logic previously observed. This time, the photograph portrays Montemiletto (Italy), but it is accompanied by geolocation, caption, and tags referable to Monte Bulgheria (Italy), therefore, two different places in the same country. Again, the post collected a large number of interactions (88 likes, 2 comments, and 12 visits to the profile), generating a total of 935 impressions on Instagram. Here too, the numerous likes came from the territory mentioned by the tags and the caption of the post—therefore falling into error—and, also in this case, none of the post viewers noticed or reported anomalies (Fig. 4).

The last example shows a glimpse of the Þingvellir Park (Iceland), accompanied by geolocation, caption, and tags referable to the Conza Lake (Italy). Also in this case, two baits have been inserted in the hashtags (i.e., #pingvellir and #pingvellir-nationalpark) and the post received 101 likes, 7 comments, and 2 shares, generating 1175 impressions. Resoundingly, it is interesting in this last example to report that one of the Italian tagged pages—which has 2.5 thousand followers—has shared the

secondo_giampaola
Monte Bulgheria

♡ ◯ ▽   ☐

◐🎵🎵

secondo_giampaola "Non entrano nei fatti vostri; vi
rivolgono di rado la parola, ma non perché timidi o
privi d'eloquenza, ma perché assenti in propri
pensieri. Ma basta che esprimiate un desiderio, ed
eccoli farsi a pezzi per accontentarvi: lo fanno per
inclinazione a farsi benvolere, e mi pare ormai
civiltà assai rara. Terra ospitale, terra d'asilo!"
(Ungaretti)

#cilento #campania #likers
#montebulgheria #italia #italy
#cilentolandia #salerno #landscapes
#cilentogram #travel #cilentocoast
#igerscilento #nature #instacilento
#palinuro #scario #cilentolovers
#benvenutialsud #yallerscampania
#baiadegliinfreschi #loves
#picoftheday #cilentanodoc
#parconazionaledelcilentoevallodidiano
#live #instagood #travel #montemiletto
#photooftheday

Fig. 3 Second example of the experiment via social media: Montemiletto/Monte Bulgaria

secondo_giampaola
Conza della Campania

♡ ◯ ▽   ☐

♪🎵🎵

secondo_giampaola Ed è con questo stesso spirito
che il viaggiatore moderno dovrebbe affrontare un
percorso, reale ma anche dell'anima, nella terra
d'Irpinia, e scoprire un mondo altrove ormai
perduto e qui presente nei colori, nel vento, nei
suoni, nel silenzio, nelle albe, nei tramonti, nel cielo,
nei panorami, che si perdono a vista d'occhio.
Potrebbe scoprire così l'Irpinia romana di
Aeclanum e più a Sud di Compsa (Conza della
Campania), quella preromana di Carife, Bisaccia,
della Mefite…
(Viaggio letterario nella Terra di mezzo)

#conza #oasiwwf #visitirpinia #igersavellino#italia
#borghi #irpiniaeventi #nature #italy#fotoitaliane
#avellino #campaniache#campania #natura #cam
panialandscape#pingvellirnationalpark
#paesaggi #panorami #acqua#landscapes #ig_ca
mpaniaunita #pingvellir #picoftheday
#photooftheday #landscape #naturephotography
#naturepic #campaniadavivere #natura
#igerscampania

Fig. 4 Third example of the experiment via social media: Þingvellir park/Conza Lake

image, promoting the beauty of the Italian landscape. Paradoxically, again, no fake reports were received.

These three examples show some suggestions related to the attitude of the followers toward a fake image. Of the ten images posted in ten days, only one profile among the approximately 20 thousand viewers expressed a doubt about the truth of a photo. This represents an alarm signal regarding the behavior of the stakeholders and the critical or non-critical way in which the posts on social media are observed.

3.2   The Qualitative Approach

In the next step, the qualitative approach adopted in administering the semi-structured interviews had the aim of verifying whether the same cognitive biases were found in the communication process. More specifically, questions were oriented at understanding digital native university students and young employees' behaviors assumed in relation to posted images (e.g., reactions, comments, messages).

Even in this phase, it has been chosen to report the results of a single sample which authors consider significant based on the answers from respondents, that is Fig. 2. As previously described, this image represents Reykjavík, nevertheless it has been proposed as Naples. In this case, most respondents opted for a "like" interaction (69%) in the face of the non-like action (25.8%), therefore, acting as "active" followers. The 2.4% would be commenting on the post, and the 1.4% would also leave a like reaction. The remaining percentage (1.4%) is distributed in different responses that somehow resume the same actions. At that point, participants who had opted to leave an interaction were asked to explain which aspect had attracted their attention the most: The majority of them reported their attention has privileged the beauty of the picture, the location, and the photo composition rather than the selected tags, the account, and the caption of the post. Figure 5 shows the most frequent responses in terms of attention captured by a post on the social media Instagram.

Subsequently, it was possible to quantify the percentage of interviewees who, based on the content posted by the leader, would have decided to become its "follower" or, to better say, a stakeholder. Based on data analysis of all posts and interviews, the results show that in most cases (69%) individuals tend not to want to become followers of the leader; indeed, the range of choice to become stakeholder settles around 30–35% for each post. As a consequence, respondents were asked about the reason they decided to become a follower or not. Interestingly, under no circumstances their answered concerned the validity/validation of the post. In other words, none of the respondents questioned if that place was really the exact location proposed by the authors. On a sample of 77 answers, reasons concerned the quality of the image, its beauty, personal interests, geographic location, and so forth. An example is represented by a student who said he wanted to become a follower of that Instagram page since it published photos of Naples, fully falling into cognitive bias.

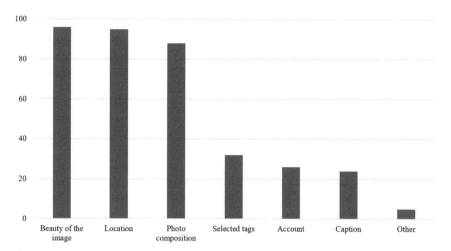

Fig. 5 Answers from respondents. % values are reported. *Source* Our elaboration

The results therefore suggest that the followers do not carry out a critical analysis of the contents posted online, so it is possible that confusion may arise in the transmission and above all in the receipt of information by the interested actors.

4   Discussion

Nowadays, communication takes place more and more online, often through social networks and the Web. Indeed, with this spread of social networks, it is precisely on the Internet that we prefer to communicate, and it has also increased with the advent of smartphones, which have made it possible to connect online even without staying at home in front of the computer [47–49]. Information is changing rapidly, hand in hand with society, and consequently it is necessary that those who carry out, or intend to carry out, the profession of communicator (and especially of leader) update themselves and become aware of all the new elements that regulate this innovative way of communicating [50–52].

Based on these assumptions, the goal of this study was to identify how communication in social networks works, and how the relationship between leadership and followership at work changes accordingly. Communication that is online or offline has a heavy impact on our lives, and it is an essential aspect of relations within society, of any type, from work to the sentimental spheres, even if the aspects related to digital followership in relation to work environments are still little investigated in the literature [17, 18].

Social networks have changed the way we understand communication and have created a sort of new code that is differentiating itself from the generally recognized models. Immediacy is at the same time a distinctive trait and a necessity. Being there and communicating an event when it takes place is of paramount importance and, given the social democratization brought by social networks, every moment of our life is important and likely to become the subject of this new communication.

In the world, on Instagram, 55 million new photos arrive every day with descriptions and attached comments. The world of social networks is a reality that, even just looking at the numbers, we cannot ignore. Now there is no shop, brand or character, real or imaginary, that does not have at least a couple of profiles on the most used social networks, and these profiles are often in at least a couple of languages to reach a wider audience [53]. Also, by observing the type of content that is posted, it is clear how communication on social networks is decreasing in the number of words, and instead is growing in the amount of "alternative" contents [54]. The reduction of words used, however, if on the one hand, it seems to diminish the value of the text as a significant means of communication, on the other, it makes the few words that are chosen and used fundamental.

The advent of these innovative platforms has drastically changed our life and our way of relating to the world around us. The comments, the likes, the tweets, and the shares have supplanted the old communication systems, also making the phone obsolete: Why should I call you when I can send you a message on Facebook? Social platforms have undoubtedly speeded up and in many cases improved our lives: With the use of social networks, we can keep in touch with people distant from us, re-establish old friendships, find work, or create our work of the future [55].

This study, in addition to investigating these aspects and enhancing their positive outputs, also surprisingly suggests that communication via social media may not work as it should. Through this exploratory study based on a content analysis [31], the results suggest that followers on social media do not use a critical spirit to evaluate the contents of the communications they access.

From the practical point of view, both the online experiment and its subsequent validation by the interview showed that it is not precisely correct assuming that individuals' attention is uncritical, since interviewees followed their own logic to answer the question, albeit bias-oriented. Rather, it is this new form of communication (marked by immediate consumption times, dictated perhaps by the unconditional trust in the account/leader role, characterized by the repetitiveness of actions and gestures) that leads, in fact, to the consequential flattening of users/followers critical thinking. Moreover, our results open a new debate on the consequences that this followership style would generate within organizations. In fact, the communicative experiment via social media reveals a commonality between social and organizational followership, thus suggesting the possibility of reviewing the five categories of organizational followership hypothesized by Kelley [23, 24] in a modern key.

This study has some limitations. First of all, the sample, chosen randomly among students and young workers, is certainly not representative of the universe to be investigated, but it could represent a starting point to deepen the still little investigated topic of digital followership at work. Furthermore, the qualitative study lends itself to easy cognitive distortions: Although the coding process was carried out by two of the authors, clearly a quantitative study could have given greater rigor to these results making them generalizable; future studies on the subject could close this gap.

Finally, it is important to underline that it is only an exploratory study and that it is not based on a well-established scale of questions on the topic of digital followership, even since there are no complete ones in the literature; it might be useful to further investigate these issues in order to create, for example, a scale for a quantitative survey or a plan for a structured interview that can investigate the perception of leaders' communication via social media by followers.

5 Conclusion

Communication via social networks is configured as something new and innovative, especially in the workplace. Words, images, sounds spread and punctuate the Net in a way that seems disordered, but that actually follows the infinite possibilities and needs, real or imaginary, of those who produce and search for the contents.

Although there is no doubt that, over time, we will be able to witness further changes in communication, this study places a first small step in the research on digital followership at work, identifying the presence of cognitive biases in the reception of information by employees and suggesting a new leadership style to be adopted in the context of online communication.

References

1. Gu, F., & Widén-Wulff, G. (2011). Scholarly communication and possible changes in the context of social media: A finnish case study. *The Electronic Library, 29*(6), 762–776. https://doi.org/10.1108/02640471111187999.
2. Lam, H. (2016). Social media dilemmas in the employment context. *Employee Relations, 38*(3), 420–437. https://doi.org/10.1108/ER-04-2015-0072.
3. Stieglitz, S., Mirbabaie, M., Ross, B., & Neuberger, C. (2018). Social media analytics–Challenges in topic discovery, data collection, and data preparation. *International Journal of Information Management, 39*, 156–168. https://doi.org/10.1016/j.ijinfomgt.2017.12.002.
4. Miller, R. (2002). A prototype skills audit for marketing communications professionals. *Marketing Theory, 2*(4), 419–428. https://doi.org/10.1177/147059310200200410.
5. Wilson, C., & Irvine, K. N. (2013). Bottom-up communication: Identifying opportunities and limitations through an exploratory field-based evaluation. *Energy Efficiency, 6*(1), 91–104. https://doi.org/10.1007/s12053-012-9161-y.
6. Kim, K. W. (2019). The new definition of creative leadership in the communication design industry-focused on the 4th industrial revolution. *International Journal of Contents, 15*(2), 53–58.
7. Men, L. R., & Jiang, H. (2016). Cultivating quality employee-organization relationships: The interplay among organizational leadership, culture, and communication. *International Journal of Strategic Communication, 10*(5), 462–479. https://doi.org/10.1080/1553118X.2016.1226172.
8. Ballantyne, D., & Varey, R. J. (2006). Creating value-in-use through marketing interaction: The exchange logic of relating, communicating and knowing. *Marketing theory, 6*(3), 335–348. https://doi.org/10.1177/1470593106066795.

9. Velentzas, J. O. H. N., & Broni, G. (2014). Communication cycle: Definition, process, models and examples. In N. E. Mastorakis (Ed.), *Recent advances in financial planning and product development* (Vol. 17, pp. 117–131). Wseas LLC.

10. Xu, S., Yang, T., Guo, R., & Zhang, W. (2019). The antecedents and consequences of employees' followership behavior in social network organizational context: A longitudinal study. *EURASIP Journal on Wireless Communications and Networking, 2019*(1), 259–273. https://doi.org/10.1186/s13638-019-1565-3.

11. Leonardi, P. M., Huysman, M., & Steinfield, C. (2013). Enterprise social media: Definition, history, and prospects for the study of social technologies in organizations. *Journal of Computer-Mediated Communication, 19*(1), 1–19. https://doi.org/10.1111/jcc4.12029.

12. Russo, A., Watkins, J., Kelly, L., & Chan, S. (2008). Participatory communication with social media. *Curator The Museum Journal, 51*(1), 21–31. https://doi.org/10.1111/j.2151-6952.2008.tb00292.x.

13. Kent, L. M. (2013). Using social media dialogically: Public relations role in reviving democracy. *Public Relations Review, 39*(4), 337–345. https://doi.org/10.1016/j.pubrev.2013.07.024.

14. Robertazzi, T., & Sarachik, P. (1986). Self-organizing communication networks. *IEEE Communications Magazine, 24*(1), 28–33.

15. Prehofer, C., & Bettstetter, C. (2005). Self-organization in communication networks: Principles and design paradigms. *IEEE Communications Magazine, 43*(7), 78–85. https://doi.org/10.1109/MCOM.2005.1470824.

16. Buchegger, S., Mundinger, J., & Le Boudec, J. Y. (2008). Reputation systems for self-organized networks. *IEEE Technology and Society Magazine, 27*(1), 41–47. https://doi.org/10.1109/MTS.2008.918039.

17. Floreddu, P. B., & Cabiddu, F. (2016). Social media communication strategies. *Journal of Services Marketing, 30*(5), 490–503. https://doi.org/10.1108/JSM-01-2015-0036.

18. Schivinski, B., & Dabrowski, D. (2016). The effect of social media communication on consumer perceptions of brands. *Journal of Marketing Communications, 22*(2), 189–214. https://doi.org/10.1080/13527266.2013.871323.

19. Grabowicz, P. A., Ramasco, J. J., Moro, E., Pujol, J. M., & Eguiluz, V. M. (2012). Social features of online networks: The strength of intermediary ties in online social media. *PLoS ONE, 7*(1), 1–9.

20. Shirky, C. (2011). The political power of social media: Technology, the public sphere, and political change. *Foreign Affairs, 90*(1), 28–41.

21. Keller, M., & Halkier, B. (2014). Positioning consumption: A practice theoretical approach to contested consumption and media discourse. *Marketing Theory, 14*(1), 35–51. https://doi.org/10.1177/1470593113506246.

22. Romero, D. M., Galuba, W., Asur, S., & Huberman, B. A. (2011). Influence and passivity in social media. In D. Gunopulos, T. Hofmann, D. Malerba, & M. Vazirgiannis (Eds.), *Machine learning and knowledge discovery in databases* (Vol. 6913, pp. 18–33). Springer.

23. Kelley, R. (1988). In praise of followers. Harvard Business Review, Boston (US). Retrieved from https://hbr.org/1988/11/in-praise-of-followers.

24. Kelley, R. (1992). In praise of followers. In R. L. Taylor & W. E. Rosenbach (Eds.), *Military leadership: In pursuit of excellence* (pp. 99–109). Westview Press.

25. Kelley, R. (1992b) The power of followership: How to create leaders people want to follow, and followers who lead themselves Doubleday/Currency, New York, NY.

26. Kelley, R. (2008). Rethinking followership. In R. E. Riggio, I. Chaleff, & J. Lipman-Blumen (Eds.), *The art of followership: How great followers create great leaders and organizations* (pp. 5–16). Jossey-Bass.

27. Hayes, L. A., Caldwell, C., Licona, B., & Meyer, T. E. (2015). Followership behaviors and barriers to wealth creation. *Journal of Management Development, 34*(3), 270–285. https://doi.org/10.1108/JMD-09-2013-0111.

28. Goffee, R., Jones, G. (2013). Cameo: Authentic followership in the knowledge economy. In D. Ladkin, & C. Spiller (Eds.) *Authentic Leadership* (pp. 208–2019). Edward Elgar Publishing. https://doi.org/10.4337/9781781006382.00025..

29. Carsten, M. K., Uhl-Bien, M., West, B. J., Patera, J. L., & McGregor, R. (2010). Exploring social constructions of followership: A qualitative study. *The Leadership Quarterly, 21*(3), 543–562. https://doi.org/10.1016/j.leaqua.2010.03.015.
30. Zoogah, D. (2016). *Strategic followership: How followers impact organizational effectiveness.* Springer.
31. Elo, S., & Kyngäs, H. (2008). The qualitative content analysis process. *Journal of Advanced Nursing, 62*(1), 107–115. https://doi.org/10.1111/j.1365-2648.2007.04569.x.
32. Lauri, S., & Kyngas, H. (2005). *Developing nursing theories.* Werner Söderström, Dark Oy.
33. Guthrie, J., Petty, R., Yongvanich, K., & Ricceri, F. (2004). Using content analysis as a research method to inquire into intellectual capital reporting. *Journal of Intellectual Capital, 5*(2), 282–293. https://doi.org/10.1108/14691930410533704.
34. Salleh, S., Hashima, N. H., & Murphy, J. (2015). Instagram marketing: A content analysis of top Malaysian restaurant brands. *E-Review of Tourism Research, 6,* 1–5.
35. Ting, H., Ming, W. W. P., de Run, E. C., & Choo, S. L. Y. (2015). Beliefs about the use of Instagram: An exploratory study. *International Journal of Business and Innovation, 2*(2), 15–31.
36. Agung, N. F. A., & Darma, G. S. (2019). Opportunities and challenges of instagram algorithm in improving competitive advantage. *International Journal of Innovative Science and Research Technology, 4*(1), 743–747.
37. Konstantopoulou, A., Rizomyliotis, I., Konstantoulaki, K., & Badahdah, R. (2019). Improving SMEs' competitiveness with the use of Instagram influencer advertising and eWOM. *International Journal of Organizational Analysis, 27*(2), 308–321. https://doi.org/10.1108/IJOA-04-2018-1406.
38. Miles, J. (2013). *Instagram power.* McGraw-Hill Publishing.
39. Virtanen, H., Björk, P., & Sjöström, E. (2017). Follow for follow: Marketing of a start-up company on Instagram. *Journal of Small Business and Enterprise Development, 24*(3), 468–484. https://doi.org/10.1108/JSBED-12-2016-0202.
40. Duncan, D. F. (1989). Content analysis in health education research: An introduction to purposes and methods. *Health Education, 20*(7), 27–31. https://doi.org/10.1080/00970050.1989.10610182.
41. Graneheim, U. H., & Lundman, B. (2004). Qualitative content analysis in nursing research: Concepts, procedures and measures to achieve trustworthiness. *Nurse Education Today, 24*(2), 105–112. https://doi.org/10.1016/j.nedt.2003.10.001.
42. Dey, I. (1993). *Qualitative data analysis: A user-friendly guide for social scientists.* Routledge.
43. Polit, D. F., & Beck, C. T. (2004). *Nursing research principles and methods.* Lippincott Williams & Wilkins.
44. Burnard, P. (1991). A method of analysing interview transcripts in qualitative research. *Nurse Education Today, 11*(6), 461–466.
45. McCain, G. C. (1988). Content analysis: A method for studying clinical nursing problems. *Applied Nursing Research, 1*(3), 146–147. https://doi.org/10.1016/s0897-1897(88)80029-6.
46. Cavanagh, S. (1997). Content analysis: Concepts, methods and applications. *Nurse Researcher, 4*(3), 5–16. https://doi.org/10.7748/nr.4.3.5.s2.
47. Subrahmanyam, K., Reich, S. M., Waechter, N., & Espinoza, G. (2008). Online and offline social networks: Use of social networking sites by emerging adults. *Journal of Applied Developmental Psychology, 29*(6), 420–433. https://doi.org/10.1016/j.appdev.2008.07.003.
48. Cheung, C. M., & Lee, M. K. (2012). What drives consumers to spread electronic word of mouth in online consumer-opinion platforms. *Decision Support Systems, 53*(1), 218–225. https://doi.org/10.1016/j.dss.2012.01.015.
49. Laghi, F., Schneider, B. H., Vitoroulis, I., Coplan, R. J., Baiocco, R., Amichai-Hamburger, Y., Hudek, N., Koszycki, D., Martin, S. M., & Flament, M. (2013). Knowing when not to use the Internet: Shyness and adolescents' on-line and off-line interactions with friends. *Computers in Human Behavior, 29*(1), 51–57. https://doi.org/10.1016/j.chb.2012.07.015.
50. Heide, M., & Simonsson, C. (2011). Putting coworkers in the limelight: New challenges for communication professionals. *International Journal of Strategic Communication, 5*(4), 201–220. https://doi.org/10.1080/1553118X.2011.605777.

51. Huffaker, D. (2010). Dimensions of leadership and social influence in online communities. *Human Communication Research, 36*(4), 593–617. https://doi.org/10.1111/j.1468-2958.2010. 01390.x.

52. De Vries, R. E., Bakker-Pieper, A., & Oostenveld, W. (2010). Leadership=communication? The relations of leaders' communication styles with leadership styles, knowledge sharing and leadership outcomes. *Journal of Business and Psychology, 25*(3), 367–380. https://doi.org/10. 1007/s10869-009-9140-2.

53. Ho, J. Y., & Dempsey, M. (2010). Viral marketing: Motivations to forward online content. *Journal of Business Research, 63*(9–10), 1000–1006. https://doi.org/10.1016/j.jbusres.2008. 08.010.

54. Ludwig, S., De Ruyter, K., Friedman, M., Brüggen, E. C., Wetzels, M., & Pfann, G. (2013). More than words: The influence of affective content and linguistic style matches in online reviews on conversion rates. *Journal of Marketing, 77*(1), 87–103. https://doi.org/10.1509/jm. 11.0560.

55. Coyle, C. L., & Vaughn, H. (2008). Social networking: Communication revolution or evolution? *Bell Labs Technical Journal, 13*(2), 13–17. https://doi.org/10.1002/bltj.20298.

Reducing Cognitive Biases Through Digitally Enabled Training.
A Conceptual Framework

Samuel Collino and Giancarlo Lauto

Abstract Since cognitive biases impair decision-making processes, organizations strive to reduce their effect. Training sustains such effort, especially when innovative learning approaches are adopted. The introduction of digital technologies, such as those related to Industry 4.0, challenges firms to upskill and reskill their employees. At the same time, these technologies offer a new set of tools for training. This paper proposes a conceptual model that disentangles the effect of the form of training and its reliance on digital technological tools, on the reduction of cognitive biases and performance in tasks related to digital transformations.

Keywords Cognitive bias · Training · Technology

1 Introduction

Disruptive technologies will bring significant shifts in the labor market requiring workers and management to develop a completely new set of skills [43]. Technologies enabling automation, artificial intelligence, and machine learning, often labeled as Industry 4.0 [20], are fostering an evolution of the social and industrial environment with huge impacts on production systems, creating the possibility to disrupt an increasing number of tasks. The digitalization of product and processes appears even more urgent now, in light of the unpredictable consequences of the COVID-19 outbreak on the organization of work and of global value chains [44].

This rapid technological shift is bringing a great productivity increase potential, but also opening a transition phase. It seems that competence creation processes can take place at a slower speed when compared to technological change. This would result in gaps between skills required by firms and skills possessed by the workforce. Therefore, it emerges a need for reskilling, that is possible through innovative forms of training [4, 10, 13].

S. Collino · G. Lauto (✉)
Università degli Studi di Udine, 33100 Udine, Italy
e-mail: giancarlo.lauto@uniud.it

179

Digital technology-enabled forms of training promise to endow employees with the skills needed to operate effectively in this new industrial setting as well as to enhance their existing skills. In this paper, we focus on the latter, by outlining a conceptual model that disentangles the effect of digital technology-enabled training on the impact of cognitive biases on decisions within the setting of operations management.

The study of cognitive biases is gaining relevance for operations management as this filed is embracing a more human-centered view in its investigation, which entails the full recognition of the bounded rationality of actors and the emphasis on behavioral dimension of the process. This field appears therefore open to fruitful contamination with a well-established stream of studies in Psychology and Organization.

In this piece of research, we study the cognitive biases not only by the adoption of a new heuristic more unlikely to lead to a severe systematic error, but with the adoption of new technologies. Training and specifically innovative forms of training have been shown to be effective in reducing and preventing cognitive biases. But may technology play a role in this relation, by means of reducing cognitive biases when performing a new task?

2   Including the Human Side in Operations Management

2.1   Toward a Behavioral View of Operations Management

The field of operations management is changing toward the inclusion of behavioral factors into its scope of analysis. From being a niche subfield, behavioral operations research has more than doubled the number of scientific publication between 2006–2012 and 2013–2017 [15], evidencing a growing interest on the topic, a vibrant methodological pluralism—leveraging on an experimental approach—and expanding from the original topics of supply chain management, product development, quality and production, to new areas of investigation [12] such as retail, healthcare operations, and social and sustainability decisions [15]. What links together these studies, and differentiates them from the earlier streams of operations management research, is the deviation from a hyper-rational conceptualization of decision making in the context of operations management that has long characterized the field [12].

Traditionally, operations management studies have assumed that decisionmakers, problemsolvers, and workers are rational or that can be induced to behave rationally [18]. As [17] put forward, rational or intentionally rational decision making rests on tools such as logical reasoning or statistics, and operations management research as much emphasized mathematical modeling as statistical testing as a way to advance our knowledge about production systems and to offer managers sound operational tools. However, it has also been suggested that in operations management "…techniques and theories ignore important characteristics of real systems, and therefore are perceived to be difficult to apply in practice. A common factor in this breakdown is people" ([5]: 737). To address this shortcoming, the study of operations management has added to its analytical models factors such as people's actions, emotions, reactions, and intentions [15]. Behavioral operations management is a multidisciplinary branch of operations management that explicitly considers the effects of human behavior in process performance, influenced by cognitive biases, social preferences, and cultural norms [26].

The idea of a non-hyper-rational individual is not new in Organization Studies, at least since Herbert [35] development of the notion of bounded rationality. However, the field of operations management seems to be lagging behind in the adoption of such perspective, as, still recently, [12] suggested that any behavior that deviates from the hyper-rational is a candidate for research in that field of studies.

Simon's well-established notion of economic agents is incapable of acquiring, processing, and deploying information with complete mindfulness that has revolutionized management scholarship as it offered a more compelling alternative to the dominant conceptualization of the "homo oeconomicus" that still characterizes much of operations management research. Furthermore, Simon's contribution has emphasized that agents are not capable of always taking rational decisions due to unavailability of complete information (informational limit), and inability to correctly interpreting and processing (computational limit) the limited information available, due to boundaries in time and cognitive limitations of their mind.

2.2   The Role of Cognitive Bias in Operations Management

Deviating from the tenets of perfect rationality, it is essential to acknowledge that decisionmakers adopt other tools, in addition to logic and statistics, such as heuristics. Building on a wealth of studies in behavioral sciences ([17]: 454) offers a definition of heuristic as "*a strategy that ignores part of the information, with the goal of making decisions more quickly, frugally, and/or accurately than more complex methods.*" With specific regard to psychology, [24] defined psychological heuristics as formal models for making decisions that:

(i) rely heavily on core psychological capacities (e.g., recognizing patterns or recalling information from memory);

(ii) do not necessarily use all available information and process the information they use by simple computations (e.g., ordinal comparisons or unweighted sums);

(iii) are easy to understand, apply, and explain.

Figure 1 offers a comprehensive view of the conceptual linkages between the notions of bounded rationality, heuristics, and cognitive biases.

Simplified heuristics, such as representativeness, availability and adjusting and anchoring have been shown to potentially lead to a series of cognitive biases, which in evolutionary psychology are meant as "*cases in which human cognition reliably produces representations that are systematically distorted compared to some aspect*

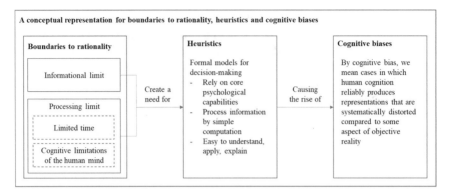

Fig. 1 A simplified conceptual framework on boundaries to rationality, heuristics, and cognitive biases

of objective reality" and systematically hinder someone's ability to rationally perform a task or set of tasks ([19]: 968).

A famous example of cognitive bias is this experiment performed by [38] related to decision-making task, that highlights the relevance of information visualization, and specifically of framing in describing a problem outcome in the decisions patterns of two identical problems. Participants were posed the following problem:

Imagine the U.S. is preparing for the outbreak of an unusual Asia disease, which is expected to kill 600 people. Two alternative programs to combat the disease have been proposed. Assume that the exact scientific estimate of the consequences of the programs are as follows:

If Program A is adopted, 200 people will be saved.

If program B is adopted, there is 1/3 probability that 600 people will be saved, and 2/3 probability that no people will be saved.

Program A was preferred by 72% of participants.

The authors then presented the same problem to a different sample with the following outcomes to choose:

If Program C is adopted 400 people will die.

If program D is adopted there is 1/3 probability that nobody will die, and 2/3 probability that 600 people will die.

Program D was chosen by 78% of participants.

This simple, yet powerful experiment, shows how choices involving gains are risk averse and choices involving losses are risk taking. The two problems are though identical from a probabilistic point of view, yet they achieve opposite results, where the only difference comes from framing the outcomes in a positive or a negative way.

The seminal contribution by [37] identified three bias categories originating from heuristic processes, namely representativeness, availability, and anchoring, which affect decision making. Then, the researchers grouped them based on the hypothesized heuristic strategy that the individual follows in taking the decision.

The representativeness heuristic implies that during a judgment process, probabilities are evaluated by the degree to which A is representative of B, for example by the degree of similarity between them. However, several factors needed to assess likelihood do not play a role in judgments of similarity. Availability refers to the tendency to assess the frequency of an occurrence based on the easiness of recalling an event or topic in mind. Adjustment and anchoring bias the person making an estimation toward the initial value that has been anchored, for instance building on previous data or a partial estimation, where the following adjustment is not sufficient to lead the judging person to the real value.

Since the 1970s, many cognitive biases have been found [23], and efforts have been made in reviewing and categorizing them (e.g., Baron, 2000, [2]). Interestingly, [14] recently built on in a comprehensive task-based taxonomy that appears particularly useful to identify the biases that might occur when performing different tasks. In this analysis of cognitive biases in information visualization, the authors categorized a broad range of 154 biases into bias "flavors" and "task categories." The "flavors" build on the heuristic concept and try to capture the phenomenon behind the bias, as much previous studies do. These flavors are [14]:

(1) Association, where cognition is biased by associative connections between information items.
(2) Baseline, where cognition is biased by a comparison with (what is perceived as) a baseline.
(3) Inertia, where cognition is biased by the prospect of changing the current state.
(4) Outcome, where cognition is biased by how well something fits an expected or desired outcome.
(5) Self-perspective, where cognition is biased by a self-oriented view point.

The biggest contribution in this piece of research was the identification of six defined "task categories" in which systematic biases found in the previous literature can be divided. These tasks are:

(1) Estimation, where individuals are asked to forecast the quantity or the probability of an occurrence. Biases in this task category include, for example, anchoring, availability, and spotlight effect.
(2) Decision, or choice tasks, refer to situations in which people make choices on a set of alternatives and tend to be systematically biased toward one of them. Examples of biases in this category are framing, automation bias, and status-quo bias.
(3) Hypothesis assessment tasks refer to cases in which people needs to confirm or reject a hypothesis conducting an investigation. This category includes a smaller number of cognitive biases, but nevertheless very relevant to the field, such as the confirmation bias, in which people tend to confirm previous hypothesis rather than disprove it.
(4) Causal attribution tasks are also prone to cognitive biases. In this situation, individuals are asked to find root-causes and effects of phenomena, where the bias induced derives from their view of themselves, their empathy toward

the part involved in the situation, or their belonging to one group over another. Some biases categorized in this task include the group attribution bias, in which group traits are attributed to an individual belonging to this group, or egocentric biases, in which the own contribution is perceived as disproportionately higher in comparison to others.

(5)   Recall tasks are those in which individuals seek to remember past experiences or knowledge after some time has passed since the event, and misinterpretation or other factors have had the time to occur. Some of the biases occurring include, as an example, digital amnesia, that makes it more difficult to retrieve data easily available thanks to digital solutions. On the opposite, the bizarreness effect makes it easier to remember facts and situations when they are out of the perceived normality. Also, the misinformation effect is an example of bias in this category. In this case, memory is enriched with new pieces of information that were not included in the original experience or knowledge.

(6)   The last category of systematic biases includes the biases occurring when asking individuals to report others' opinions, mostly on situational sensitive topics. It has been observed that often participants to studies on such biases misreported others' opinions according to specific biases, such as stereotyping, which makes an individual attribute to someone some traits associated to a group he belongs to, or the focusing effect, for which reported beliefs are based on the main and most spoken portion of a message.

Cognitive biases affect a number of different areas related to operations management such as process assessment and risk assessment [28]. Various field and laboratory experiments, e.g. [3, 7], confirm the relevance and vast diffusion of this potentially dangerous downside.

3   What Training for Developing Operation Management Skills

Training has been demonstrated to be an effective mean to reduce the occurrence and effects of cognitive biases in different tasks and settings [27, 34]. Many debiasing strategies have been proposed through training, such as rising awareness on biases, their directionality, and the importance of feedback and coaching. However, the efficacy of training in addressing these biases is associated with the design of the interventions.

Training can be conceived as a learning and development process aimed at increasing organizational performance by endowing people with the knowledge, skills, and competencies need to carry out their work effectively and successfully (Armstrong & Taylor, 2020). The main domains affecting training efficiency concern [25]:

- Trainee characteristics
- Training design

– Training transfer climate
– Work environment.

For what concerns the training design, it is useful to distinguish traditional, scenario-based cases, and problem-based experiential learning. The two latter forms of training are particularly effective in achieving the purpose of knowledge transfer in a perspective of reskilling and upskilling [34].

Traditional forms of training take the form of frontal lectures in classrooms and apprenticeship for repetitive tasks with the demonstration of an activity to trainees, until they become able to perform it [21]. One of the assumptions of traditional teaching methods is the predictability of tasks in a stable environment, while in an evolving situation with growing uncertainties it is necessary to create adaptive expertise.

Such adaptive experiences may be offered by exposing trainees to cases portraying different scenarios in a real setting, to "learn during their experiences while addressing desired goals" [32, 33]. The development of goal-based scenarios seems to have risen from a critic of traditional training methods concerning the drift toward an excessive emphasis on verifiability and standardization of knowledge, where facts are considered as basic notions with no real-life meaning or implication. To create a scenario-based case study, namely a "learn by doing course," it is necessary to combine simulation and case-based reasoning. The learner has a role to play, which can vary according to observed, real interests of the student, avoiding artificial world problems [33].

The development of problem-based learning training modules entails the following activities [8]:

– Description of the problem provided to the student. The problem may be described either in neutral, clear, non-contradictory, realistic terms and refers to a fairly common setting [8], or in an ill-defined fashion with the aim of involving trainees into the development of a complex solution and stimulating the analytical skills of participants [1]. Realism, complexity, and contradiction are on the other side probably characteristics of the working environment in which the trainees will have to apply the skills acquired during the learning.
– Definition of the scope for the problem solving activity.
– Time management. The time allocated to training activities is generally insufficient to address all the issues raised by the problem. A need for prioritizing the activities and allocating the cognitive effort emerges. It should be noted that participation is positively related to the sense of urgency for the problem.
– Design of cognitive conflict and social negotiation opportunities, that should be seen as a stimulus for learning through the evaluation of viability of individual understanding. To this purpose, it is important to encourage to test ideas rather to accept alternative views.

Problem-based learning is probably the most widely adopted experiential learning method within executive development programs [45]. Indeed, live projects, a concept very similar to experiential learning, have the highest positive result in terms of successful skill transfer, and, in general, teaching methods that trigger the student to acquire additional knowledge on his own may result in a more positive outcome [29]. Although it is a very effective and motivating technique, it is very time-consuming, and therefore not particularly efficient [8].

4 How Industry 4.0 Technologies May Attenuate Cognitive Biases

Some of the technologies that are part of the broad Industry 4.0 landscape promise to help to remove or attenuate both the causes of cognitive biases: the unavailability of information and the human capacity to process information.

In 2013, a group of practitioners and academics at the yearly Hannover Messe enshrined in a Manifesto a set of recommendations for implementing what was called "Industrie 4.0" [20]. The trend of automation and smart system development in both physical and intellectual contexts emerged decisively, interpreting and linking different new technologies that grew in the beginning of the new millennium, ultimately aiming at keeping competitiveness high, also through an optimized decision making.

For instance, the Internet of things allows for the collection of data through sensors and stacks that contribute to the creation of big data and data lakes constituting an organization's backbone for a data-based decision making. It is a new paradigm of interconnection of final goods exchanging information to provide data, optimization, and self-control in the most advanced examples, which are transforming the business world [30]. This concept shares many of the characteristics of "smart factories," where Xia [42] points out ubiquity, interconnection, glocalization, and traceability as core enablers and constituents of this new paradigm made possible by the low costs of these new technologies and their miniaturization. A further step has been the interconnection of production facilities to this network, captured as the paradigm of the industrial Internet of things [16]. This further step creates significant implications not only for strategic and marketing-related activities, but also for areas of the field of operations management, for example in production, capacity management, and supply chain decisions.

Building on the same technological ground, also lean-empowered product life-cycle management [22] can now provide an increased and improved amount of information feeding the product development process, leveraging on big data [41] and cloud to facilitate the exchange and usability of the collected data and information. Many examples of successful industrial implementation of these concepts now exist from aerospace, automotive [9, 39], and prove the advantage provided by an enriched base for data-driven decision making.

While some technologies help to solve the information availability issue, others address problem of information processing. For instance, one of the key principles identified in Industry 4.0 is the adoption of knowledge tasks automation systems, such as Robotic Process Automation systems [40] and smart assistance systems, which have the scope of releasing workers from having to perform routine tasks, enabling them to focus on creative, value-added activities [20]. In this, Industry 4.0 promises to grant more time for individuals inside organizations to take decisions of higher quality, reducing the information processing boundary to rationality.

At the same time, other technologies allow for a better use of this information during the allocated time, enhancing an individual's ability to select, acquire, and process relevant information. This is the case of wearable technologies, able to convey information in more ways than traditional, static visualization, and of virtual reality (VR) when compared to traditional monitor visualization, thanks to its vividness and interactivity [36] and by immersing the individual in a new, safe to experience of reality, recognizing the need for a better intermediation tool to enhance the cognitive abilities of humans [11].

Augmented and mixed reality go further on this, by bridging the physical and cyberworld [31], enhancing human comprehension and information processing abilities by adding additional layers of information on the reality they see. The application fields are broad, as are the potential gains, that include an improvement of visualization, for example allowing for the inspection of internal components otherwise difficult to see, adding the possibility to test in a safe environment even complex tasks for operators, giving instructions, training, and coaching [31]. Further applications included the use of augmented reality for prototyping and product testing [6], demonstrating their usefulness as technological tools able to enhance humans' information processing ability.

5 How Training and Advance Technologies Help to Offset Cognitive Biases. A Conceptual Model

The inclusion of human factors into operations management has been a necessary step toward a better understanding of the real-world issues by overcoming the well-established hyper-rational conceptualizations. Embracing the perspective of bounded rationality implies the necessity of acknowledging the effect of cognitive biases on task results. Various studies have then analyzed how tasks in different fields of operations management can be prone to such biases, but training has proved to be an effective way to impair their effect.

The introduction of new technologies—such as those brought by the digitalization of production processes according to the Industry 4.0 paradigm—demand a reskilling and upskilling of employees who are asked to perform new, richer, and more complex tasks. Training is therefore an essential activity to perform in this new industrial setting.

On the ground of such considerations, we propose the model portrayed in Fig. 2 to study the relation among training, cognitive biases, adoption of new technologies and task performance.

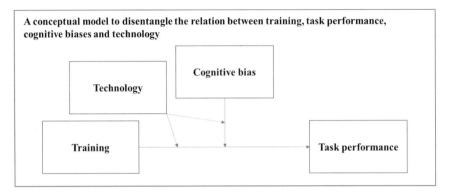

Fig. 2 A conceptual model for the study of the relation between training, cognitive biases, technologies, and task performance

Our model posits a direct relationship between training and the performance of operators in carrying out both existing tasks and new tasks introduced by the adoption of novel technologies. In the latter case, the training effort is more substantial, as employees need to learn completely new skills, competences, behavior, and attitudes, since their job may be redefined. However, training is essential even in the case of established tasks, as the adoption of new technologies may alter the context in which such task is performed. An example may be the activity of safety check in a production plant that adopted Industry 4.0 technologies. In such an environment, old and new hazards coexist and the tasks of employees who perform safety check change and potentially become more complex.

We expect that innovative forms of training—such as problem-based scenarios, simulations, and role-play—are powerful in improving the operators' performance in carrying out a task, by virtue of their ability of delivering knowledge through a more engaging approach.

However, as previously discussed, operators are prone to cognitive biases while making the decisions required by the task. Through training, operators may learn to be aware and recognize such biases and therefore their effect may be attenuated. We expect that different models of training have a different level of efficacy in attenuating the effect of the biases.

Furthermore, we acknowledge the role of technology as a support for training provision as well as the object of the training. On one hand, the use of technology could enhance the training, offering a richer learning experience. For instance, the use of VR tools that simulate a shop-floor where hazards such as wet floor or incorrect storage are present may offer trainees a more realistic experience, improve the delivery of content, and make trainees more aware of the biases that they may incur when they are evaluating the hazards of a real shop-floor. In this sense, digital technologies contribute to debias complex tasks and eventually improve task performance. On the other hand, the use of digital technologies for training may induce other series of biases, associated with the very use of such tools. Trainees may show a different performance in the training and in their operative activities, due to the fact that the training has relied on a specific medium for the delivery of the content. Indeed, the performance in the training may be due to the novelty for the subject of new technological tools, while it might fade away if the technology is repeatedly used.

Such conceptual model can be empirically tested in an experimental setting. In such experiments, trainees may undergo different forms of training, such as frontal lectures, cased-based simulations, and digital supported training. Training may address either a task that has been improved thanks to the application of digital technologies or a completely new one. Trainees can be induced different kinds of cognitive biases (e.g., anchoring or overconfidence) through scenario-based manipulations. The joint effect of training method and cognitive biases should be appreciated in terms of learning as well as in terms of change of behavior in the long term.

Disentangling the relationship between new digital technologies, training and cognitive biases on task performance would contribute to the development of the field of behavioral operations, as outlined by [18]. This effort would also provide evidence of the benefits of the adoption of new technology-based tools when performing tasks that might be prone to cognitive biases, even when debiasing training has been put in place.

Acknowledgements Research for this paper was supported financially by a doctoral scholarship from the University of Udine (Doctoral program in Managerial and Actuarial Sciences) and by Lean Experience Factory Scarl.

References

1. Allen, D. E., Donham, R. S., & Bernhardt, S. A. (2011). Problem-based learning. *New Directions for Teaching and Learning, 2011*(128), 21–29.
2. Arnott, D. (2006). Cognitive biases and decision support systems development: A design science approach. *Information Systems Journal, 16*(1), 55–78.
3. Ancarani, A., Di Mauro, C., & D'Urso, D. (2016). Measuring overconfidence in inventory management decisions. *Journal of Purchasing and Supply Management, 22*(3), 171–180.
4. Balsmeier, B., & Woerter, M. (2019). Is this time different? How digitalization influences job creation and destruction. *Research Policy, 48*(8), 103765.
5. Bendoly, E., Donohue, K., & Schultz, K. L. (2006). Behavior in operations management: Assessing recent findings and revisiting old assumptions. *Journal of Operations Management, 24*(6), 737–752.
6. Billinghurst, M., Clark, A., & Lee, G. (2015). A survey of augmented reality. *Foundations and Trends® in Human–Computer Interaction, 8*(2–3), 73–272.
7. Bisin, A., & Hyndman, K. (2020). Present-bias, procrastination and deadlines in a field experiment. *Games and Economic Behavior, 119*, 339–357.
8. Boud, D., & Feletti, G. (1998). *The challenge of problem-based learning.* Psychology Press.
9. Borsato, M. (2014). Bridging the gap between product lifecycle management and sustainability in manufacturing through ontology building. *Computers in Industry, 65*(2), 258–269.
10. Callan, V. J., Bowman, K., Fitzsimmons, T. W., & Poulsen, A. L. (2020). Industry restructuring and job loss: Towards a guiding model to assist the displaced older worker. *Journal of Vocational Education & Training.* https://doi.org/10.1080/13636820.2020.1744693

11. Chavan, S. R. (2016). Augmented reality vs. virtual reality: Differences and similarities. In *International Journal of Advanced Research in Computer Engineering & Technology, 5*(6).
12. Croson, R., Schultz, K., Siemsen, E., & Yeo, M. L. (2013). Behavioral operations: The state of the field. *Journal of Operations Management, 31*(1–2), 1–5.
13. David, H. (2015). Why are there still so many jobs? The history and future of workplace automation. *Journal of Economic Perspectives, 29*(3), 3–30.
14. Dimara, E., Franconeri, S., Plaisant, C., Bezerianos, A., & Dragicevic, P. (2018). A task-based taxonomy of cognitive biases for information visualization. *IEEE Transactions on Visualization and Computer Graphics, 26*(2), 1413–1452.
15. Donohue, K., & Schultz, K. (2019). The future is bright: Recent trends and emerging topics in behavioral operations. In K. Donohue, E. Katok, & S. Leider (Eds.), *Wiley series in operations research and management science. The handbook of behavioral operations* (pp. 619–651). Wiley-Blackwell.
16. Gilchrist, A. (2016). *Industry 4.0: The Industrial Internet of Things*. Apress.
17. Gigerenzer, G., & Gaissmaier, W. (2011). Heuristic decision making. *Annual Review of Psychology, 62*, 451–482.
18. Gino, F., & Pisano, G. (2008). Toward a theory of behavioral operations. *Manufacturing & Service Operations Management, 10*(4), 676–691.
19. Haselton, M. G., Nettle, D., & Murray, D. R. (2015). The evolution of cognitive bias. In D. M. Buss (Ed.), *The handbook of evolutionary psychology* (pp. 724–746). Wiley.
20. Kagermann, H. (2015). Change through digitization—Value creation in the age of Industry 4.0. In: H. Albach, H. Meffert, A. Pinkwart, R. Reichwald (Eds), *Management of permanent change* (pp. 23–45). Springer Gabler.
21. Kraiger, K., Ford, J., & Salas, E. (1993). Application of cognitive, skill-based, and affective theories of learning outcomes to new methods of training evaluation. *Journal of Applied Psychology, 78*(2), 311–328.
22. Hines, P., Francis, M., & Found, P. (2006). Towards lean product lifecycle management: A framework for new product development. *Journal of Manufacturing Technology Management, 17*(7), 866–887.
23. Kahneman, D. (2011). *Thinking, fast and slow*. Farrar.
24. Katsikopoulos, K. V. (2011). Psychological heuristics for making inferences: Definition, performance, and the emerging theory and practice. *Decision Analysis, 8*(1), 10–29.
25. Kontoghiorghes, C. (2004). Reconceptualizing the learning transfer conceptual framework: Empirical validation of a new systemic model. *International Journal of Training and Development, 8*(3), 210–221.
26. Loch, C. H., & Wu, Y. (2007). *Behavioral operations management*. Now Publishers Inc.
27. Ludolph, R., & Schulz, P. J. (2018). Debiasing health-related judgments and decision making: A systematic review. *Medical Decision Making, 38*(1), 3–13.
28. Murata, A. (2018). Cross-cultural difference and cognitive biases as causes of gap of mindset toward safety between approach based on hazard detection and that based on firm safety confirmation. In: J. Kantola, S. Nazir, T. Barath (Eds.), *Advances in Human Factors, Business Management and Society. AHFE 2018. Advances in Intelligent Systems and Computing*, vol. 783. Springer.
29. Narayandas, D., & Moldoveanu, M. (2016). *Executive development programs enter the digital vortex: I. Disrupting the demand landscape*. Harvard Business School Working Paper, No. 17–020, September 2016. (Revised June 2018).
30. Porter, M. E., & Heppelmann, J. E. (2015). How smart, connected products are transforming companies. *Harvard Business Review, 93*(10), 96–114.
31. Porter, M. E., & Heppelmann, J. E. (2017). Why every organization needs an augmented reality strategy. *Harvard Business Review, 95*(6), 46–57.
32. Schank, R., Fano, A., Bell, B., & Jona, M. (1994). The design of goal-based scenarios. *The Journal of the Learning Sciences, 3*(4), 305–345.
33. Schank, R. C. (1996). Goal-based scenarios: Case-based reasoning meets learning by doing. In *Case-based reasoning: Experiences, lessons & future directions* (pp. 295–347). AAAI Press/The MIT.

34. Sellier, A. L., Scopelliti, I., & Morewedge, C. K. (2019). Debiasing training improves decision making in the field. *Psychological Science, 30*(9), 1371–1379.
35. Simon, H. A. (1955). A behavioral model of rational choice. *The Quarterly Journal of Economics, 60*(1), 99–118.
36. Steuer, J. (1992). Defining virtual reality: Dimensions determining telepresence. *Journal of Communication, 42*(4), 73–93.
37. Tversky, A., & Kahneman, D. (1974). Judgment under uncertainty: Heuristics and biases. *Science, 185*(4157), 1124–1131.
38. Tversky, A., & Kahneman, D. (1981). The framing of decisions and the psychology of choice. *Science, 211*(4481), 453–458.
39. Vezzetti, E., Alemanni, M., & Macheda, J. (2015). Supporting product development in the textile industry through the use of a product lifecycle management approach: A preliminary set of guidelines. *The International Journal of Advanced Manufacturing Technology, 79*(9–12), 1493–1504.
40. Van der Aalst, W. M., Bichler, M., & Heinzl, A. (2018). Robotic process automation. *Business & Information Systems Engineering, 60*, 269–272.
41. Zhang, Y., Ren, S., Liu, Y., Sakao, T., & Huisingh, D. (2017). A framework for Big Data driven product lifecycle management. *Journal of Cleaner Production, 159*, 229–240.
42. Xia, F., Yang, L. T., Wang, L., & Vinel, A. (2012). Internet of things. *International Journal of Communication Systems, 25*(9), 1101.
43. World Economic Forum. (2020a). *Jobs of Tomorrow. Mapping Opportunity in the New Economy.* Cologny/Geneva.
44. World Economic Forum. (2020b). *The Impact of COVID-19 on the Future of Advanced Manufacturing and Production.* Cologny/Geneva.
45. Wuestewald, T. (2016). Adult learning in executive development programs. *Adult Learning, 27*(2), 68–75.

Printed in the United States
by Baker & Taylor Publisher Services